Sally discovered that visualization and imagination are indeed powerful forces. She inspired me to do more with my life than I had been doing. She inspired me to not be afraid to reveal my fears and my weaknesses and my vulnerabilities, for when we truly see ourselves—the weaknesses as well as the strengths—and when we are not afraid to reveal them to others—then we can truly see ourselves and the real world around us. —Ed Bernard Jr., Texas

Seeing Myself Seeing the World is truly a remarkable story of strength, courage, determination, and inner spirit. It is awesome the many countries that Sally traveled to and was able to experience. Her story shows us that we are all capable of taking risks and challenging ourselves, we just need to believe we have the inner-strength and courage. Sometimes we simply need to try, and the courage and strength come, as it did for Sally. —Linda Racicot, Spokane, WA

This story demonstrates that the power of the mind is limitless.
—Jose Silva, Founder of the Silva Method of Mind Development, Texas

I was just mesmerized by this story. Wow what an impressive journey, both spiritually and physically.
—Christana Gnehm-Boyle, Liberty Lake, WA

Just could not put it down, you helped me reflect on my travels in a positive manner. —Mark Fromm, Singapore

Your book and your presentation gave me the inspiration to begin looking at my life with new insight and help me with daily choices.
—Rosalyn Chamberlin, Claremont, CA

...A fasinating Odyessey! —Pat Raup, Timken, KS

... I am awed by your experiences. You are truly a remarkable person ...
　　　　—Jayne Murdock, May-Murdock Publications, Ross, CA

... What a fascinating book! It gives women a tremendous tool.
　　　　—Mary Florey, Florey's Bookstore Pacfica, CA

... I was deeply moved by your physical and emotional strength, Sally. I cried all the way from New Zealand to Aptos.
　　　　—Gary Harold, Aptos, CA

Sally! My daughter leaves for Thailand in 2 days. For a year! To meditate and explore. I'm excited and scared for her but if I hadn't read your book I don't think I would have been able to cope with this adventure. Thank you for your inspiration.
　　　　—Nicole Lund, Spokane, WA

SEEING MYSELF
SEEING THE WORLD

SEEING MYSELF
SEEING THE WORLD

A Woman's Journey Around the World on a Bicycle

Sally Vantress-Lodato

Copyright © 2017 by Sally Vantress-Lodato
All rights reserved.

Published by Vantress-Lodato Enterprises/SMSW Publishing
4903 W. Howesdale Dr, Spokane, WA 99208

Co-Writer: Martin Krieg
Editor: Larry Pearson

Map Design: Karla Hutton
Photographs: Sally Vantress-Lodato

Cover Art: Electric Art Studios
Interior Design: Russ Davis / Gray Dog Press

Third Edition: Updated & Revised
ISBN-13: 978-1-880101-01-8

Library of Congress Control Number: 2017918493
    Subject Index:
        1. Voyages around the world
        2. Bicycle touring
        3. Women travelers

Previously published under:
    ISBN-10: 0-9611490-3-5 First Edition
    ISBN-10: 1-880101-07-6 Second Edition SMSW Publishing

CONTENTS

PART I
New Zealand and Australia

Chapter One:	*Seeds of the Journey*	3
Chapter Two:	*Learning the Road*	15
Chapter Three:	*Breaking Away*	33
Chapter Four:	*Travelling Within*	37

PART II
Hong Kong, China and Russia

Chapter Five:	*The Center of Attention*	75
Chapter Six:	*Russia by Rail*	111

PART III
British Isles and Europe

Chapter Seven:	*Family Ties*	139
Chapter Eight:	*Unwinding in the Rhineland*	165
Chapter Nine:	*Pasta, Problems and Pests*	177
Chapter Ten:	*Siesta Time*	197

PART IV
United States

Chapter Eleven:	*Back in the USA*	215
Chapter Twelve:	*Only My Body Not My Soul*	229
Chapter Thirteen:	*The Rhythm of Cycling*	247
Chapter Fourteen:	*Coming Home*	259

Acknowledgments

I am humbled and eternally grateful for everyone who has been a part of contributing to my bike ride, the books and my journey's forward. It is with sincere thanks for your insights, generosity and support over the past 30 years. I could not have done this without you!

To all the people around the world who opened their hearts and homes to me, thank you. Your selfless love, trust and kindness inspired me to keep going.

To my parents, family and friends who gave me their love and encouragement throughout my trip, thank you. To Mark Fromm for our chance meeting that took my life in another direction. And to Martin Krieg and Larry Pearson who contributed hundreds of hours, my sincere thanks. You helped me put meaning on paper!

To my niece Lynn Thompson who edited this edition, what a gift to work with you. Lynn traveled on book tour with me for two months when she was just nine. She has been the perfect person to help bring this story back thirty years later. Thank you for your insight and perspective.

To my husband Jim for your unconditional love and support that has always allowed me to pursue my passions while raising a family. My desire to be adventurous blended well with the traditions of family and motherhood because of your selflessness.

To my children Brian and Michelle, you are the greatest gift of all. What a privilege it is to be your mom. I love you with all my heart.

To God and the universe for directing me to share this story in ways that serve so that these experiences never end, but live on through others.

Prologue

Sweat was pouring down my face as the sun beat its brutal rays deep into my skin. My heart pounded against my chest from exertion and excitement. There was a graceful rhythm as my arms and legs worked in harmony to move my body with speed and agility across the terrain. My bare feet landed ball to heel onto the hot sandy dirt yet I did not feel the rocks or the thorns. I felt alive and free as I drifted in and out of sleep, dreaming of running across Africa.

It seemed a lifetime of waiting for this day to come. Not because I thought about cycling around the world, but because I dreamed about adventure. I longed to escape, to be free and without obligation. I was just turning thirty, yet it felt as if I had lived beyond my years and often wondered what my life was to be. I did not feel called to the normal direction most would take, yet I was raised to follow those traditions and expectations. I felt conflicted about these feelings deep inside of me. My dreams and visions were about being free, like my all time favorite movie, *Born Free*.

As with many college graduates, I wanted to take a year and travel. My urge was strong, but again the pressure to follow tradition was even stronger. Perhaps my upbringing and values influenced me more than I wanted to admit. Guilt was overwhelming at times and frequently drove my decisions to do the responsible thing. So I followed this pattern for years rising to success in a world of shoulds and have to's.

In 1987, after leaving the family business, I accepted an offer to work in banking again. Although I was genuine in my desire to return to Corporate America, I think I was driven by money; something I had never done before.

Looking back three decades later, I think my feeling of entrapment was blamed on money, but it was really my inner spirit that needed a change. The desire to acquire things can be mistaken for fulfilling goals. The problem is that this type of satisfaction is a temporary fix. A pattern is established but the long term need inward is not achieved.

Learning to fly was so unusual and far removed from my predictable life. Buying an airplane was even more off character. Looking deeper into these events, I am convinced that it was not about flying or wanting to acquire possessions, but a desire inward to disrupt tradition. And possibly validation to myself and my family that I could actually depart from the norm and take such a risk.

My professional life came easy for me. Yet my personal life did not. As a result, I moved in and out of relationships lacking direction and inner growth. It's clear to me today that I lacked self-love and confidence and expected relationships to fill that gap.

Being a runner has always nurtured my spirit and eased my mind. This constant for now nearly forty years has helped me cope with stress, solve problems and tap my creative thinking. This place I go in my mind ignites a fire and drives me forward. Preparing for my trip, I ran every day listening to positive thinking tapes. My cycling prep was minimal. I counted on my mind to help me through, as I still do today.

Becoming a pilot was not an image or idea in my dreams. It never occurred to me that I would even like it. But when I hired a bookkeeper to help me automate the family business, she was learning to fly and insisted I come along one day. I expected to be watching from the ground, but her instructor not only invited me to take a ride, he put me in the pilot's seat! It was that moment where my hands felt the power at full throttle and the wheels left the ground that I felt free. Like a bird we flew away from the airstrip and followed the beach along the Monterey coastline. To see the world from this vantage point was accelerating and empowering. There was an undeniable connection to something deep inside of me that I had to pursue. Ultimately flying would awaken my spirit and test my boundaries.

In my typical fashion, I poured my heart and soul into learning to fly. Passion drives me and this was no different. My left brain also directed me; I was always smart with money and this decision was not logical. Committed to making this work, I studied every day and flew multiple days a week. This would help me learn quicker and get my ratings in the most economical way possible.

Flying also gave me courage to challenge my life. Every time I stepped into the cock-pit I knew there was a risk of crashing and somehow I was willing to continue. I took this responsibility seriously and did everything in my power to be a proficient pilot. I took my friends and family flying and I had to be sure I mitigated as much risk as possible.

This diligence gave me the strength to overcome my fears. It forced me to think about self-talk and imagery. I had to train well, but even more important, I had to be positive and visualize successful flights and safe landings every time I went out. This reminded me of running marathons and visualizing the completion before even starting. It's really the same skill and one used all the time with athletes. Our mental screens are like watching ourselves on TV.

Looking back, flying initiated the course correction to my life. The bike ride provided notoriety and a platform to publish a book I had not planned to write. My book led me to become a public speaker, which terrified me. While traveling and speaking, I met my husband. We were married and that led me to a new career direction. Each event was life changing because it was something I never thought of doing. Nor did I think I could.

These examples demonstrate that we can choose a life we want, even when we have no clue what that means or what it might be. We can awaken our inner being and begin to listen. It can be a feeling, a connection or intuition that seems familiar but we don't know why. This voice is there but often times we are too busy to hear it or believe its truth.

And so almost thirty years later, as I relaunch my story about my bike ride around the world, I can look back and see the impact people have had on my life. The urge to travel was not about a destination but a hunger for learning and sharing. The connections are difficult to express, yet they are real. These encounters are glimpses into life beyond our own. They give us an appreciation for how love, kindness and joy are found and shared regardless of our economic status, culture, language and race. That we are all connected by something more powerful than ourselves.

When we aspire to bring meaning into our lives we no longer fear traditions or routines that might entrap us. Having nice things does not mean we are materialistic. Working an 8-5 job does not confine us. Relationships and families are not at the expense of adventure and a sense of freedom. We make the choice to enrich our lives in ways that serve others, at home, at work and in our day to day exchanges with people. Making a difference cannot be measured nor does it end. It's a way of life, an attitude and a daily habit. It takes little thought, it just is. Yet the impact is everlasting.

As I re-tell my story, I hope to bring forward how this trip began a lifelong realization that fulfillment and purpose comes from within. That our inner spirit is nurtured when we serve a greater need. That life is about people and that our interactions with each other are at the core of all we are and all we can become. Without relationships we cannot grow, we cannot love and we cannot truly live life. I hope that my journey inspires and motivates others to follow their dreams and aspirations and that new stories and new circles will be born. That our connection to one another will continue to expand in ways that can only serve a greater good.

Introduction

When I left home in January 1988, I knew it was gamble to put everything on hold and interrupt a successful career. By selling my home, car, airplane and other personal possessions, I would be forced to continue my trip when times were tough. This would give me little temptation to return home and it would force me to find solutions rather than giving up in the face of fear and adversity.

As it turns out, this trip was just the beginning of my quest. By writing this story, I began to understand more about the catalyst this trip became in rebuilding my future. That every bit of triumph, sadness, pain and at times suffering taught me more about myself. That I could not have completed this trip and learned what I did without the people who came into my life on my bike ride and the people that worked with me on this book. To put into writing your most intimate thoughts and try to make sense of them seemed at times more difficult than the bike ride itself. On the bike, I only had one job, that was get through each day. While writing this book I had to put those days into thoughts and uncover feelings that I buried just to survive. Ultimately this painful process helped me grow and better understand myself.

My journey demonstrates that each and every one of us chooses the limits which govern our lives. Through my trip, I learned that love and truth begin with one's self. If we are true to ourselves and we love and accept ourselves, then we can be anyone, or do anything, we wish. And so we begin . . .

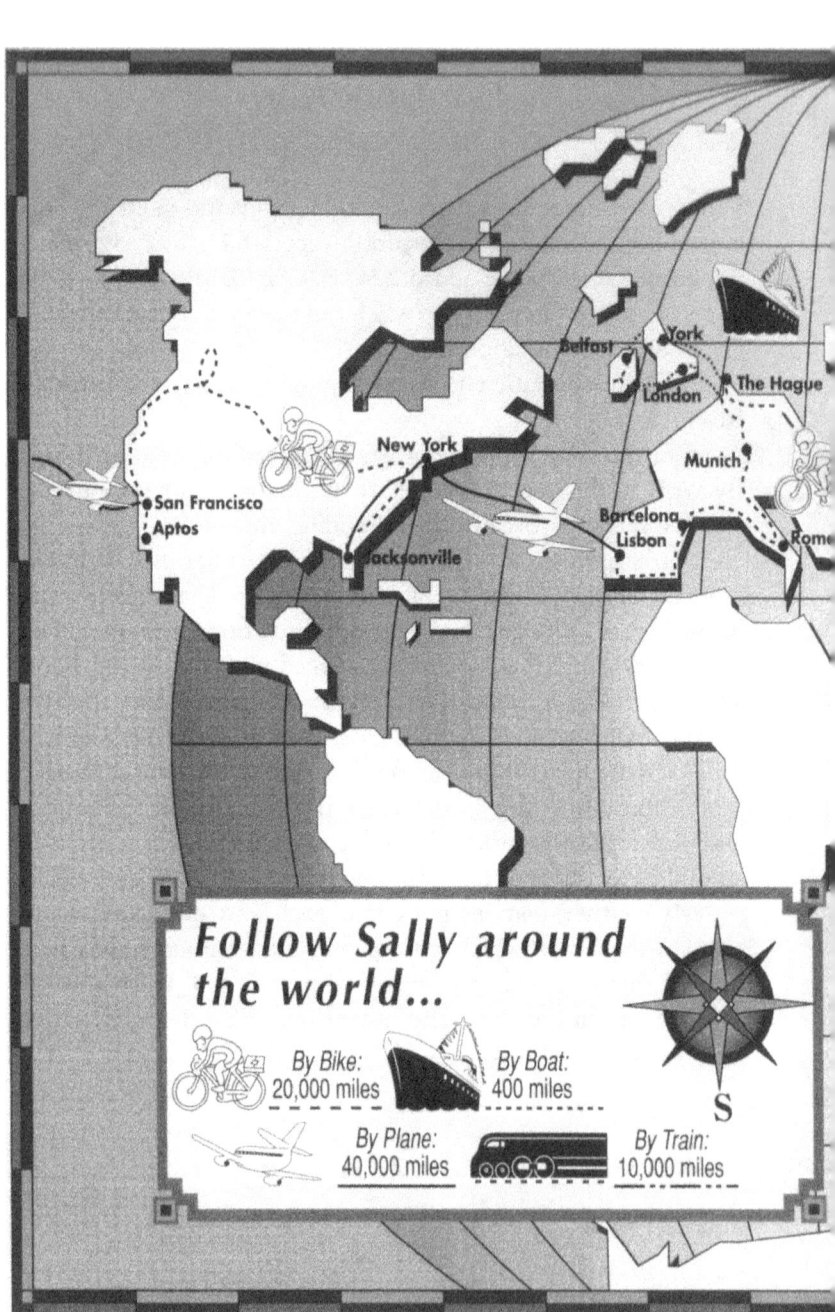

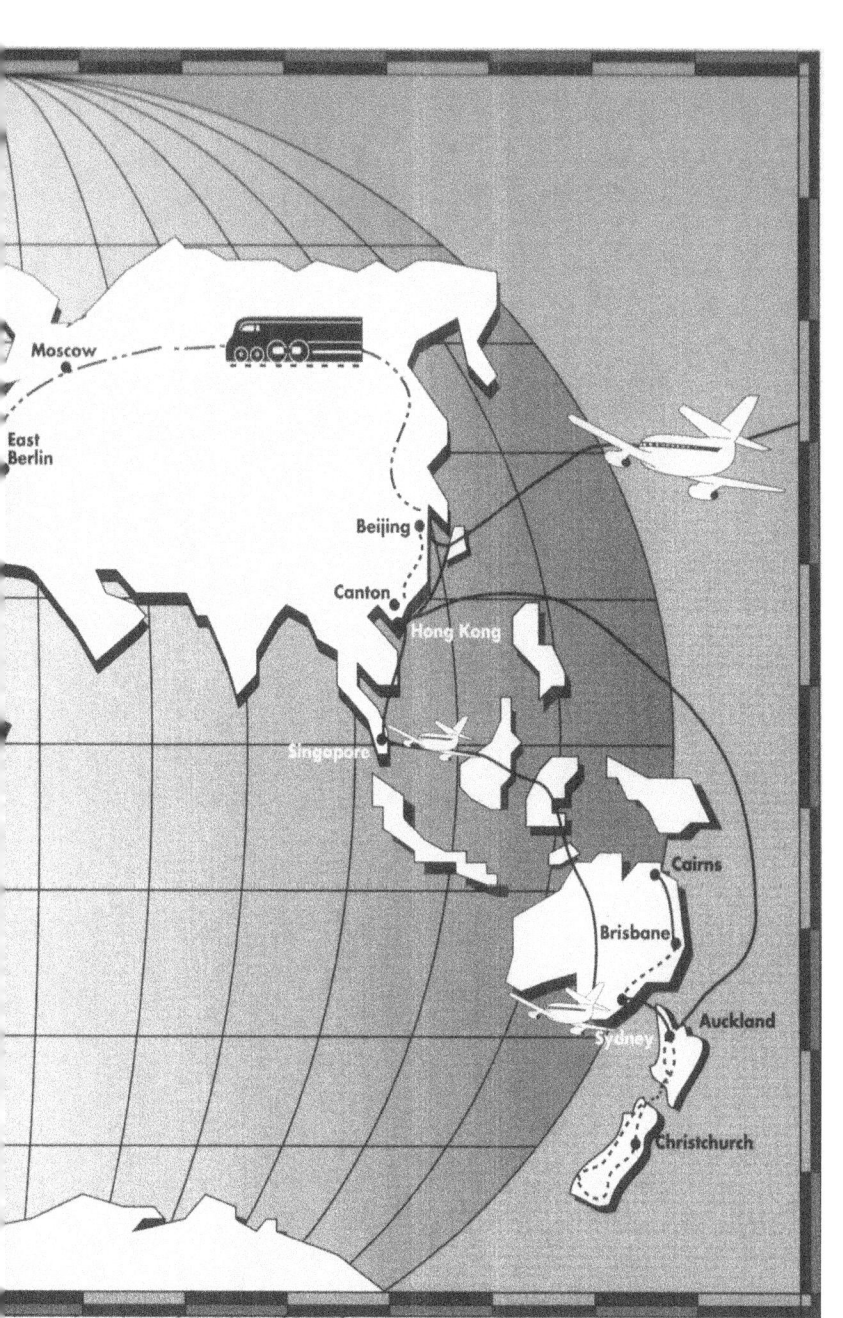

PART 1
New Zealand and Australia

CHAPTER ONE:
Seeds of the Journey

CHAPTER TWO:
Learning the Road

CHAPTER THREE:
Breaking Away

CHAPTER FOUR:
Traveling Within

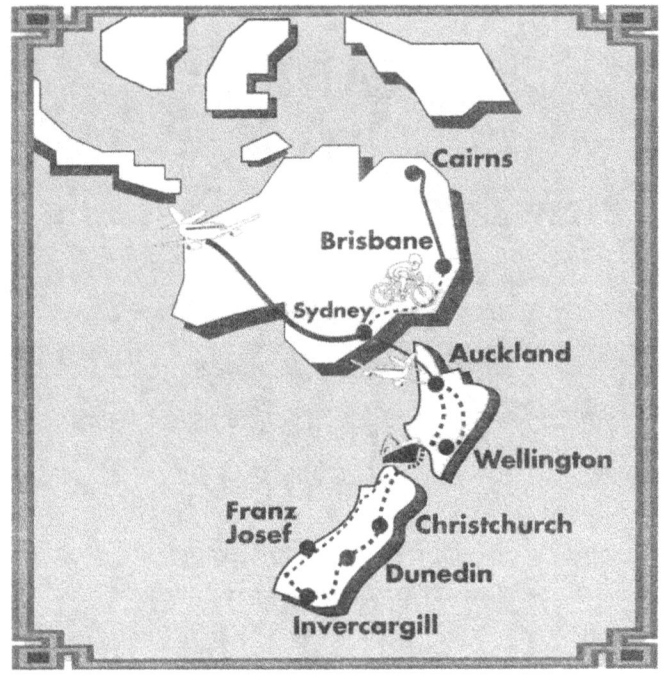

Date: *January* 14, *1988-June* 16, 1988
Bike Miles: 5,137
Route: *New Zealand: Auckland, Wellington, Franz Josef, Invercargill, Dunedin, Christchurch.*
***Australia:** Sydney, Brisbane, Cairns, Sydney.*

Chapter One

Seeds of the Journey

Cycling along an edge of the world, I was captivated by the scenery around me. Emerald vineyards climbed a steep mountain on one side of the road; cliffs dropped hundreds of feet to the ocean on the other. I could hear the surf pounding on rocks far below. I listened to the wind in the trellises above me. Ahead stood a nearly vertical wall.

"Come on," I told myself, "no walking." I began to feel adrenaline pumping through my veins. The muscles in my arms began to bulge as I braced against the handlebars. I used strength in my back to pull my legs through each laborious revolution of the pedals. My speedometer read two miles per hour.

The cars that passed me weren't doing much better. Their engines strained as they, too, tried to conquer this mountain. As they crept by, the drivers beeped their horns and shouted encouragement. I passed a group of bike riders who were having a difficult time walking their bicycles up the steep grade. They looked at me and the camping gear strapped on my bike in disbelief. Sweat covered my body; I felt like I was conquering the world as I assaulted the summit. Nothing was going to stop me.

After six miles and three hours of this exhilarating ascent, I reached the top. I yelled. I celebrated. I jumped up and down. But unfortunately, not for long.

Four more miles of up-and-down gravel road awaited me. As I wound around one switchback after the next, nobody passed. I had this deserted world all to myself.

I was pushing beyond any limits I had known—or ever dreamed I would reach. All I had experienced as a businesswoman were boundaries that kept me safe and secure. But this journey was showing me that the heights and depths my life could encompass extended far beyond my wildest imaginings. This trip was proving to me that limitations are self-imposed. I could be anyone or do anything that I wanted. I need only believe in myself…

Just a few months ago I was completely oblivious to bicycle touring. During a two-week vacation between jobs, I flew my airplane to the San Juan Islands in Washington State. This trip was a huge adventure for me. First, I had not flown alone this far away. My flights involved taking people places they needed to go. To prepare, I took extra lessons on how to land on grass and dirt runways since I did not know what islands or airstrips I would end up at. I was nervous and excited. This was way beyond anything I had ever tried before. Equipped with a bicycle, a sleeping bag and an ice chest backpack, I was alone and without a plan. I ended up in Friday Harbor, a thousand miles from my home in California.

I met Mark the next day while boarding a ferry to Orcas Island. Mark stood six feet tall, had brown eyes, thick dark hair and a three-month summer tan from bicycling. He spoke with a New York accent. We talked over coffee on Orcas Island, and then set off for a day's ride together. We pedaled through gorgeous rolling fields sprinkled with wild flowers. Although I wasn't a cyclist, Mark encouraged me, and I began to feel a whole new sense of rhythm and freedom as we pedaled along the undulating terrain. I was completely taken by the outdoors and the beauty that surrounded me. Traveling on a bicycle gave me the opportunity to be close to nature, people, and myself. There were no barriers: no windows or car doors that kept me from seeing, smelling, and feeling the beauty of the land.

We talked throughout the day, covering many subjects we both enjoyed. I felt exhilarated and alive. We spoke confidently about our dreams.

Mark was completing a bicycle trip across the US. A former engineer and salesman for a chemical supplier, he had left the working world and placed his belongings in storage for this three-month trip. "You know, Sally," said Mark as we cruised along, "if you can pedal 20 miles over these hilly roads on Orcas Island with that crazy pack on your back and old 12 speed bike, there's no reason you couldn't cycle across the country."

After a day of cycling, we wanted to spend more time together. We were in a natural paradise and infatuated with each other. The real world was forgotten while we covered one Island after the next, cycling, hiking, running, and laughing.

A few days into our travels, I suggested a sunset flight over the islands. "Yeah! " Mark exclaimed. "I've never been in a small plane before. I'd love to go."

We returned to Friday Harbor and saw two cyclists we had met on Orcas Island. We invited them to join us. They excitedly jumped on their bikes and we all pedaled to the airport where my plane was parked. My three passengers—all first-time flyers in small planes—smiled nervously. Everyone watched intently as I went through my checklist. I could feel their anxiety. I turned to them with a smile and said, "Here we go! It's going to be beautiful up there." Tension eased as I pushed the throttle to full speed, sending us hurtling down the runway.

As we lifted into the air, excitement replaced fear and my companions began to take photographs. We were like a bird, gracefully flying in one direction, then turning and flying in another. With each bank, the plane offered perfect aerial views of the islands. Clouds formed whimsical shapes and displayed dynamic blends of reds and oranges as the sun worked its way toward the horizon. When dusk arrived we turned west, taking one final look at this heavenly setting. After landing, we stood talking about our adventure in the sky. We had seen the San Juan's from a spectacular vantage point.

For 10 days Mark and I cycled around the islands, flew to Canada, and took ferries to various destinations. Somehow I sensed this was only the beginning; I was gaining a whole new perspective on traveling. It was becoming clear why I had met Mark. He had planted the seed that would take my life in a new direction.

After returning home to the workday world, I couldn't focus on my new job. My mind continually drifted back to the San Juan Islands and forward to the possibility of traveling. Mark cycled down the Pacific Coast and stayed with me off and on during his forays around California. This accentuated the restlessness I was already feeling. Mark came home excited one day. "Sally!" he exclaimed waving a letter in his hand. "I received a response from my friends Audrey and Tom in China. They're anxious for me to visit for a month. Yeah! But why stop in China? Why not circle the globe?"

When Mark got the idea to cycle the world, I knew my life would change. How could I watch him plan such a trip while I continued to live a structured and regimented life? My urge to travel was derailed before. All these feelings inside and desires to travel were awakened in the San Juans. It wasn't about Mark or riding a bike, it was so much more. It was this deep feeling of adventure and freedom without knowing anymore.

Meeting Mark was more than a coincidence and it was not about the relationship. It was a way out. This urge to travel was much too important and I had to do this for me, not for anyone else. When I dreamed of travel, I had not considered how or where I would go. That did not seem important, but a meaningful trip did. Now meeting Mark, it was clear, I could use a bicycle as my mode of travel. I would pedal around the world even though the the furthest I had ever cycled in a day was 30 miles!

The great adventure I was now embarked upon had been deferred twice. After graduation from college in 1980 I wanted to travel, taking six months to a year, but my teachers and family warned me of a coming recession and the probability of scarce employment when I returned.

Heeding their advice, I went to work for Crocker Bank two days after commencement. In my usual gung-ho way, I spent five ambitious and rewarding years with the bank, obtaining the title of assistant vice-president. I became deeply involved in advancing my career, looking for happiness through my achievements. These efforts only provided short-term satisfaction and did not nurture my deeper needs. Inside I was questioning my happiness.

Eventually, the confines of banking became increasingly frustrating. Due to the high interest rates, high debt and poor company performance, banks were unwilling to take risks. I loved working with companies and strategizing on how to help them grow their business. It became impossible to get loan credits through the systems as bank leadership began to play the CMA game. This environment was stifling with no end in sight. My mother had been recruiting me for a few years to help her grow her commercial design business. Finally, I left banking and agreed to help her for a few months. A two-month stay turned into a three-year career, as I once again ignored my inner urge to travel.

During this time I could see myself getting more restless. I stumbled on the chance to fly. This was not a life dream or something I ever thought I could do or afford. Somehow, I felt called to fly and so I went after it with conviction and purpose. This endeavor rattled many inner beliefs.

School and testing was not easy for me. I did not have good study habits or desire. Yet when I decided to obtain a real estate license in college I aced my written exam. It felt like I was another person walking out of the exam room so quickly and confidently. The flying exams were the same way. I know I had to study much harder than the average person, but I learned when a subject was something I cared about, testing came much easier.

Flying taught me a lot about myself. It gave me a sense of freedom and passion. I would come to learn so much from this seemingly extravagant endeavor, that ultimately it kept me diverted while life prepared me for the world journey to come.

Even though I had always enjoyed working for educational and personal growth, my lifestyle began to own me and this made me feel anxious and unclear about my future.

My life had become more materialistic. Working for money and spending it on possessions made me feel like I had lost touch with what was important in life. Even though most people viewed me as happy and successful, in reality, I felt lost and did not have a sense of direction or purpose.

Cycling in the San Juans had whet my appetite. It seemed my time to travel had finally come. I still doubted it. So I decided to test my decision to go and put all my belongings up for sale. If everything sold easily, I reasoned, then it was meant to be. But if selling my possessions became difficult, then perhaps this was still not the right time to go.

Excited, scared, and very thankful—everything sold easily and quickly! My home went for full asking price in less than a week, my Piper Arrow plane sold over the phone, and people flocked to buy my furnishings and even some clothes. Suddenly, anxiety set in. What had I done? All my hard work to accumulate and settle was gone overnight. Soon, however, my doubts were replaced by excitement and a sense of freedom. It was happening, I was going to ride a bicycle around the world!

How was I going to do it? I wasn't much of a cyclist nor did I know the first thing about fixing a bike, camping, or living on the road. The odds were against me. I couldn't speak another language, was afraid of the dark, had not changed a flat tire or even pumped up my own tires! But an old Chinese proverb reminded me that the longest journey begins with but a single step.

It was probably best that I had not put a firm plan together where the scope and details would have discourage me from going. Compared to my safe and secure life, this seemed crazy. Plunging into something new generally meant figuring it out as I went. Preparing for this trip was no different except that the consequences were far greater. My mind had to be strong. All the preparation in the world would not matter if my mind faltered.

Using a bicycle-touring checklist and some help from Mark, I bought my gear, but lacked any knowledge on how to use it. In fact the first attempt to set up my tent at home failed. It made for a great laugh with my friend as the new tent collapsed to the floor. But that was nothing compared to the new portable stove. Regular gas stoves make me nervous, but this gasoline burning camping stove was positively hazardous in the hands of someone like me! Using a stove that was fueled by gasoline was needed overseas but risky for a beginner like me. Reading and following the directions was essential.

I went through numerous iterations of packing and reducing my equipment to a light, manageable assortment that would fit on my bike. Still there was too much stuff.

We would need an itinerary. Mark and I decided to begin in New Zealand and Australia because it was winter in the United States and summer in the Southern Hemisphere. We also felt that an English-speaking country where bicycling was common would help us get acclimated to the road.

From the South Pacific, my plan was to go to Asia, then Europe. It was not clear where I would go for the winter. I packed for summer hoping to keep moving west, following warm weather. Then the plan was to cross America in the spring or summer. Although my time was virtually unlimited, I had mentally set a year-and-a-half guideline keeping flexible about stopping to work or live for awhile in another country. Next it was necessary to figure out the money and travel visas. Traveler's checks were the safest and preferred method to carry funds along with a Visa card if cash advances were needed. It was a choice to only carry a few hundred in currency at any one time.

Next was the airline ticket. Not satisfied with the restrictions and prices of American flights, I purchased a one-way ticket to Hong Kong. Once there, it would be cheaper to buy a round-trip ticket to New Zealand/Australia and return to Hong Kong to enter China.

My final step was to buy a bicycle. After some research, I chose a mountain bike because it was one of the few bicycles that would fit my small body (5'1" and 115 pounds)—and it was known as a good "beginners" bike, which in my case was totally appropriate. At the bike shop I was a little embarrassed asking for help. After telling him what I wanted it for, I'm sure he worked hard to keep from laughing. I didn't even know what a derailleur was—the shift mechanism on the rear axle—and he knew it!

After packing my new Univega mountain bike with the 65 to 70 pounds of gear, I prepared for the last phase of my departure—saying good-bye at the farewell party my friends Nancy and Evelyn had arranged.

Nancy's home overlooking Monterey Bay buzzed with conversation as 30 of my family and friends talked with Mark and I about our trip. There was such extreme emotions in everyone: from wonder to sadness to fear to the uncertainty of not seeing me again. I felt my family's concern as they tried to celebrate my final night with me. We had shared so much together. They had seen me grow frustrated with my life, yet they could not feel my pain inside. And therefore they didn't fully understand my need to go. But as always, they supported me.

The mood changed to gaiety as I opened gifts. The ways in which people wanted me to remember them ranged from a cushioned bike seat cover to money for phone calls to playing cards and a mini flashlight Mark and I said our goodbyes and I embraced everyone for the last time. Inside my heart felt sadness for those I was leaving behind; many would live vicariously through my trip. It was an adventure of a lifetime for me and they were returning to work on Monday. Still, I was too excited to sort out my emotions and wanted to stay strong—convincing myself I really knew what I was doing this for. "You take good care of her," my family and friends warned Mark. They didn't want to contemplate that we would separate.

The party ended and a sleepless night followed. Anticipation of what lay ahead kept me awake for hours.

In the morning, it was time say goodbye to my best friend Toshia. My loyal Australian shepherd mix was my devoted sidekick, roomy and jogging buddy. For the past nine years she was the most dedicated, smart and loving dog. Leaving her behind was heartbreaking. It was time to load our boxed up bikes into my mother's station wagon and head for the San Francisco airport.

I could sense Mom's embattled heart. It was always clear that she loved me and wanted the best for me. She also knew that she had to let me follow my heart. But at this moment she didn't know whether to offer encouragement or concern. Little was said for the next two hours en-route to the airport.

While checking in our bikes, we found that they were still eight pounds overweight (the U.S. weight limit is 70 pounds per person). We raced the clock unpacking boxes and stuffing the excess into our carry-on luggage as Mom nervously paced the lobby. The hour we had planned for visiting turned into an anxious weight-checking game. We finally finished moments after the last boarding call was announced.

Excitedly, Mom kissed me good-bye. "I love you Mom," I said looking into her eyes. There was so much still to say but our time was up. It was a race across the terminal to get to our waiting plane. Five minutes later we were fastened into our seats and soaring off the ground. It was the beginning of a new year—January 1988—and certainly the beginning of a profound new experience in my life.

Once off the ground, I breathed a huge sigh of relief, yet a ten-hour flight to Tokyo and another four hours to Hong Kong lay ahead. I passed the time reading Shirley MacLaine's *Dancing in the Light* and another book entitled *Centering*, which discussed meditation and focusing one's mind. It was clear to me that mental strength would be just as important as the physical endurance to get me through my journey. The month before leaving the majority of my time was spent prepping my mind. I read *Silva Mind Development*, a book that Mark recommended, which described accessing the right side of the brain. I considered taking a course on Silva Mind Development during my trip if the timing worked out.

We finally arrived in Hong Kong and walked down a huge ramp that deposited us in the middle of the terminal. Immediately we were pounced on by throngs of solicitors offering everything from rooms to souvenirs to clothing. The airport was crowded and very confusing. Foreign voices called out over loudspeakers. Bells sounded. The smell of a new country filled my nostrils. It was a challenge to find our way through the swarms of ambitious salespeople who anxiously waved their business cards each claiming a better rate than anyone else.

We had to choose our hotel carefully; many inexpensive places were tucked far away in the countryside, required long ferry rides or stood at the top of endless stairways. Because I had been to Hong Kong on a business trip, I knew there were hotels on Nathone Road. We left our bikes and luggage in airport storage facilities and boarded a local bus headed for Nathone on the Kowloon side of Hong Kong. (Like New York City, Hong Kong is made up of an island that comprises the financial district, and a mainland side. The mainland, or Kowloon, attaches to the New Territories, the part of Hong Kong which backs upon communist China).

At the Kowloon Hotel, a low-budget facsimile of the plush and beautiful Kowloon Hotel known the world over, we were greeted by Mr. Li, the owner. A tall, well-dressed man, he offered us a room for 90 Hong Kong (about $24). We took it; the shower and bathroom were down the hall.

The bathroom was a prefabricated fiberglass unit no bigger than an outhouse. The floor slanted downhill. Using the shower required skill. I was sandwiched between the sink and toilet as water sprayed recklessly throughout the entire bathroom. Somehow I managed to keep my clean clothes dry and stay upright.

I suspected this was luxury compared to what lay ahead.

After consulting a resource book on travel in China (referred to by travelers as the *Lonely Planet Green Book*), we went to look for cheap airline tickets to New Zealand and Australia. Hong Kong was much as I had remembered it. The streets were as busy as ever and the alleyways were filled with merchants all selling cheap products. It was slightly cooler and less humid than during April when I had previously visited, but the January humidity still tired me.

After hours of searching and talking with various student travel centers, we discovered that the information in our book was outdated. Frustrated, we returned to Kowloon to work with Tony, a middle-aged Chinese travel agent we had met while sitting in a cafe. Tony would become a friend and good contact for me during my trip.

Although all the other travel agents told us it would be 30 days before we could book a flight to New Zealand, Tony somehow moved us to the top of a 26-person waiting list. He even got us 10 extra kilos weight allowance for our bikes! We had left the States unaware of the overseas weight limit for luggage of 20 kilos per person (44 pounds).

On the following morning, we took a taxi to the Hong Kong airport, picked up our bikes, and repacked them down to what we thought was 30 kilos. I put my bike tools, stove and other small heavy items in my day pack. We checked in after waiting in the usual long lines for international flights, only to find that we were still five kilos (10 lbs) overweight. That would cost us $80.

We urgently ripped the bicycle boxes open once again and repacked them. The clock was ticking as our boarding time closed in. Luckily, this time the bikes passed. Struggling down to the gates with all the extra luggage in my hands and on my back, I faced a problem of my own creation. With some tension building between Mark and me, my negative energy must have filled the room.

Mark walked through security without a hitch, but as I walked by the security checkpoint, all the bells rang. Busted, I thought. Everyone looked at me as I was escorted to the side where I set down my pack. I felt like a criminal as the security people searched through my bags. They inspected my tools one by one, looking for secret compartments. Eventually they gave up and sent me on my way.

This episode taught me the advantage of projecting myself in a positive and unthreatening way to people. I never was searched again during my trip, even though the same tools and gear accompanied me at all of the other security and border checks throughout the world.

We arrived in Singapore at 1:30 pm. During our eight-hour layover before the flight to Auckland, we took a city bus tour. It seemed as though we would never reach New Zealand. With so much anticipation, the adrenaline flowed and yet we could not burn it off. We waited some more.

Finally, we boarded the Singapore airliner headed for Auckland. Nine and one-half hours later, we touched New Zealand soil! We had spent 30 hours in the air since leaving San Francisco 72 hours earlier. And yet, the waiting was still not over.

New Zealand requires all arriving airplanes be sprayed to prevent the spread of insects. So a half-dozen agriculture inspectors wearing fumigation suits boarded our airplane and proceeded to spray us down. I buried my head and held my breath. After a minute I gave up, but they kept spraying. We sat in the mist for 10 minutes.

Once off of the plane, it took three more hours to assemble the bikes, change money, and clear customs, immigration, and agriculture inspections. Tired but excited, I walked my loaded bicycle out the doors of the airport and inhaled my first breath of New Zealand air. I had arrived!

Chapter Two

Learning the Road

Straddling my bike, I secured my right foot in the toe clip and raised my leg for the first downward stroke. Pushing on the pedal reminded me of lifting weights back home. This can't be, my thoughts raced. The resistance was startling. My focus on each pedal stroke, only propelled me inches forward. Overwhelmed by this, I wondered how was I going to ride up a small hill let alone a mountain pass!

My new red bike and bright red touring packs wobbled left and right as I cycled away from the airport. My face registered fear and determination. Gripping the handlebars and locking my jaws I focused was on the road ahead.

Why hadn't I practiced riding this bike loaded with gear? What had I been thinking? My inner voice began debating this. Yet practicing first with all this gear might have convinced me about how difficult and unprepared I was to make this trip. My thoughts raced from one scenario to another, questioning my predicament. Calming down I thought about other events in my life where I had just plunged forward without considering the alternatives. Flying was certainly a good example. I pondered how many things would not have happened if I had analyzed everything. As a doer, not a thinker this worked to my advantage and other times not; but it was my pattern, part of my personality.

Mark rode ahead, excited to be on the road again. The heavy load on my bike convinced me that the white line was not really painted on straight. My bike rocked and swayed and it felt like I was learning to ride all over again.

To add to this confusion, everyone was driving on the "wrong" side of the road. It was necessary to switch my mirror to the right handlebar, but each time I glanced into it, my hand simultaneously turned my bike toward the direction of traffic. This would surely cause an accident.

Totally confused by the direction of travel, I turned into the oncoming cars at the first intersection. Quickly pulling to the side of the road to safety, I walked my bike across the street, remounted and pedaled off.

The first major town we arrived in was Manukau, 10 miles from the airport. We bought a map of New Zealand there and began to study the country.

Two major islands, called simply the North Island and the South Island, make up most of New Zealand. The entire country compares in land mass to the State of Colorado. Over-population isn't a problem: three million people and 60 million sheep live in all of New Zealand. More than half the people are in the Auckland area of the North Island. Only 650,000 people inhabit the beautiful South Island.

Following a tip we had received from a local cyclist, we looked up Danny, the owner of the Cycle Warehouse. Danny, who regularly bicycle-toured on both islands, mapped out our route and gave us the names of friends and family to call and possibly stay with. What luck! Just hours into New Zealand and we were off to a great start! Leaving Manukau, we arrived at our first "round-a-bout". Mark pedaled confidently into the maze of circling cars. I watched this procession of vehicles, each jockeying for the best position to leave or enter the swirling mass of confusion. I was trying to figure out how to make it through. After about five minutes, I summoned enough nerve to venture into the crazy intersection and turn off in a southerly direction toward Drury.

It was getting late and we needed at least an hour of sunlight to cook dinner and pitch our tent. We began looking for a place where there was running water. We stopped at a rugby field next to a restaurant. The fish and chips owner gave us all the water we needed. There was a nice picnic table to cook on too. This was our first day in New Zealand and we celebrated over a bottle of champagne. Reminded of the good times in the San Juan's, we laughed with each other.

Awaking full of energy the next morning, my excitement propelled up as I wondered what the first full day on the road would bring. After drinking a cup of coffee and packing my gear onto my bike, it was time to cycle. The sun was rising into the clear blue sky.

Pedaling along the quiet country road, gave me a chance to think. It was hard to believe I was really here. Back home at this time in the morning, I would be finishing my daily run. Soon after, dressed in a suit, equipped with a briefcase, and among the hordes of commuters inching their way to work. This morning was different. Wearing what would become my uniform, red jogging shorts and a T-shirt, a grin stretched from ear to ear as I thought about my reality. There was no going to work today this was the start of an adventure to see the world!

Cycling under the morning sun in rolling terrain warmed me quickly. The birds singing and lush greenery were treasures. There were no cars, just my bike and me. Sitting up tall and proud, my legs work through each revolution; I looked over my sparkling bike and was proud of my partner, we went well together. In the months ahead, my appreciation would grow for my bike and I would cherish the experiences and adventures that we soon would face as a team. Naming my bike "Buddy"; he would be my constant and important companion. More than just a machine, Buddy was beginning to develop a personality-at least in my mind.

After stopping for fresh blueberries and a New Zealand treat, vegetable pies, I left quiet country riding and turned on Route 2, where Mark was waiting for me. Mark frequently rode ahead. He was a stronger cyclist, and not only had he traversed America, he had cycled all his life. Mark had another advantage. He rode a touring bike which had a lighter frame, a more aerodynamic sitting position, and narrow, high-pressured tires which gave him more road speed.

Mark had stopped to show me the effect passing trucks have on cyclists. Up ahead, a big semi was headed in our direction. As it neared, I gripped my handlebars and felt a strong surge of turbulence hit me. The blast of air threw me off balance nearly launching my bike to the ground.

"Let's go; be careful though," Mark, said calmly.

Frightened, I yelled back, "What do you mean, let's go? No way am I cycling next to those trucks."

"Sally, you don't have a choice." He showed me the map and said, "If you just keep riding it's not so bad you now know what to expect. See you down the road."

Standing next to Buddy on the side of the road I wondered what to do as Mark pedaled away. There was absolutely no shoulder to ride on and navigating a straight line was still impossible. There was no doubt in my mind that my bike and I would join the ranks of dead possums that never made it across the road. Inhaling a deep breath, I patted Buddy's handlebars and said, "Oh well, here we go."

Although I returned to the saddle, I jumped off my bike every time a truck passed me. This went on for 30 minutes before summoning enough courage to follow Mark's advice. Actually, sitting on my bike was less traumatic than standing beside the road holding it. The key was to focus on riding a straight line and not veer toward the trucks. After much practice and relentless focus, it became easier and a normal part of cycling in traffic.

Looking back, it was clear to me that my fear and dislike for riding next to trucks created an adversary relationship. Changing my attitude would change the outcome. So, when a truck approached, I smiled and waved. After awhile, they began to cheer me on with a friendly honk and a wave through headwinds and during strenuous climbs.

Just as evening approached, we found a peaceful spot along the river near Karangahake, a gold mining area. We walked our bikes about a mile and then through a train tunnel to a private area where we would camp for the night. After dinner I sat watching the stars. At home I would be indoors, collapsed on the sofa, watching the evening news. My eyes began to tear as I contemplated my situation. What a privilege to be able to take a break and explore the world.

Learning the Road

During my first three days of cycling, I had averaged 64 miles a day. Each mile required intense concentration because there was so much to learn about riding a loaded bike. While cycling, my knees and neck ached. Since a friend bought me a cushioned seat cover, there was little discomfort with sitting so long even with nylon running shorts. It was important to stop every 10 to 20 miles, however, just to stretch. Counting down the miles to complete each day helped me meet my goal. But when the end was miscalculated, or there was not a place to stay, continuing on was extremely hard.

Each night when my head collapsed on my makeshift pillow, fatigued and exhausted, I wondered if cycle touring was for me. Because jogging was a daily routine, I thought this was enough to begin the journey. Each day, more aches and sore muscles appeared. I couldn't imagine a year and a half with such discomfort. Would my body get strong enough so the daily grind would be replaced with enjoyment as my adventure unfolded. It was encouraging to think back on my running days and the time it took to develop my endurance. This too reassured me that my body would adapt to cycling. It was amazing to feel so exhausted and beat at the end of each day, yet every morning my body was rested and ready to go again.

Enroute to Lake Rotoma I encountered my first stretch of gravel roadway. In New Zealand they're called metal roads. I stared down and studied the large pointed stones. I was thankful for the fat tires on my mountain bike, but wondered if even they would be wide enough. "Well, on with it," my inner voice commanded, as I inched forward.

Gripping the handlebars tightly, my bike bounced and swerved and there was little traction to steady my bike. Out of nowhere a loud roaring came from behind and there was a huge dust bowl heading my way. Yikes, this speeding car was heading right for me and I don't even know if they see me! This is it I will be swallowed up for good!

Damn, this makes the trucks easy as I scrambled to the side

of the road. In the process my bike slid out from under me as I left the hard pack in the middle of the roadway. We went toppling down into the thick, mushy gravel. Rock chips and dirt went flying everywhere as the car passed, leaving me feeling like Buddy and I had just survived a rock storm. After the deafening roar subsided, I cursed the driver and got back on my bike.

My bike was fishtailing back and forth, when I heard the sounds of another rock storm approaching. This time the car was coming right for me! I felt like I was in the middle of a racetrack. Again I swerved to the side and lost traction in the soft gravel a second time. The wind from the car covered me with dirt and another shower of small pebbles. Damn! I stood up shaking. What was going on? Nervously, I straddled my bike once again.

This went on for four miles until rejoining the pavement. Settling in again knowing the metal road was behind me, I looked up and gasped. Ahead there seemed to be a major climb. Oh, this can't be, this is not good timing. But there was no time to rest. The sun was setting and my destination was still miles away.

I searched deep within to find the mental strength to undertake what lay ahead. The evening sun continued to bake dirt into my back as I surged forward.

"Come on," I told Buddy, "we can do it."

Operating out of fear, I didn't feel at one with my body. Blood engorged my legs while my arm and chest muscles somehow managed to keep my sweat-covered hands attached to the handlebars.

Flashing back on my marathon days reminded me what it felt like at 20 miles and how another 6 miles seemed impossible. Pretending the passing cars were cheering spectators helped me believe I could make the top.

This pretend game and positive attitude kept me going. Eight tortuous miles later, I narrowed my sights on the summit.

It was true, my persistence and courage paid off. The view was breathtaking. Inhaling incredible fresh air deep into my lungs, I savored my conquest. Rejoicing my victory and shedding some tears, it became clear to me the depth it took to break through this barrier.

I hugged my bike and together we charged downhill, cruising happily at 25 to 30 mph. The warm breeze quickly dried me, leaving a layer of dirt and sweat all over my skin. I felt totally exhilarated as we raced downhill, taking the entire roadway to lean into the turns. I pretended I was on a motorcycle, maneuvering my load with care and precision. Gracefully, we leaned right and then we leaned left, enjoying a rhythm of S-turns down the mountain.

My throbbing legs and cramped knees reminded me how hard I had pushed myself. A sense of freedom overwhelmed me. I felt strong and confident. Pedaling onto a sandy road by Lake Rotoma—our destination! I parked my bike and jumped into the water clothes and all. The cold mountain lake refreshed me, adding to my happiness and excitement. It felt like I had just packed a lifetime into one day. Mark came from the campsite and gave me a big hug.

"Congratulations," he said, smiling. "You made it." He knew what it took to reach another level of cycling skill. It was another important day of learning the road.

From Lake Rotoma, we pedaled to the town of Rotorua. Located near the middle of the North Island, about midway along a volcanic fault line, Rotorua was a world-famous tourist destination. We visited its geysers and thermal springs until rain forced us into a coffee shop for two hours.

When the rain finally let up, we left town and discovered the Whakarewa National Forest about 15 miles down the road. This was a beautiful, exotic rain forest, completely isolated. We hiked down a trail and camped by a lake for the night. I was totally captivated by the life surrounding me. My eyes seemed to find any moving activity. I even watched troops of ants making their way from one tree branch to another.

The next morning hundreds of singing birds awakened me. A symphony echoed through the trees sending a chill down my spine. I pinched myself. Was I really here?

It was now a week into my trip, and the sun, which traded places with the rain, began affecting me. My fair skin had always been sensitive to sun, and my cycling attire red nylon shorts and a running jersey—gave me little protection. Fair skin and freckles were a bad combination. Thinking it would be fine, it was not and the damage was done.

My thighs glowed bright red while the tops of my hands were covered in peeled skin. Although I was miserable, I had to laugh at myself. As a child, I disliked my freckles so much that I would spend hours in the bathtub scrubbing them, praying they would go away. My brunette hair was also turning red, a color I had previously refused to acknowledge. This fair haired, freckled woman was turning into a weathered cycle tourist. Happily, it was much easier to accept my coloring now and laugh at it than in my teen years.

After an enjoyable day cycling through rolling terrain, we pulled into the Chateau Tongariro. Tucked between three mountains in the Tongariro National Park about halfway between Rotorua and Wellington, the imposing Chateau Tongariro stood several stories high. The surrounding meadow was filled with fall flowers and the warm mountain air blew softly through my hair.

That evening we decided to splurge for dinner at the plush Chateau restaurant. Inside a different reality greeted us. Freshly scrubbed waiters scurried about busily. Classical music wafted through the air. We ordered from the gourmet salad bar. As we dined, we talked about the temptations such a soft life-style could bring.

We left the fine linen, crystal, and rich paneling of this famous resort centerpiece and embraced an evening of flashlights, ground tarps, and mosquito nets. We camped in the fields below feeling rugged and free.

Finally, after 10 days of camping, pedaling, and bathing in lakes, we spent our first night under a roof. We arrived at the home of Danny's mother, Lima, in Titahi Bay, at the base of the North

Island. From our telephone conversation with Lima we had expected a spot on the floor in her converted garage.

Lima opened the door and invited us in. A pretty brunette woman in her mid-50s, she offered us some cold lemonade and a seat in her living room. She looked at my burned hands and thighs.

"Sally," she said, "you poor girl, don't you have anything to cover yourself with? How long have you been cycling "Ten days," I replied.

"The sun is very intense here," she said. "Many people come down with skin cancer. Do me a favor," she continued in a supportive motherly way, "promise me you'll be careful?"

It was touching that she was concerned; she reminded me of Mom.

We talked for an hour sharing stories about our journey down the North Island. Lima insisted that we stay in her guest room and sleep in warm beds. She showed us the hot shower and gave us full use of her home while she went out for the evening.

"Please make yourselves at home," Lima offered, "I'm sorry I already have plans tonight. I would have loved to stay and visit, but we'll talk over breakfast in the morning."

Lima showed me the house. She gave me instructions on using the appliances, TV and stereo.

I reached for her hand. "Thank you so much for sharing your home with us," I said.

The next morning Lima put us in contact with her good friend Barney, who worked for a freight company that ran a boat between the North and South islands. Barney gave Mark and I a ride to the South Island. We spent the four-hour trip eating and talking with the crew. They filled our bags with food, including a huge leg of lamb they strapped onto the back of Mark's bike. They laughed and cheered as we pedaled down the plank toward our next adventure, the South Island.

The Marlborough Sounds served as a backdrop as we cycled through the northern tip of the South Island. In the distance, sheer vertical cliffs rose powerfully from the ocean floor. Bathed in mist, these mountains surely hid great treasure. Few cars interrupted the quiet and wonder the peaks inspired. This stretch of road reminded me of the beauty and serenity I had enjoyed in the San Juan Islands. This is what I thought my days would be like when I planned my world journey. I hadn't envisioned the trucks, gravel or continuous climbing that contributed to my more difficult challenges. But each obstacle gave me a chance to learn something new about myself and for that I was grateful.

As evening approached, we found a campsite near the beaches of Cloudy Bay. A group of campers nearby busily tugged and pulled clumps of jumbo, palm-size mussels from the rocks. They put the mussels in a jar full of a special marinade. A man from the group came down to our campsite and offered us this local delicacy. Hesitating, I said "Oh, why not," as I reached my hand into the jar.

Mark looked at me in disbelief.

This reminded me about the last time I ate a raw mussel, nearly 10 years ago in college. I'd had too much vodka and had thrown up.

Closing my eyes I took a bite of the raw, slimy mussel. Surprisingly, it tasted great and I gobbled the whole thing down.

Later that evening we sang around the campfire, drinking beer and wine and eating kiwi sausage. I felt as if I was back home sharing a warm campfire with friends and family. What a day and what a combination of food! The ferry ride had included lamb, potatoes, vegetables, bread and dessert, and evening brought the raw mussels and kiwi sausage we now consumed.

I enjoyed being with the locals. It gave me a sense of belonging.

When Mark and I returned to our tent, we found it surrounded by clouds of sand flies. The Northern Islanders had warned us about these pesky biting flies, telling us that an insect repellant of some sort was an absolute necessity. We didn't believe them.

For several nights thereafter, I woke up in scratching fits, my legs covered with red spots from the flies that invaded our tent. Even during the daytime we couldn't escape the black clouds of sand flies unless we moved at a brisk pace. They even swarmed around our bikes when an uphill climb slowed our progress to only a few miles per hour.

Everyone had remedies to keep the sand flies away including "Shoo" repellent and excess vitamin B; nevertheless, they always came back for another bite. It was impossible to sit outside in peace. Many times the natural beauty, fresh air, and clean water of New Zealand nearly hypnotized me, but the sand flies were that little reminder of reality that kept me from drifting into paradise.

Enroute to Nelson we visited a local museum, swam in the Pelorus River, and pedaled two passes, stopping to rest and play backgammon between the climbs. We met Monika and Uli again, a bike-riding couple from West Germany we had seen earlier near the Chateau Tongariro. We agreed to join them at a local pub for dinner. They stayed in a bed and breakfast inn while Mark and I camped in the garden of a local church.

In Nelson a delivery man offered us a free bag of sandis (sandwiches), sausage rolls, and all kinds of pastries. I overate and ended up spending the night running from my tent to the garden, sick with diarrhea. I never thought the night would end.

I woke up feeling drugged and exhausted from the effects of all those pastries. It was January 27, my 30th birthday. Something was different about Mark. He was distant. Finally, he confronted me with his feelings. He said he felt trapped, claiming I had coerced him into traveling the South Island together. He forgot that only two days earlier he had suggested that we leave some gear at Lima's. Thinking this meant he was comfortable with our arrangement, I had left my gear. What had changed in two days? We argued for more than an hour and got nowhere. I was angry at him and wanted to get away.

We could have traveled back to the North Island at a cost of two days to get my gear, but neither of us wanted to do that. We felt a bit pressured to keep moving south and complete the circumference of the South Island before it became too cold.

Knowing we would probably part after traveling the South Island, I decided to learn everything I could from Mark about camping, map reading and survival before I was on my own. Our decision to continue south forced us to be together for the next month. We would learn some important lessons.

Riding up, down, and around the island's west coast cliffs was challenging but very rewarding. Millions of sheep occupied this premium real estate. A few simple houses stood in the middle of idyllic green pastures. We made our way to Punakiki, home of the famous Pancake Rocks and active blowholes. The Pancake Rocks with ridges that look like a stack of pancakes, rise from the bottom of the sea and reach toward the sky. Such a wonder!

We continued our roller coaster ride along the scenic west coast bluffs through Greymouth to Shanty Town. Rain replaced the flies as we pedaled toward Franz Josef, an active glacier about halfway down the west coast of the South Island. Soaking wet, we pulled into a campground, pitched our tent in the rain, took a hot shower, and headed for the laundry room. We spent the rest of the day in the kitchen, reading and trying to warm up. Happily, most of the campgrounds in New Zealand feature full kitchens and laundry rooms.

The next morning we each paid $18.75 (New Zealand dollars) for a guide and pair of heavy boots, and set off on a five-hour hike that would take us to the base of Franz Josef. The sky darkened, but it looked as though we could make it before another storm hit. I took my first few steps in what felt like army boots. I walked clumsily, wondering if these hiking boots were all that good. Not having any previous hiking experience and looking at the sheer ice walls we were about to climb, I considered backing out. But then I remembered my first mountain pass and how much it had challenged me. I decided to hike the glacier.

At times we walked quickly and softly over the crunching ground; at times we inched slowly through narrow passageways. After a morning of carefully obeying our guide's instructions, we arrived to our turn-around spot. Franz Josef seemed close enough to touch and yet it was still distant. I stood on a plateau with the cool wind blowing through my hair and I found myself absorbed by its power almost as though it would sweep me away.

After a few peaceful moments the guide told us we needed to leave because a storm was approaching at full speed. In minutes the glacier was hidden in the clouds. Feeling renewed by some unknown energy, I slid down a section of sheer ice as rocks tumbled all around us. I felt like a child as I raced to the bottom before anyone. Hiking the glacier was another glimpse into self-discovery and facing fear. Would my bike adventure continue to help me overcome fear?

I felt exhilarated and energized, ready to cycle the 24 miles to Fox Glacier. Three climbs lay ahead, each steeper than the previous one. Mist and rain began to fall after the first climb. My body felt strong pedaling through each revolution that would bring me closer to the top. It was interesting to witness my sheer determination to attack this mountain rather than pace myself. There was only 24 miles to go before dark. Approaching the last of three climbs, I pulled myself out of the saddle and raced for the top.

At the top, Mark came over to me smiling, "where did you get all your energy?"

We chuckled; neither us of had the answer. It just felt great to feel so strong.

We camped at Mirror Lake, famous for its reflections of Mt. Cook. After rising early to witness a picture-perfect reflection of the snowcapped mountain, we headed for Haast Pass in the Southern Alps.

Along the way, nearly every cyclist we encountered told us stories about the steep climb and the flat tires caused by 25 miles of gravel roads. By this time, I'd found that most everyone complained about steep passes. Sometimes it was better for me not to know what was up ahead. This would cause me to worry about the climb rather than enjoy the adventure of it. This mindset helped me overcome the anticipation of steep climbs and begin to appreciate their contribution to my journey.

As I cycled toward Haast Pass, I bucked strong headwinds while I pedaled up a constant incline for 40 miles. My reserves were drained. Mark felt strong and kept pushing ahead. My body was weak and fatigued. I had woken that morning with flu-like symptoms. Feeling defeated, I inched along wondering where Mark was. Finally he was stopped for lunch. I pulled over, got off my bike and collapsed on the grass. It was frustrating at times to keep up with someone who was much stronger and experienced. I wished my gear and supplies were with me rather than counting on keeping pace with Mark. I was pissed at him for pedaling so far ahead and not stopping earlier to eat. He wanted to carry the lunch supplies, but it was inconsiderate of him to go so far ahead before taking a break. On an average day, not being sick, riding a mountain bike was harder especially in a headwind. Mark rode a touring bike and was more aerodynamic. My handlebars perched me upright without any options to adjust my position. There were times like this I wished I didn't have a mountain bike. It was demoralizing and exhausting.

A few hours later we arrived at the base of Haast Pass. Mark went on and I stood there staring at the wall-like climb. Wishing for a motor, I had no choice but to start pedaling.

The wind was relentless and continued to blow in my face as I stood on the pedals pulling my loaded 110-pound bike forward. With each stroke, the pain sunk further into my body. My stomach tightened. Pushing down hard on my pedals and pulling up on my handlebars, my speedometer read one mile per hour. I swayed my body from one side to the next with every stroke. The road was narrow and cars passed close by. It was difficult to stay in a straight line and have enough momentum to avoid falling over. My arms quivered and my hands were losing their grip; my head was pounding and my knees just couldn't take anymore.

Quickly I squeezed my brakes and released my feet from the toe straps. It's incredibly difficult to stop on such a steep ascent without just falling over. Discouraged and exhausted, I leaned forward and mustered the strength to push Buddy the last hundred yards on foot. The two-mile climb peaked at 1,740 feet. Steeper passes surely lay ahead, and they would no doubt get easier as my body and my mind grew stronger.

After a few more days of riding, we stopped for a two-day rest in Te Anau, a popular place for taking day trips to Milford Sound. We toured the visitor's center. There in front of me was a poster-size photograph of travelers hiking through Fiordland National Park, my heart stopped and I gasped for air. No, this can't be, as my head turned away for a few seconds and then turned back to look once again. Sure enough, my best friend, Evelyn, and two of her friends looked down upon me in this almost life-like picture. A free-lance photographer had taken this photo of Evelyn when she was here in 1984. I grabbed Mark, and we both stood there in disbelief. My eyes watered as I thought about home and my friends and family. Knowing Evelyn was unaware of the photograph, I bought a copy and mailed it to her.

It was hard to leave the visitors' center knowing I was leaving my best friend behind once again. Evelyn and I had shared a lot together. We ran on the beaches back home, went on bike rides, played racquetball, windsurfed, water skied, and flew in my plane. We believed in a lot of the same things. Seeing her also reminded me of my dog, Toshia. Evelyn was taking care her for the first part of the trip.

There were days like this that I felt lonely and homesick. I pondered how much I had given up to make this trip. There would be times that I would feel as if I was just surviving. But somehow I was learning that the tough and lonely times would be outweighed by the adventure and changes in my life that I was seeking. I felt that change occurring inside of me.

Turning back one last time to say goodbye to Evelyn, I wiped the tears from my eyes.

Rain would become my new adversary. For the next week, the cold wet weather dampened our spirits and made every task a chore. After pedaling down through Invercargill on the southern tip of the South Island, we headed to the Catlins State Forest area. Hoping for better weather, we decided to cycle an 80-mile stretch of gravel. The rain never stopped and neither did we. With my jacket zipped to the top and my hood covering all but my nose and eyes, we tackled the mud and thick gravel.

Surprisingly, I stayed positive and upbeat. People along the way served us hot tea and biscuits, giving us a warm place to take a break from the rain. Even so, we ended each day setting up camp and cooking dinner in the rain. Each evening we looked into the gray sky hoping for a brighter tomorrow. We went to sleep each night to the sound of rain hitting our tent. The rain had imprisoned us. It was a shame not to be able to really see one of the most beautiful and secluded areas in New Zealand.

After a while, my skin began to shrivel. With so much rain, it was impossible to dry out. I started and ended each day putting on wet clothes. At times, my bicycle crank would hardly turn because it had so much mud and grit around it. Slowing down or stopping stained my wheel rims with mud.

We kept going, knowing we had a warm house waiting for us. Finally, we arrived in Dunedin, a town on the southeast coast of the South Island. We stayed with some college students referred to us by a family in Invercargill. We spent the next four days drying out and recharging ourselves. We toured Dunedin and the surrounding areas by bike.

Dunedin was a college town full of beautiful old buildings. It had a Scottish flavor with immaculate streets, many trees and colorful flower gardens. Ducks, geese and pigeons begged for food from passers-by. We enjoyed hot, home-cooked meals and watched the Olympics on television. Our stopover was a pleasant change of pace.

We left Dunedin and climbed five miles right into a cloud. The local folks along the way stood in their front yards cheering before I disappeared into the fog. The eerie quiet was fascinating. My view and surroundings disappeared as I ascended up. My body felt strong and ready for the road once again. It seemed that no matter how miserable the weather became or how fatigued my muscles got, a short break recharged me. More than just a break, the kindness of people everywhere inspired me to keep going. I crested the summit and coasted slowly down the other side to prevent hypothermia and to keep from skidding or losing traction in the water and puddles. Because I wore shorts in the sun and rain, the wind-chill traumatized my legs. In time, I would learn the value of long cycling tights.

Cycling yet another day in the wet, I pleaded for the rain stop. Please, anything but rain, I hollered. Well the rain quit, only to be replaced by eight days of strong northwesterly winds from the east coast through the Canterbury district. The prevailing crosswind tested my ability to ride straight and stay upright. Thinking about my flying days, I recalled the technique of tipping the wing of the plane into the wind, to keep the plane tracking straight. Leaning sideways into the wind helped keep my bike parallel to the edge of the road. I survived eight grueling days of howling wind by distracting myself with positive thoughts, singing and whistling.

Eventually, nature's fury won out. As I was climbing a four-mile mountain pass toward Blenheim, the closer I came to reaching the top the stronger the wind blew. Trying to ignore the force of the wind, I sang louder. Approaching the final corner near the top, the roaring and howling wind felt like a tornado. My hands squeezed tightly around the handlebars bracing Buddy with all my might. Suddenly, a tremendous gust of wind hit us from the side blowing me off my bicycle and sending Buddy crashing to the ground!

Scrambling to my feet in disbelief, I was scared to get back on my bike. After three false starts, I successfully stayed on. Finding every ounce of strength, I pedaled down the hill fighting this incredibly strong headwind. Typically a descent like this would be a reward of coasting at 25 mph. Not today and not on this hill. Pedaling into the wind my odometer registered only five mph.

As I came around the base of the mountain, I turned and bucked a strong crosswind that continually blew me into traffic. It was impossible to hold a straight line, and the unpredictable gusts sent Buddy and me out of control once again.

After a few near misses with cars, I surrendered and jumped off. I walked for two miles, leaning my bike close to the ground so that the wind wouldn't pick it up. Finally I was able to get back on my bike and ride. Wondering where Mark had gone, I found him waiting on the side of the road muttering about the day. Collapsing to the ground, I felt defeated.

Chapter Three
Breaking Away

By the time we took the ferry back to the North Island, Mark and I stopped trying to "be nice" to make our journey together somewhat pleasant. It was time for me to travel solo. Leaving my gear behind was a poor decision on my part. It forced me to travel with Mark for too long.

After arriving at Lima's, I excitedly yet nervously gathered my gear and began packing my bike. My mind began churning out a series of questions. Why had our relationship turned so sour? Why couldn't Mark express his feelings about the friction that had developed? Why did I stay, I could have turned back? It was always the plan to go alone, but I did not anticipate the adversity we both felt. What would it be like to continue alone where all my decisions and consequences would be mine to own. I would be responsible for my days, my achievements and failures.

I was looking forward to being on my own. But at the same time I was scared. There was a lot of unknown ahead and a woman traveling alone added more complexity and logistics. It could get lonely too.

I knew it was going to be a long journey ahead. I prayed for strength, insight and safety.

When it became clear I was leaving, Lima objected. "You're not going anywhere in this weather," she said. Looking at Mark, she continued, "You just let Mark keep taking care of you."

Even though I wanted to scream, I smiled and replied, "I can handle a little wind and rain. Besides, Mark and I will do OK on our own. But thanks Lima."

I felt bad for Lima, she would certainly worry; as a mother, it would be difficult not to. I'm sure she thought of sending her own daughter out in such conditions and it upset her. I stayed positive, giving her assurance that it would be fine and it was time to go alone.

Mark quietly packed his things. Nothing much was said.

"Well, you just be careful and make sure you keep me posted as to how you're doing," Lima said as we hugged each other. Mark left the room; he couldn't say good-bye. It was a curious and unsatisfying end to our time together. We didn't know when, or if we would see each other again.

I left late in the day and pedaled through a fierce storm as I began my journey alone. My mind drifted back to the marathon I had run in Sacramento a month before this trip started. It was a stormy December day. Rain pounded the streets while thunder roared and lightning cracked across the sky. My friend Evelyn and I nervously watched from the bus as we approached the starting line. This would be my third marathon and Evelyn's first. Running in these conditions were concerning, but it was important for me to stay upbeat for my friend.

With our jackets zipped up and hoods over our faces, we took off at the sound of the gun. We were drenched in minutes. We paced each other, disciplining ourselves to keep an 8-1/2 minute mile. The wind blew through my ears sending a chilling pain to my head. I squinted to focus on the road as the rain spattered against my face. My shoes squeaked and squashed with every step.

Ten miles into the marathon, we turned from a headwind to a crosswind and had more challenges to deal with. The wind blew my heels against my calves with every stride, making me feel like I was not coordinated. I constantly kicked myself, eventually causing bruises all down the backs of my legs. I felt like I was running drunk, and at times I wished I was.

We passed the time picking subjects to talk about. Evelyn and I had trained so much together we knew when conversations were needed to distract us from the constant pain. This was certainly a time to get involved in such discussions. We kept up our conversations for the entire 4-1/2 hours.

Crowds of people stood with their umbrellas cheering us on. Their encouragement was touching and energizing. I was wet, miserable, soaked, and shriveled, but at least I stayed warm while I ran. The spectators clapped while they were shivering. I felt blessed that they had come out to support the runners. They were there when we really needed that extra energy; it kept us going. With each cheer, I threw my fist in the air yelling "Thank you."

My mind raced ahead to my approaching around-the-world adventure. Weather like this would no doubt be present during the day as I cycled, and at night when camping. Thinking about these conditions motivated me to stay upbeat and complete the marathon despite the temptation to quit.

At 22 miles, my mind labored to stay alert and positive. Again, I contemplated quitting. My body ached, my thighs throbbed. But then I thought again about my upcoming bike ride and knew it would test me far beyond this marathon, so I pushed on.

Suddenly, the finish line was in sight and excitement filled our bodies. The crowd grew louder. Finding the last bit of energy, Evelyn and I picked up our pace. Pounding hard against the pavement we pushed our legs has hard as they would go. We grabbed each other's hands, held on tight and raced through the finish line like warriors. The crowd was screaming with excitement. We hugged each other with all our might. We had finished an incredibly difficult run by staying positive even though we both were dying inside. I would not forget this day and would look within for the drive and determination needed to survive my upcoming adventure. It was certainly a day to remember.

I arrived at the riverbank park where Mark and I had camped on our way through Wellington. The rain subsided but the wind howled. I swam in the river to wash off the road grime, then, cooked dinner under a picnic table to protect my stove from the wind. It took me forever to pitch my tent alone. I thought about how much easier this task was with two people. Anxious to spend some time with myself, I climbed in my tent. Moments later a pair of headlights illuminated the whole area.

A tall man got out of his car and said, "Hello in there."

I peeked out of my tent and saw that he was a policeman.

He asked, "Are you in there alone?"

"Is that OK?" I answered.

I was not breaking the law, but he spent the next 10 minutes lecturing me on the dangers of camping alone. Then he left. About half an hour later, he returned with a couple in a large motor home he had relocated from another area of the park.

"I want you all to camp together," he instructed. Once again, he left.

My neighbors parked so close to my tent that I thought the wind might blow their motor home on top of me. And instead of spending time with my thoughts about Mark, we visited until late. I did, however, enjoy having company. It felt good to laugh and be happy. The next morning we had eggs and toast together.

I rolled out of the park into a beautiful sunny day and allowed my mind to drift. Because the weather no longer occupied my every thought, I could begin think about my past relationships and the patterns.

It was obvious that when I met Mark I was ready for a change. My travel plans had been deferred for eight years. When he appeared in my life, I sensed it was my time to finally let go. Even though we both set off on our trip with an understanding of our individual needs, what we said we could do and what we actually did (or how we handled it) was much more difficult than we both had anticipated. Intimacy and emotion complicated our relationship, causing us both to expect things from one another. During this period, however, we had both learned some valuable lessons. In the process, unfortunately, I had allowed myself to loose some self-esteem. This was not the first time this had happened. It can be easy to give up a part of yourself in a relationship. I think that can be difficult and common for women. This caused me to be cautious about relationships and I think it contributed to my view on not wanting a traditional life.

But that, too, was something for me to explore.

After a month and a half on the road, and 2,500 miles of pedaling, my body felt stronger than it ever had. My days were enjoyable and I could begin to look forward to mountain passes and undulating terrain. My skin had adapted to the sun and I was getting a dark tan on my freckled body. My legs had grown strong and muscular. My knees and neck were beginning to heal and the pain was minimal. My bike and I began to feel like one machine; we were an inseparable team. I felt a great sense of relief being free to go on alone.

Enroute to Hawea, a car full of teenage boys pulled up alongside me.

"Hey lady," they called.

As I looked, one of the boys pulled his pants down and stuck his bare butt out the window. As they sped off, laughing, it occurred to me that this type stunt might happen more often as a woman traveling alone.

My route wandered through peaceful countryside as I headed to Mt. Egmont National Park. Cycling along a two-lane road surrounded by dairy pastures, I watched the snow-capped volcanic mountain grow larger with each approaching mile. I had stopped on the side of the road to pet some dairy calves, when a car drove up. A long-haired woman stepped out and walked toward me excitedly.

"Hey!" she exclaimed. "Where are you heading so late in the day?"

"Up the mountain to Dawson Falls to camp for the night," I replied.

"You can't pedal all the way to Dawson by nightfall, it's all uphill, ya know. Listen, my name is Shirley, and my home is only a few miles from here. It would be fun to have you stay with me and my husband. I'm on my way home to fix dinner and it's no trouble to cook for one more."

"Oh, it fine," I said. "I need to be in Auckland for a class in a few days. I was hoping to get a few more miles in tonight."

"You have more than a few more miles to the falls," said Shirley "Stay with me and get a fresh start early in the morning."

"OK, thanks for the invitation," I said gratefully. Shirley wrote down the directions and drove off.

It was just a few miles before the turn to head down her road. Shirley had an old white house with a white picket fence around it and there was laundry hanging off the veranda. I stopped in front and could see an American flag on the mailbox along with a white scroll that said "Sally" in huge letters. I was touched.

No sooner had I walked in then she laid out the ground rules.

"I cannot or will not make you feel at home," she said. "You must make yourself comfortable and make this home your home while you stay."

Her house was quaint yet warm. She and her husband, Arnie, were simple people living a simple life. They cooked on a wood-burning stove and hand-pumped water from their well. They were essentially self-sufficient and ate vegetables from their garden, eggs from their chickens, and meat from their farm animals. Remembering how complicated my life at home had become, I felt comforted to see people living a simple but very happy life.

Looking around the house, I saw that Shirley admired airplanes. Her dream was to fly on a Concorde someday. I couldn't satisfy that dream, but I could share an hour of flying with her in a small plane. "Shirley," I said, "I'm a licensed pilot. Is there an airport nearby where we could rent a plane?"

Shirley shrieked, "You really fly planes?" She turned to Arnie, her eyes beaming.

Smiling, I nodded my head. I didn't seem to care about the money; it was just more important to give something to Shirley.

"Yes, we have a small airport about 20 minutes from here," she replied.

Arnie watched the two of us excitedly planning our flight. The next evening Shirley returned from work with her boss who also wanted to come along. Our simple airplane ride had become known throughout the town. Soon, the three of us charged down the grass runway and lifted into the air. Shirley's excitement filled the cockpit as we circled high above the dairy farms in this area along the west coast of the North Island. She asked me questions about all the instruments and the flying terms that she could hear me speak into the microphone. She wanted to know everything.

It felt so good to make someone happy while sharing a part of myself. This flight made me realize how much I had missed flying. On the road, I sometimes practiced flying while cycling. I would visualize the control panel and go through take off and landing steps mentally. I had never dreamed of actually flying overseas. It was great!

The next morning we stood outside saying good-bye. In only two days, Arnie and Shirley had claimed a part of my heart. As I pedaled away, I thought about how much fun we had and how easy it was to share stories about our lives. The connection recharged me even though I would probably never see them again.

Heading east to Stratford watching Mt. Egmont was in my view all day. First, along its southern border and then while heading north toward Inglewood, I passed its eastern side. The sun was warm and the beautiful surroundings and the friendly people kept me energized throughout the day. It was becoming clear to me that my encounters with people were playing an important role in my trip. Although I traveled alone, I was rarely alone.

Reaching the coast northeast of the volcanic mountain, I pedaled along to the small town of Onaero. It was a daily routine to stop to buy groceries before camping for the night. Suddenly remembering that there were five fresh eggs in my pannier that Shirley gave me I raced out the door to inspect the damage. The eggs had been with me all day on rough roads and in hot weather, packed in my cooking pot.

Carefully, I lifted the lid off, took a deep breath, and looked inside. "They survived!" I shouted, as I threw my arms high over my head. "I can't believe it, not even cracked!" The shopkeeper came out with a customer to see what was going on. We laughed as we thought about what could have been.

As a female traveling alone and by bike, it was easy to meet people. From a passing hello to staying overnight, I was rarely alone. Cherry, the shopkeeper was another of those wonderful people that just wanted to be helpful. After my shower, she not only reduced my camping rate to half price, she invited me to have tea with her and her family. Dinner is called "tea" in New Zealand and Australia and originally comes from the Britain traditions. "Sally," Cherry said, "what you're doing is amazing. You've exposed yourself to every element by traveling on a bicycle. Your bravery is rare. You'll find many folks like us who'll help you along because of your faith. I wanted my children to meet you and listen to your stories. Thanks for sharing with us."

I was touched by Cherry's words. It was good to hear that my stories inspired people and that my trip helped others.

As we feasted on potatoes, a roast, salad and bread, a car pulled into the driveway. Cherry got up to answer the door. I heard a man's voice ask for me. Who knows I'm here and who do I know halfway around the world, I wondered?

It was Shirley and Arnie! They had driven 70 miles to find me and return the little blue coin purse that I had left on their couch. The purse had less than two dollars in it.

"Sally," Shirley said, "we searched in bushes and down dirt roads for you. I can't believe you came this far in one day."

"Shirley, you didn't need to return my coin purse," I said. "There was hardly any money in it."

"It was so hard saying goodbye this morning, and after work tonight Arnie could see I was upset that you were gone," Shirley said. "So he offered to drive me here. But we were getting worried that we came all this way and wouldn't find you. Finally, we spotted your bike in the yard."

As darkness approached, everyone exchanged good-byes and I rolled Buddy over to the adjacent campground where I would be able to sit in my tent, write in my journal and relax after such a busy day. I no sooner pounded my last tent stake into the ground when another couple insisted that I eat with them.

Joan and Ashley begged me to come to their motor home for tea, chocolate cake, and white bait, a rare New Zealand delicacy. White bait is a transparent pollywog about the size of a small peanut. It can only be found in certain waters of New Zealand. Mixed with scrambled eggs, they tasted great! Hours later I finally rolled myself into my tent and crashed.

By now it seemed that wherever I went or whatever I was doing, people appeared. Being a woman alone, it was easy for people to approach me all the time. Maybe the "umbrella effect" that I had heard other travelers talk about was beginning to come into play. The umbrella effect, they claimed, was a rule that the more people you travel with and the more you are surrounded, the more difficult it is for new people to break into your circle. So, the smaller your group, the more people you could expect to meet. According to this theory, a solo traveler could expect to involve the greatest number of people in his or her journey.

Traveling on from Onaero early the next morning, I pedaled along Mimi Gorge. It was quiet and cool as I made my way through fascinating vegetation and terrain. The trees kept the road shaded and the wind blew lightly. After a few climbs, I arrived again on the coast. It was hot and muggy. I cooled off by taking brief swims in the many rivers I encountered throughout the day. I pedaled through another gorge, and pumped through two steep climbs before I arrived in Te Kuiti, marking a record day of 87 miles.

My intuition told me not to free camp or knock on anyone's door here. Beer cans littered the side of the road leading into town and many young adults loitered in the streets. So I decided to stay in the city campground. Once there, something told me this wasn't right either, because neighboring campers confined themselves to their caravans (motor homes) with the curtains drawn. I rarely saw curtains drawn. In fact, I was impressed by the wide-open windows common to the caravans. I locked my bike and took a quick shower in the cinder block building located in the middle of this small green area.

When darkness fell, the campground became a cruising zone for low-rider cars that now slowly prowled around. A few slowed down near my tent, their occupants looking at my bike. I decided to bring it inside to prevent someone from figuring out that I was a woman traveling alone. Whenever I did share my tent with Buddy, I didn't feel alone. Sometimes during rainy nights, I would feel sorry for my traveling companion and would bring him in. It's strange but I felt better when he was inside with me, even though it was crowded and I worried that he might tip over on me.

I should have known better than to be in town on a weekend night. But calendars and watches no longer entered my mind. Happily, I was far removed from the pressure-filled days of deadlines, next-day deliveries and payment due dates. The only times that mattered anymore were sunup and sundown. I would, however, have to be more mindful of which day of the week it was.

I snuck out of the campground early the next morning. Disgusted with the conditions and lack of order, I didn't pay. Instead, I retreated to a bus stop on the other side of town where I could plan my day. Suddenly, out of the semi-darkness, a man's voice startled me. I looked up to see a tall black man with thick, curly dread-locked hair. He was a Maori, one of the people native to this land. His dark eyes looked right through me as he offered me his hand. He wanted to welcome me to the ranks of the other street people.

I tried not to act scared and looked for the good he had to offer. He had already asked me where I was from and why I wasn't married when his friend showed up. As both of them stood over me, I smiled and tried to make light of the situation. I asked them questions about New Zealand. I asked for directions. I complimented them for the freedom that their lifestyle gave them. I tried to be a friend and acted like this was a normal encounter.

When they asked me if I was afraid to be alone, I told them how great people had been and how everybody had good in them, that it was up to me to find that good. I'm sure this answer was a change for them.

"Good luck, sister, you keep on doing it," one offered as they walked off.

"Another victory," I said to myself.

It began to drizzle as I approached Te Awamutu and began to rain while I sat under an umbrella-covered metal table. I fired up my stove and drank coffee to warm up as I prepared for more wet riding. After I pedaled 40 miles in pouring rain, incredible crosswinds began to team up with the unrelenting deluge. The plastic trash bags I used to keep the gear and clothes inside my panniers dry began to leak. I turned and picked up an even stronger tailwind. It terrified me. Gripping my handlebars tightly, I studied the white line as cars and trucks sprayed dirty water all over my face.

I looked down at my speedometer. It registered 24 mph and I wasn't even pedaling! I wondered when my bike would start to hydroplane. I was beginning to panic when I recalled how flying taught me to relax in tense situations like this.

So I did what any normal person would do. I sat upright, loosened my grip on the handlebars and began to humor myself. I sang to release the tension. I laughed because this was the first time I had moved so fast without pedaling. I put my face up into the rain and began to enjoy the wonderful storm.

It worked. Just as the storm took another turn for the worse I stopped at a dairy farm. A woman I had met earlier in the day suggested I call her sister, Bev, who lived on this farm, if the weather prevented me from making my destination. The wind picked up its pace while I hurried down the driveway toward the farm. The owners, Max and Bev, came out to greet me. We raced inside as the wind howled and tree branches fell. I spent the next four days with them waiting out what would become Cyclone Bola.

My bike and I roomed together in a small cottage in the back yard. I showered and came inside to help the children, Debbie and Robin, fix supper while Max and Bev milked the cows. It was a nightly tradition: one team milked and the other fixed dinner. They rotated their chores throughout the week.

I sat in the kitchen, watching the storm through the window, grateful to be indoors. Where would I have gone in such a storm? Surely not camping. I worried about Mark. Was he OK and did he find a safe place for shelter?

Max and Bev came in drenched and muddy. After they cleaned up, we all sat down for dinner. We ate pot roast with potatoes and vegetables.

"So, Sally," Max said. "Bev's sister says you're on an around-the world trip alone. Is that true?"

"That's right, Max," I said. "I did start out with a friend who is probably in the area, but we just recently split up."

"Why aren't you scared?" Bev asked. "What about your mother? She must be worried sick."

"My parents are both doing OK with it. They've supported my need to make this journey. But they don't know yet that I'm alone. In my next letter I'll tell them."

"But what about your friend?" Bev said. "Why don't you want to be with him?"

"Mark is a neat person and we had a good time for the most part," I replied. "But I gave up my career in banking and sold my home, car and airplane because I wanted to change my life. I had proven I could be successful, yet inside I was not fulfilled. By selling everything, I knew I would continue forward even when the times got tough."

"But why alone?" Max asked.

"Because I will learn more about myself and grow more independent if it's just me. Mark also felt he needed to go on alone because it would help him understand his life and goals better."

"Wow," Max exclaimed, "you had an airplane?"

"Flying is part of why I'm here today," I replied. "I learned a lot about addressing fear and building confidence. Although I had no business owning a plane financially, I did learn some valuable lessons."

Max, Bev, and the girls sat around the table listening to me in total amazement. They didn't quite know what to make of me.

By the second day I was feeling useless. "Bev," I begged, "please put me to work. I can't just sit here and be waited on. I want to help out. You know I raised steers, pigs and sheep back home in my high school agriculture program."

"OK," Bev agreed, "come with me. You can help milk the cows." I grabbed my rain jacket, borrowed Debbie's rubber boots, and ran excitedly to the barn.

The storm had not eased a bit during the previous 24 hours. Trees Max had nourished for 18 years had been flattened. Fences were down and the animals were miserable.

The cows all lined up for their turn on the milking machine. Each one had a name; they even had an order for milking. I watched Max and Bev wash their udders. Then with their right hands they lifted the cups to the cow's teats and with their left hands put the nozzles on one at a time. Moments later I could see milk funneling through the clear plastic tubing.

I thought about my first steer, Sam. He was a cross between a Hereford and a shorthorn with brown circles around his eyes that gave him a devilish look. And sure enough, he was one of the wildest steers on the school farm. During my first day at the school farm, I was walking out to the paddock with a rope around my shoulder looking for Sam. The ground was soaked and slippery from the rain and cow manure. There was some commotion in the barn, so I headed in that direction. Suddenly I heard my name called.

"Sally, block the door!"

"No problem," I yelled back.

But I had a problem: a big black Angus that everyone was trying to catch charged right at me!

"Oh no!" I yelled, waving my hands wildly.

There was no stopping him. He put his head down and aimed for my stomach, sending me into the air and face down in the slimy manure. I lay still until my rescuers came to lift me up. I was alive, but was covered in wet manure, head to toe.

Bev's voice interrupted my daydream. "Go ahead and milk the two in front," she said.

"OK," I replied. I grabbed a suction cup in one hand and patted the cow's rear with the other.

"Now you be nice to me," I instructed my first volunteer.

"I'm new at this y'know." The cow turned and looked at me. "OK, ready? Here we go."

The poor cow. I tried to aim the nozzle for her teats but somehow always missed. After a while, I got better. Max and Bev were careful what cows they gave me; some would have had little patience.

My confidence grew, and without waiting for instructions, I took the liberty of picking my next cow. Unfortunately, I picked the wrong cow and got a hoof to the side of my head.

Max turned quickly, "You OK, Sally?"

"You bet," I replied, rubbing my head. "I'm sorry, Max," I apologized. "I was too impatient."

I became one of the family while we worked, ate and played together. Every spare moment was spent sharing stories of our lives and our countries. I felt a growing affection for my special friends. This stay gave me a new awareness and appreciation for life on a farm. I always wanted to live in the country surrounded by animals. My dad and I shared this dream, but my mother, a true city girl, did not.

I began to see how much of myself I had given up because of my ambitious quest to reach one goal after another. It was also clear how different our respective cultures were. Max and Bev couldn't begin to comprehend my previous achievements, including this trip around the world.

After four very happy days, I found myself standing in the driveway saying goodbye to these wonderful people. We stood for several minutes, none of us wanting to be the first to say good-bye. Finally they took my picture and it was time to go. I embraced Max and Bev as if I was leaving my family all over again. I pedaled down the driveway as they waved one more time.

Now heading for Auckland I was approaching a new phase of my trip. A month earlier I had registered for the Silva Mind Development course. The Silva course is one of many programs that teach people how to develop the intuitive right side of the brain. Through meditation and other techniques, the creative, nonlinear part of the brain is accessed. I felt that this two-weekend course would help me learn more about myself and also help me cope with those episodes that would challenge me both physically and mentally. Mark had taken the course in California and had highly recommended it. The Silva book had increased my interest, and now I was ready to develop those skills in more depth.

The cyclone was over but the storm continued. The visibility dropped and the rain increased as I started down Route 2, the same road where Mark had shown me how dangerous the trucks were. That seemed so long ago!

I pointed my handlebars in the direction of the wind and rode strongly and confidently. The trucks sprayed mud all over me and the wind buffeted my forward progress, but I kept moving.

Six miles from my destination, Cycle Warehouse, I was pedaling along a busy suburban street when suddenly I felt my bike sink and wobble. I stopped and jumped off. Damn, it was a flat tire.

I looked around to determine what I would do next and spotted a gas station up ahead. What luck! "Come on Buddy," I said, "someone will help us out."

The attendant greeted me. "This is not a good day to be cycling," the man said jokingly. "And it looks like you have a flat."

"It's good and flat and my first one in three thousand miles," I replied.

"I don't have any bicycle parts or tools," the man responded.

"Oh, that's not my problem," I said. "I have all the tools, tires, and tubes, but I don't know how to use them. I was shown once how to change the front tire, but I don't think I remember a whole lot. I'd like to stay inside the garage while I figure it out. It might take me all afternoon. "

By now his partner had walked up shaking his head. "You all alone in this horrible weather, dear?" he said.

"Listen," the first man interrupted, "you sit here while I fix you a hot cup of tea. We'll fix your bike, don't you worry."

He left and heated the water and brought another jacket to

keep me warm. Then the two men began. After taking all the gear off, they removed the tire and began looking for the cause.

"Ha Ha, we have it," said one of the mechanics. He pulled out a huge piece of glass, which had put a non-repairable gash in my tire. I retrieved a new tube and tire and watched intently while they quickly revealed the art of tire repair. Surprisingly, I even remembered a few points Mark had shown me back in California.

I knew that God was helping me out this time; he'd given me these men to show me how to do the repair. Gratefully, I shook their hands. I felt more confident about being alone now that I had one flat tire under my belt. I was certain, however, that my next flat would not be in front of a gas station!

Before leaving I called the Cycle Warehouse. Danny answered and sounded surprised that I was in town and had bicycled in such terrible weather. Knowing I couldn't make it to Auckland before dark under these conditions, he offered me a place to stay for the night.

I thanked the garage attendants, gathered my things, and pedaled into the rain. Following Danny's directions, I arrived at the Cycle Warehouse without delay. Cold, wet, and shriveled from the day's rainy ride, I changed into dry clothes and drank some hot coffee.

During the next three days, the first weekend of a two-weekend course, I attended the Silva class in Auckland. The timing was perfect. It was now a chance to begin searching for answers about my life. Employing an approach very different from that of my orthodox education-and completely opposite from my left-brain banking days-this course helped me to see the limitations I had placed on myself by ignoring the power of the right brain. New revelations were unfolding for me as the weekend came to an end. I couldn't wait for the open road.

Feeling like a new person, I happily pedaled north toward the Bay of Islands 240 miles away. Danny had told me about the great scuba diving there on the northeast coast.

Now with my new attitude and positive right-brain techniques, it seemed I was meeting more people. I was getting so many offers to stay overnight that I wondered if I would ever make it to the Bay of Islands. Determined to keep going, I declined several offers and kept on pedaling, anxious to see the underwater world that awaited me.

Just before dusk I arrived in Wellsford, only to find that there were no campgrounds. Eager to camp, I found a group of trees in a local park. I could hide myself there when it got dark.

Since I couldn't use any lights or fire up my stove in my hiding place, I returned to the main street to cook dinner. The owner of a fast-food diner gave me permission to use the table outside. I thought about all the nights Mark had insisted we wait until dark to pitch our tent. I appreciated the importance of this now, as a woman traveling alone.

After dark, I hopped on my bike and rode back to my secret campsite. I felt like a spy as I surveyed the area. Quickly, I jumped off, and ran into the group of trees, hoping no one would see where I went. Quietly, I pitched my tent by feel and crawled inside with my bike. Just as I settled into my sleeping bag, I heard footsteps. I lay still, careful not to move. I held my breath and listened. Recalling a new Silva technique, I closed my eyes and counted my way into a meditative state. I visualized my tent and my surroundings, seeing everything safe. I completed my exercise by placing a light around my tent as a shield of protection, and went right to sleep.

I began to practice Silva methods daily. I used their awake control system for getting up in the morning. Finding that it worked, I tried perfecting my wake-up time to the minute. I meditated three times a day even though the mosquitoes and sand flies made it difficult. This daily ritual produced a new awareness in me. I felt more at peace with myself.

Arriving in Pahia, I called Stewart, the bespectacled, fun-loving, fifty-year-old brother of a Silva classmate. He managed the Bay of Islands Swordfish Club and had been expecting me. I took a 10 minute ferry ride across the bay to the town of Russell, where I sat for a few hours in the bar of Stewart's club talking with the locals. We drank beer and ate several trays of fish and chips. Everyone was friendly and hospitable. They entertained me with stories about the famous fishing and yachting trips that keep this area alive.

The next morning eight of us plunged into the sparkling blue waters of the South Pacific. While those familiar with the area expressed disappointment at how the cyclone had stirred up the water, I had rarely seen better conditions. Since most of my diving had been done on the northern California coast where 25 feet visibility was good, this was outstanding.

I studied the many different species of tropical fish and watched curiously while this entire panorama of sea life unfolded around me. Because cycling improved my lung capacity, I could stay down after all the others had given up, and I explored more of these waters with the dive master. Once, after a sudden scare that I had lost my dive buddy, he reappeared holding a white fish. He signaled me to watch while he shook the fish back and forth gently. Immediately the little white fish blew itself into a huge ugly ball, it's skin covered with sharp points. We played a few rounds of underwater volleyball with this porcupine fish.

Seeing the underwater world of New Zealand added another dimension to my appreciation of the world's richness. It felt great to be underwater again.

I returned to Auckland in the back seat of Simon and Sharon's small car. They were a couple whom I met on the dive boat. The car had no trunk so I took off my bike's wheels, seat, handlebars, and pedals. I climbed in and Simon and his wife wrapped the bike around me for the four-hour drive south.

Simon drove like a man possessed. I didn't like all the swearing, honking and weaving. Then I remembered how I drove at home. Maybe I wasn't quite as demonstrative, but I wasn't a lot different either. I always seemed to be rushing from one appointment or class to another. I had never seen myself this way before, and promised myself that I wouldn't drive in such haste ever again.

We arrived in downtown Auckland where Simon and Sharon dropped me off on a steep hill in the downtown financial district. I took up the whole sidewalk as I tried to reassemble my bike in the midst of neatly dressed business people scurrying about with briefcases. I used to be one of them, I thought, as I stood there using a greasy rag to wipe the oil stains off of my leg. While I knew they felt sorry for me, I felt sorry for them. At this point in my journey, I viewed the business world as one of limited flexibility and entrapment.

Because I knew mail would be important for me to receive on the road, I arranged drops through American Express. So after I finished assembling my bike I raced over to the local office, anxious to pick up my mail. Excitedly, my fingers ripped open one letter after the next. It felt like Christmas.

I usually picked up mail every 30 days. Even though I looked forward to reading these messages, sometimes the letters would make me feel homesick, especially when my travels got tough. Most of the time, however, I could sit back happily crying as I read about how my old world was changing. It seemed life at home was escalating: people getting married, changing jobs and even having children. It was fun for me to watch from so far away and with such a new perspective. At this distance I could really ponder the significance of these life changes.

After completing the second Silva weekend, I headed back to Max and Bev's. Because Cyclone Bola had prevented me from seeing the Coromandel Peninsula two weeks earlier, I decided to return to explore this incredible coastline before heading north again for my final week in New Zealand. This was also the perfect excuse to pay Max and Bev a surprise visit.

During the next few days, I learned a lot about bicycle repairs. First, after just completing three hours of challenging terrain through some of the most beautiful country I'd seen yet, my gears began to slip. Just outside of Tairua on the Coromandel Peninsula, they became a lot worse. When I took a closer look at the problem, I noticed that the cable that attached my derailleur to the shifting mechanism had frayed. Even though I had an extra, I didn't know how to change it. I pressed on. Then the cable broke completely and my gears automatically slipped into their hardest-to-pedal combination.

After switching the front derailleur to low, I pedaled into town and looked for someone who could help. Of course, I thought, nothing on my bike broke while I was with Mark. It all waited until after we separated.

I found an auto mechanic who gladly helped me change the broken wires. I studied his every move so that I could perform the needed surgery when there was a next time.

That afternoon I arrived in Whitianga ahead of the schedule I had set for myself, so I went to the local bike shop to clean my chain. When I told the owner I was on an around-the-world bike ride, he gladly volunteered his tools thinking that I would know what I was doing. He worked on other repairs while I broke my chain apart and cleaned it with a brush and gasoline.

Everything was going great. I sat outside in the warm afternoon sun scrubbing my chain. Then I spent over a half-hour trying desperately to put the little rivet that I had removed back in its place. But it just wouldn't go back where it came from. The rivet seemed out of place. Then I remembered Mark telling me something important about the chain: "Never remove . . ."

Trying to recall what Mark had told me, I walked over to the owner with my chain in one hand and the tiny rivet in the other and said, "Excuse me, but I can't seem to get this little stopper back into the hole to close my chain."

His eyes grew large and he bellowed, "Oh, no! You're never supposed to take that out!"

I dropped my head and looked at the floor.

"I'll tell 'ya, it's damn near impossible to get them back in, but I'll give it a go. And if that don't work, you're 'gonna need a whole new chain."

Fumbling with the chain in his huge hands, he managed to get the rivet back in place between phone calls and dealing with customers. He struggled with it for an hour. Then he wouldn't let me pay him. I felt terrible. Blushing with embarrassment, I thanked him and quietly slipped out the door.

The next morning I awakened early so that I could pack and meditate before pedaling the monster hills that stood between my destination and me. As I approached the top of one of them, a car pulled alongside me. The gray-haired man inside watched me as I pulled toward the summit with all my strength.

Once I reached the top, he asked, "Are you Sally?"

Shocked, I thought, who is this person and how does he know me?

A big grin came over the man's face as he explained that he had spoken with his son, Max, about this crazy American girl who was riding her bike around the world.

Charlie, who spent many of his days driving the Coromandel Peninsula looking for backpackers to pick up and drive around the beautiful coast, offered me some ice water, lemonade and a chocolate bar. I gladly accepted. The last three climbs in the dusty gravel had left me hot and sweaty.

Charlie also insisted I come to his home for lunch. I did, and he later took me for a two-hour drive along the north tip of the peninsula. He was a sweet old man, retired and very lonely. He had lost his wife several years ago.

It began to rain and blow once I finally set off on the last 40 miles to Max and Bev's house. Charlie wanted to drive me to their home, but I wouldn't let him. Tears filled his eyes as we hugged and said good-bye.

I started down the steep driveway when I felt my tire sink and wobble. Another flat tire! I will never make it to Max and Bev's before dark, I thought.

I walked back up the hill and knocked on Charlie's door. He opened it and, seeing that I was back, his eyes lit up and a huge smile came across his face.

"Charlie," I said, "did you wish my flat tire on me so I would have to come back?"

He smiled and hugged me.

Charlie drove me to Max and Bev's. As I walked through the front door with Charlie, Bev exclaimed, "Sally's back, can you believe it?"

Max and their daughters rushed into the front room as Bev hugged me. All six of us marveled at the miraculous coincidences that enabled us to share Robin's birthday together that evening.

I had already cycled from the Coromandel Peninsula to the Bay of Islands after my first weekend of the Silva course, so I decided to hitchhike at least to Auckland before catching a bus to go north.

I cycled to the main road towards Auckland, leaned my bike against my hip and held out my extra tire to attract attention. I remembered that Mark had told me this would cause more drivers to stop."Won't the driver get upset when they learn all I want is a ride?" I had asked. "No, cyclists do it all the time," he replied. Uncomfortable with this trick, I stood timidly holding up my tire. Nothing happened. The people inside cars barely looked. Then I remembered what I had learned in Silva.

I smiled and projected the most positive energy I could conjure up.

I pulled feelings from deep within to radiate my needs throughout every cell of my body. I looked within to my mental screen and role-played the outcome I desired.

It worked!

Soon, cars began to stop. Some drivers even stopped just to apologize for not being able to give me a ride because they were going just a short distance. Others told me they would go out of their way to help me if I was still there after they completed their errands. Four rides later, I made it to the Bay of Islands, excited about all the new friends I had made and the conversations I had enjoyed.

Two days later, I stopped at a campground near the tip of the North Island. This was the hottest place I'd visited in New Zealand. Along a tree-lined creek campers were enjoying the afternoon sun. A couple waved and signaled me to stop.

"Hey, dear," the man called, "where are you from?"
"California," I replied.
"And you are alone?" he asked.
"Yes, and I'm having a great time in your country."
"Well, I bet you haven't had some fresh New Zealand snapper," said the woman. "Here, take this and cook up a good meal for yourself," she said as she handed me a whole fish, head and all. Then she gave me a frying pan and oil.

I walked slowly down the path, pushing my loaded bike in one hand and carrying the frying pan with a fish hanging over the side in the other. Moments later I heard another voice.

"What do you have there, honey?" a person called. A man in his late 60s came over and introduced himself. "Hi, I'm Doug. Did you catch that fish?"

"Not hardly," I replied, "No, your neighbor down the way wanted me to try some New Zealand snapper."

"That's Bill and he goes out every day in his fishing boat. Maybe he'll take you out. Are you all alone?"

"Yes," I said, thinking this campground looked like a great place to settle for the night.

"Come pitch your tent near my wife and me, and have dinner with us. We'll cook your fish for you. They only have cold showers here, but behind that curtain we have our own hot shower and you may help yourself. I'll put the water on."

For the next three days, I ate fresh fish, and sang and partied with fellow campers. I splashed and played in the ocean and ran on the beach as if I were experiencing it for the first time. And on my last day the campers organized a fish-feed celebration in my honor. We all feasted on fresh smoked mullet, mussels, snapper and fish chowder. When I came to New Zealand I expected to eat a lot of fresh fish, but I found that the country exports most of its catch. What they do keep commands a very high price in the stores, so this feast was a real treat.

During my final days in New Zealand, I headed back to Auckland. It seemed so long ago that I arrived here and inhaled my first breath of air. And it felt like years ago that I was with Mark. I realized I had grown over the past three months both as a cycle tourist and as a person. Although Mark caused me frustration and anger at times, I knew that was part of my lessons. I was supposed to learn from Mark, and I certainly did. He was instrumental in my being here and he did teach me well. But with Mark gone, I was beginning to experience a whole other side of travel. Families were showing me love in a very caring way. People from all walks of life were helping me to make my journey successful.

Although I didn't know where this quest would take me spiritually, I knew that Australia was my next destination.

Chapter Four

Traveling Within

Storms and flooding damaged Australia even worse than Cyclone Bola had assaulted New Zealand. By the time I arrived in Sydney, more rain greeted me, complicating my travel plans. Soon I would encounter road closures and flooding.

It took three hours to put my bike together and clear customs. After cracking my tube valve twice causing two flat tires, I walked tiredly to the now-vacant customs area. The Australian officials screened me very carefully. They wanted to know how much money I had, asked me when I would be leaving the country, and studied my airplane vouchers. In Australia the government is sensitive about immigration and requires travelers to enter with a round-trip ticket, guaranteeing departure.

"Everything seems in order," said the man at the customs gate.

"But where are you going with that thing?" he asked, referring to my bicycle.

"I'm going to ride the east coast of Australia," I answered.

"That's three thousand miles in two months," he said, frowning. "You don't have enough money."

"It doesn't cost much to live on a bike." I replied. "I don't have to pay for hotels or gas."

"Please be more specific," he said. "You can't camp in the big cities. Do you have friends with addresses?"

I took a deep breath and began. "Well, from here I will go to Brisbane and there's lots of camping between here and there, and then I intend to head north to Cairns where I can scuba dive. And I've got someone expecting me here in Sydney and someone in Brisbane."

"Can you tell me who these people are, who you're staying with?" the man asked suspiciously.

I pulled my address book out of my pack. It was full of names from around the world.

"Here in Sydney I'm staying with these people, Peter and Amanda," I said as I pointed to the address.

He looked at it and nodded. "And in Brisbane?"

"Oh, that's Michelle and Glen," I said as I flipped to that page.

Surveying my bags, he said, "I don't see any scuba gear."

"I'll rent my equipment because it's not practical to carry gear around the world," I responded.

"Around the world? Is that what you said?"

"That's right," I replied.

"Well if you have enough courage to cycle around the world, then good on you. No worries, carry on."

For the next four days, I tried to carry on but the storms continued. So I caught up on paperwork and toured Sydney in the afternoon hours. It was April and winter was quickly approaching. By heading north over the next six weeks, I was sure to find better weather.

Since Peter and Amanda both worked, I explored this city of three million people by myself. Not anxious to take my bike in the rain through its winding mix of convoluted streets, I walked about 10 miles each day.

In some ways, Sydney reminded me of San Francisco. Hidden beneath its muscular skyline of bridges, towers and high-rises, I found museums, art galleries and parks. Along the shore lay a spectacular harbor full of ferries, sailboats and other pleasure craft. Empty lifeguard stations dotted the sandy beaches. The majestic wings of the famous Sydney Opera House served as a backdrop to this rich urban texture.

Finally, on my fifth day, I awakened to sunshine. Excited to begin my journey up the east coast, I cycled out of Sydney during the morning commute, a big mistake. The cars, buses and trucks forced me into the gutter with no margin for error. I couldn't even risk a glance in my rearview mirror because I had to concentrate so hard on keeping a straight line. Grabbing tightly onto my handlebars, I prayed for protection and surrounded myself in light.

I soon found myself gasping for air. I couldn't catch my breath at the stop lights because the long lines of buses billowed huge plumes of black smoke into the air. Horns honked and engines rumbled while trucks and cars added to the exhaust-filled stench. After an hour of this stop-and-go nausea, the roads began to clear as I headed northwest for Parramatta and Windsor.

I pedaled along quiet two-lane roads and began to let my mind wander a bit. I recalled my conversations with New Zealanders. Being from a country without poisonous creatures, they warned me to be careful where I sat, walked and camped in Australia. Despite understanding that this fear was theirs and not mine, I allowed myself to become paranoid. And sure enough I got what I feared! Something landed on my leg! I screamed and quickly jumped off my bike. Whatever it was had already slithered down my leg.

It was a leaf!

Feeling foolish, I took a deep breath and got back on my bike, thankful that only Buddy had witnessed this show of paranoia.

After several days of detours, intermittent rain, and camping in muddy fields, I pedaled an eight-mile dirt road to the Comboyne Plateau. While ascending, the earthy smell of fresh pine filled my nostrils and a chorus of birds sang. The tall pine trees formed a canopy to shield me from the hot sun. Once on top, I hiked another 400 meters on a dirt path to the plateau where I enjoyed a 360-degree view of the valleys below.

Feeling exhilarated by the climb, I sat down to savor both my accomplishment and the view. Glancing down toward my shoes, I noticed slimy worms covering my socks. I jumped to my feet and screamed!

I tried furiously to flick them off. I began to panic when I realized that these intruders were stuck on me! Some were burrowing into my socks while others began digging their way into my exposed legs. Now frantically tearing and pulling at them, I began to cry.

I realized it was not helping to panic. I stopped crying and took a deep breath. Closing my eyes, I visualized these creatures as friendly and harmless. I asked them to please let go of me and visualized them dropping off. I opened my eyes and carefully began to pull and pick them off. As I hiked back down the hill, a few more latched on at the ankle. This time, however, I was ready and quickly pulled them off.

Later, I learned that these were leeches! Leeches are best removed by burning them with a cigarette or match. This way they will back themselves out without leaving their waste in the victim's bloodstream.

These obnoxious creatures hang off bushes in many parts of Australia; they will attach to just about anything. I found clusters of them on the bottoms of my bicycle panniers. They dangled perilously from my rear rack and fell onto my rear tire every time I hit a bump. I spent hours cleaning dead leeches off of my bike.

When the leeches couldn't find me the ticks did. The next day, in Kempsey, halfway to Brisbane, I stopped at the visitor's' center where I asked a woman there to look at the strange lump on my neck that had been bothering me. With a pair of tweezers, she pulled out what looked like a small spider. The woman identified it as a tick. She gave me some medication and offered some words of encouragement

"You are wide open to just about anything we got here in Australia. There's snakes in the water. For that matter some snakes even live in people's attics. There's leeches. And I guess you know about the 'mosis'. These storms have made mosquitoes the worst we've ever had. Living here you just get used to all the bugs and snakes. It's really weird, but if you're not scared of 'em, they don't bother you."

OK, I told myself, I am not going to let these little creatures bother me anymore.

My new attitude would be short-lived. That evening I set up camp at Trial Bay Gaol, where an old stone prison stood next to the grassy seaside campground. As the sun began to set over the rocky beach, it painted the horizon with rich pastels of red and orange.

I sat watching this perfect vision while sipping some wine, when suddenly a black cloud of buzzing mosi's surrounded me. I sprang into action, running around swearing as I collected my belongings. I took off in a sprint with my free-standing tent above my head. I felt like I was flying a kite except for the army of mosquitoes that were closing in on me. They bit and chased me for several minutes as I raced around searching for a better site.

I took refuge inside my tent for the rest of the night, watching hundreds of these hungry vultures guard my home. They buzzed all night, and when morning came I waved off a swarm and ran to the bathroom, only to be greeted by more inside. They bit me while I sat on the toilet and attacked me while I took my shower. It seemed like the only way I could escape the Australian mosquitoes was to keep on riding.

I moved on to Grassy Head, another beach-front campground. I played in the warm Australian ocean and did laundry until confining myself in my tent before the nighttime crawlers took over. That was when the mosi's hit the hardest.

Only this time, a population of rats joined the attack. As the mosquitoes collected on the screen door, I listened to an aggressive colony of rodents as they crawled and munched outside my tent. I couldn't sleep because I thought they would bite their way through, lured by the smell of food.

The next morning I turned inland, hoping to escape the mosquitoes, cars, and noise of the coast. One night as dusk was falling, I stopped at a farm to ask permission to camp. I was invited inside by the hospitable family. Alinda fixed me a welcome dinner of eggs and toast. We stayed up late talking, laughing and drinking lots of beer with her friends. My host gave me a tip about the roads ahead.

"You've got to watch out for kangaroos," Alinda grinned, as she brushed her thick blonde hair aside. She was about my age.

"Kangaroos?" I asked.

"Yeah, why we even had one attack the paper boy the other

day," she informed me. Not sure if she was teasing or serious, I decided not to take any chances. I would stay alert.

As I pedaled off the next morning, I put another culprit on my growing list of Australian creepy crawlers: kangaroos. Far from being attacked by one, sadly, I never even saw a kangaroo the whole time I was in Australia!

After returning to the coast and doing tourist things like drinking a banana milkshake at a banana plantation, I cycled to Glenreagh and found The Dog, a pub I couldn't pass up. In addition to a man playing acoustic guitar on the outside deck and laughter from a party going on inside, there was a pool and a shower next door. After I had cleaned up, I excitedly made my way to the party. The folks inside, all locals, reminded me of the mountain people I'd seen on TV shows back home. The men wore either jeans and T-shirts or jeans and flannel shirts with rolled-up sleeves. The woman wore loose-fitting long skirts and blouses. Children ran around playing and screaming. A collection of dogs sat near the tables waiting for scraps.

These Aussies made me feel welcome, and after a few pitchers of beer, we began to discuss the US. One particularly boisterous man with bloodshot eyes walked over to our table to initiate a heated discussion.

"You Americans think you know it all." His words began to slur. "We've had these Yank school teachers come to our area. They tell us they're gonna use their experiences back home to improve the conditions in our schools. And you know what?" his voice raised, "these Goddamn temporary teachers are unwilling to learn our ways or our culture. You know what these know-it-all's do?"

I was afraid to ask.

"They disrupt the entire system and then they leave."

"Yeah, you Americans all got this big superiority complex," added his long-haired friend. "You go around and try to shove your capitalistic ways down the throats of these poor little countries all in the name of democracy. Look what you did to Vietnam. Who needs it?"

As we covered subjects from school teachers to the US dollar to politics, the crowd around our table grew as we debated the pros and cons of each issue. Finally, I managed to leave the controversial topics and began to talk about my trip. Laughter filled the air once again.

During these discussions I met Jack, a former resident of Seattle. He invited me to stay at his home. A contractor by trade, Jack built his own house as well as many others in the area. A slender man in his late 30s, he had engineered switches and buttons into every part of his luxurious pinewood home. He showed me how he controlled the lighting and stereo in different parts of the house from one electrical panel. His kitchen was an arcade full of the latest time-saving devices. A broad expanse of windows looked out on a forest of eucalyptus.

As I sat by his outdoor hot tub and listened to the crickets and other nighttime sounds, Jack confided that he was escaping a bad marriage and a rocky business partnership. "But I'll tell you," he said, "I go to the States once a year, see all the problems and I can't wait to get back. This is as good as it gets." He looked inside at the warm glow from his fireplace. The stereo played softly in the background. A plate full of cheeses, crackers and grapes sat next to us.

"I'm living life the best it's ever been for me. The people are real here. I'm not always watching my backside for the next joker to give me problems. I can really live in Australia."

I thought about Jack's comments and wondered if that's what I was doing. Was I also escaping? Yet, something inside was telling me that you can only hide for so long and that Jack might create the same issues here in Australia that he did not want to confront back home. I had become frustrated with the US, too. But I thought it may be self-inflicted. I had never really taken time to develop real opinions about issues involving politics, international affairs, or other major subjects. I hoped this trip would encourage me to understand our country more deeply.

"So, where are you headed from here?" Jack asked.

"Well, right now I'm going to World Expo in Brisbane and then I will travel to China and Europe," I replied.

"Is that right?" Jack looked amazed. "China? On a bicycle? What an adventure. Well, you sure have my support."

I called it a night, and crawled into a warm fluffy bed. It reminded me of an old grandma's featherbed. Lying there, I thought about China. It wouldn't be long before I would be crossing its borders. I wondered if they would let me in with my bicycle. How would I do alone? And where I would stay? Surely I would not be sleeping in a featherbed. My eyes closed and I fell asleep.

The next afternoon, I participated in Anzac Day at The Dog. This legal gambling holiday was created to honor Australia's World War I dead. The crowd in the pub cheered and laughed as a game called Two Up was played. I watched while I drank a beer-and-lemonade concoction called Shandys.

In Two Up, a person stands in the middle of the room and uses a special wooden tray to flip three coins at a time. For each flip, the gamblers who surround him are divided into those who call heads and those who call tails. In order to win, you must pick the correct two-out-of-three combination. A lot of money changes hands.

I followed the party back to Jack's house where the drinking continued and several of us played round-robin backgammon. Exhausted, I fell asleep on the couch.

The smell of fresh coffee lured me from my slumbers. Jack fixed fruit fritter pancakes for me before I headed down the road. I was in no hurry to leave as I shuffled around very slowly, suffering from a hangover.

"Good luck on your trip," he called, "and don't tell anyone about Glenreagh. It's great just this way."

The clear streams, earth smells and singing birds along the way made me forget about my aching head. Having this wonderful place all to myself, I decided that this would be a perfect spot to meditate—as well as a great place to camp for the night. I picked a spot for my tent beside the brook which babbled gently nearby.

I walked upstream a short way to meditate and found a perfect rock to sit on. I counted backward from ten as the birds sang a melody in the background. The gentle gurgling sound of the creek deepened my relaxed state. I began to focus on love and relationships. I asked the universe what it was teaching me. What was the purpose of my relationship with Mark? Why did it end the way it did?

"If I brought these situations to myself," I asked, "then why am I not dealing with them in a way that I can grow?"

"But you are growing," an inner voice seemed to be telling me. "You have chosen to use pain to stimulate your growth. There are other ways to grow, but you have chosen Mark to mirror the things that are painful for you to see. Your pain comes from letting your goals and purpose for this trip get lost in trying to make him happy rather than yourself. Now that he's gone, you are changing. You are growing and understanding yourself more."

I began to see the pattern in my conflicts with Mark as well as those in my past relationships. I had always believed my first goal in life was to be happy. And yet, even though I had achieved objectives and had enjoyed a successful career, I never felt the picture was complete simply because I had not found a man I wanted to share time with. In my personal life, I felt a need to compromise myself as I had done with Mark in order to be happy. But why, I wondered?

It seemed that people and institutions treated couples better than they did singles. As a single person, I know I paid more for insurance and my taxes were higher. Was even the government telling me that I was a bigger risk as an unmarried person?

For all our lives, our schools, our parents, and even our employers seem driven by an unquestioned instinct to move us toward coupling and the creation of a family. But what about the individual? How can we ever have a balanced society unless every one of its members is complete within him-or herself?

I began to wonder how I could be happy and truly love myself unless I made myself number one. How could a man ever respect me if I continually placed his desires above my own?

I was sitting on a rock in Australia and to get here I had traded my home, car, and luxurious life in California. Only now could I see how blind I had been!

Love is not a balancing act between two people. Happiness

doesn't depend on finding a "knight in shining armor" to bring love into one's life. Love comes from within. This inward process is key to feeling complete. We often don't start with ourselves and instead we chase relationships hoping to fill voids. Ultimately these gaps reappear and we typically repeat this pattern again. This cycle goes unnoticed until we take a step back and look deep into our behaviors.

I misunderstood unconditional love. I believe I responded to love and acceptance based on achievements. Striving to succeed and chasing goals got twisted up with internal values. As I thought this through I realized that my trip forced me to be happy with all outcomes even failure. And that being in the moment with my very existence was enough to be proud of.

I opened my eyes and looked around, feeling as if I had been somewhere else. Watching the water gently riffle the ferns that lived along the river's edge, a calmness settled over me. I returned to my campsite and watched the sunset, ending a day I would never forget.

The next morning, while cycling through Casino and Dygole enroute to Brisbane, I began to feel more and more at peace with myself. Discovering that I could give myself the love and attention that I previously thought I needed from men gave me a tremendous feeling of freedom.

After a few days, I arrived at Michelle and Glen's home as the lights of Brisbane flickered on the distant horizon. Michelle, who had been kneeling in her vegetable garden, stood as I approached their house.

"Sally?" she called.

"Michelle?" I returned.

"Excuse me while I wash this dirt off my hands and tell Glen you're here."

Moments later, she returned with Glen. "Sally, this is Glen. Evelyn has told me so much about you."

Michelle bubbled with energy. She and Glen both stood six or seven inches above me, yet all three of us had the same blue eyes, sandy hair and freckles. Travelers themselves, they helped me get situated and comfortable.

"So, Sally, Evelyn tells us that you were a banker," Glen said as we sat around a picnic table and sipped tea.

"Used to be," I grinned. "I don't know what I am anymore."

"Well, I'll tell you. Michelle and I like to hike and explore different parts of the world, too," Glen paused. "And there's been lots of times when I get fed up with my work and I want to just leave it all and take off. "

"What's stopping you?" I asked.

"Michelle can do it a lot easier than I can. She can find a job working with the handicapped pretty much anywhere and besides she gets one month off every year for vacation. But me, oh, I've got too much invested in my career. I can't just go become a pharmacist any old place."

"Well, Glen, what I did was OK for me. But selling everything and resigning a career isn't for everyone. Perhaps you and Michelle can find a way to travel more and retain your careers. I hope to be able to find that nice combination when I return home. I feel like this trip is only scratching the surface. There's still so much to see and many different ways to see it."

"Are you sorry you sold everything?" Glen asked.

"No," I said. "I can't put a monetary value on what my trip is teaching me. I could have rented my home instead of selling it, but by liquidating everything, I freed myself from worrying about renters and paying the mortgage. By letting go, I've opened myself up for other opportunities."

An ant crawled up my cup.

"If it's not one bug it's another," I joked as I brushed the ant off my cup. "Anyway back to accumulations. By selling everything, I have nothing to return to. That will force me to continue with my travels during tough times. And perhaps I'll find another place in the world to live. And if I don't, and I return to California to settle, it will be for the right reasons."

"That's an interesting way of viewing things," Glen said. "You're a perceptive person to see all that. Still, the way you've chosen go is pretty amazing."

For the next few days I spent my time wandering in an out of the various pavilions at World Expo. This event provides countries around the world an opportunity to showcase their resources and attractions to the general public. Many countries played a continuous multimedia slide show displaying hundreds of different photographs. The voices which boomed over the speakers kept time with that country's music.

The US exhibit showcased high-tech exercise equipment. I was surprised that I didn't recognize any of it, and the prices were well above an average consumer's budget. I found this display of technology an inadequate representation of our country and was embarrassed by its materialistic slant. I was probably a little sensitive to all of it, because I had just gone through getting rid of my possessions.

I watched water ballets, laser shows, and fireworks displays. Many pavilions offered gift shops and restaurants, tempting visitors with even more reasons to travel abroad. The international selection of food was a welcome break from peanut butter, cereal and vegetable soup, some of my on-the-road staples.

Each night Michelle cooked a different vegetarian meal. I could see her eyes light up when she talked about her travels through Nepal, Turkey, New Zealand and Great Britain. With her vacation coming up, she had already selected some literature about China. Every night she asked me a little bit more about my trip to Hong Kong and China five years ago.

Early one morning Michelle and I talked over tea. "Michelle, you know I'm planning to travel in China alone, but if you want to go I'd love your company. At this point I'm not certain I can get in with my bike, nor am I sure I want to go there alone anyway. I was thinking about storing my bike in Hong Kong and taking trains throughout the country."

Would you bike if I came?" Michelle asked.

"I think it's easier with two people," I said. "All I remember from five years ago were the long lines and mass confusion at the train stations. I can't imagine watching my bike and dealing with the crowds all alone. I couldn't stand in line with my bike, that's for sure."

Michelle's excitement about this new option grew. "Wow, we could see so much more than in these tour groups I've been looking at. Do you think we can get in?"

"I just don't know," I replied."We must believe we can and be open to any different options if our first one doesn't work. The travelers I've talked to and the books I've read all say that the key to China is persistence combined with patience."

Glen laughed as he walked into the room. He had overheard the last of the conversation. "Michelle? Patient?"

He kept laughing as he walked out of the room.

In the days that followed Michelle and I firmed up our plans for traveling together. We agreed to meet in Hong Kong.

After a ten-day visit with Michelle and Glen, I was anxious for the road once again. Winter was here and it was time to move north where the tropical weather of Cairns would be welcome. I would take my bike with me, do some cycling in that warm environment and some scuba diving, too.

"Thanks for sharing your home with me, Glen. You made me feel welcome," I said. Turning to Michelle and giving her a hug, I continued, "And as for you, I'll see you in Hong Kong."

Michelle's eyes lit up."Yeah!" she exclaimed.

Glen and Michelle waved as I pedaled off to the Brisbane airport. I felt a real friendship with them and was excited knowing Michelle would be joining me in China.

When I arrived in Cairns, the towering palm trees and singing birds of this tropical resort area signaled a welcome change from the dusty, car-laden roads of the Australian coast. As I pedaled off to Port Douglas and the Great Barrier Reef, I became more and more excited about seeing a new underwater world. I shouted, "It feels so good to be back on the road! It feels so good!

As soon as I arrived in town, I signed up on a boat scheduled to leave one hour later. Excited about diving, I raced around to meet my deadline. I had just enough time to rent my gear, lock my bike and change my clothes. I boarded the boat with moments to spare and we motored out to sea.

Sitting on the boat's edge, I took my last breath, inserted my mouthpiece, and plunged backwards into the warm tropical water. An incredible starburst of colored coral stood tall and moved gently with the current. Time seemed to stop as I let the beautiful emeralds and reds of the coral reef stimulate my imagination. Sea creatures in a myriad of different sizes, shapes and colors moved about with ease and grace. Their world almost looked too easy.

After that inspiring day of diving on the reef, I treated myself to a carefree bicycle ride along the southern coast of Cairns. Palm trees towered high above the white sands of Mission Beach where I took a rest day. The area reminded me of Hawaii and the people were exceptionally friendly. Ripe coconuts hung from the palm trees and campers ate sliced coconuts and drank the juice. I played in the surf and didn't feel pressured to be anywhere by any specific time.

From my ocean paradise, I cycled northwest of Cairns to the Atherton Tablelands. I found tranquility and beauty there each day as I discovered the blue waters of pristine mountain lakes. One particularly special day I explored a series of waterfalls, each one cascading down upon a rich carpet of flowers and lush green vegetation. I found a small village hidden within this tropical setting where produce stands and a small flea market competed for my attention. I rarely saw cars.

I flew from Cairns to Sydney, leaving myself two extra days before flying on to Singapore and Hong Kong. I called Sue and Bill, a couple I had met while camping at Trial Bay in New South Wales. They had invited me to stay at their home on Scotland Island near Sydney.

"Well, hello, Sally, we've been expecting you," Bill said. "We'll be at work tomorrow when you arrive but make yourself at home."

After he gave me directions, I hopped on my bike and pedaled toward the ferry for Scotland Island. Twelve miles of scenic cycling in the warm winter weather relaxed my every muscle. I pedaled easily as I turned onto a tree-lined boulevard approaching the ferry harbor. I arrived at the dock and sat in the sun waiting for the next boat. I reflected on my past four months in New Zealand and now Australia. I was really making this happen. At the beginning of my trip, I could only really comprehend my first country, New Zealand. Now, four months later, I was leaving Australia and heading for China. Did I really ever think I could go this far? Yet, when I thought what was still ahead of me China, Europe and the States, I immediately snapped out of my musings and focused on the present.

"Sally," I told myself, "concentrate on today. You're just about to deal with the infamous funnel spiders."

When I met Bill and Sue at Trial Bay Gaol campground, I had refused their invitation to come here, solely because of the funnel spider population which inhabited their island. This was another lesson—never say never. I said I would never come here, so of course here I was waiting for a ferry to Scotland Island, home of the famous funnels.

The ferry arrived and the captain lifted my bike onto the roof of the small wooden cabin. I watched Buddy with a worried look on my face. As the boat pulled away from the dock, the pilot assured me my companion would survive a short jaunt across the bay.

We arrived at my destination and I watched nervously as the captain lifted my bike off the roof and held it over the open water. I raced over to retrieve Buddy. Tightening my grip and flexing my muscles, I grabbed hold of my dear friend and brought him to safety. I waved the captain good-bye and sat down on the dock.

No sooner had I caught my breath then I looked straight up and saw the home I was heading for, about 300 steps away. I began my journey up the mountain, carefully choosing my path. The funnel spiders I had been so concerned about lurked underneath the rocks I was now walking on. I kept my mind busy with the challenge of carrying 110 pounds up this mountain. I didn't think about the spiders.

My fear had subsided and, of course, I had no problem. I thought about how far I had come in dealing with fear. Surely two months ago this event would have turned into a confrontation with the deadly spiders.

I had learned some important lessons about myself in Australia, and now I was anxious to move on. I felt ready for adventure to experience new horizons. No doubt China would provide challenges I couldn't even imagine.

PART 2
Hong Kong, China and Russia

CHAPTER FIVE:
The Center of Attention

CHAPTER SIX:
Russia by Rail

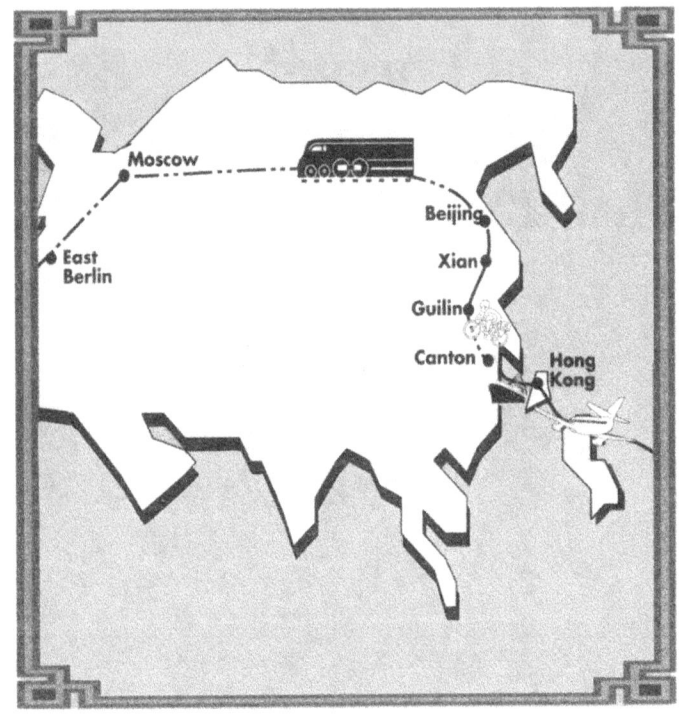

Date: *June 17, 1988–July 23, 1988*
Bike Miles: 818
Route: *Hong Kong, Canton, Wuzhou, GuiNn, Xian, Beijing, Moscow, East Berlin.*

Chapter Five
The Center of Attention

After an eight-hour flight from Sydney, I spent the night in a Singapore hotel. There I read a book called *Life and Death in Shanghai* by Nien Cheng, a Shell Oil executive imprisoned during the 1960s anti-capitalism movement in China. Cheng's experiences gave me insights on the cultural revolution and its profound effect on China. Her book helped me understand how the Chinese people see the world and relate to foreigners.

My other travel books had promised that China would challenge me. After the Soviet Union and Canada, China is the third largest country in the world. It holds one-quarter of the world's population yet was closed to foreigners for almost three decades. My excitement was mixed with the apprehension of traveling among one billion people squeezed into 15 percent of the earth's total land mass.

Suddenly doubts overwhelmed me. A series of questions raced through my mind. Would I get my bicycle in the country? What about water and food? Would the heat of summer be too extreme? What about lodging or camping? If I get sick or injured, how will I get help? Would my phrasebook be adequate to communicate? What if they confiscate my bike?

Finally, I resolved just to go, trusting that everything would work out.

I flew on to Kowloon. Michelle greeted me at the airport; I spotted her immediately.

"Hey Michelle," I called running toward her. "I can't believe it, here we are on our way to China." We laughed and hugged.

"Sally, am I glad to see you," Michelle replied. "It's been a depressing three days here."

We walked through the corridors. It was deja vu as I witnessed the mobs of solicitors offering cheap rooms and souvenirs. The familiar musty, humid smell of Asia filled the air. Yet I felt like a different person-the past four months had matured me as a traveler. I now had some miles under my belt.

After we were away from the crowds, I turned and stopped. "OK, Michelle, what happened?" I asked.

"Everyone has told me that we can't travel with our bikes in China. I went to all the places you suggested, then, I went to see Tony. He was the only person who was positive. He wants you to come see him as soon as you get in. He invited us to lunch to discuss our plans."

Tony was the miracle-worker travel agent who had helped Mark and I get tickets to New Zealand during our visit in January.

"You did a great job, Michelle," I said, patting her on the back. "And you're getting around here like a pro. I'm so glad you came. I know everything will work out. Either way we will have fun figuring it out."

We laughed with anxiety and excitement as we both thought of what lay ahead.

The two of us left the airport and pedaled among hordes of people in the suffocating heat and distinctive smell of the Orient. Wow! I couldn't believe I was really riding my bike in Hong Kong! I would have never imagined returning to Hong Kong on a bicycle. Five years ago, I found walking enough of a challenge.

By the time we reached downtown Hong Kong, the street solicitors had bombarded us with offers of cheap accommodations. We spent more than an hour walking and riding in the dark to various hotels, sampling the elevators of these bargain offers. Since most of the budget hotels sat atop commercial buildings that rose fourteen stories, we had to make sure that we could get our bikes into our rooms. All of the elevators were too small.

We finally found the Kowloon Hotel and Mr. Li. Even though his rates were a little higher than most of his competitors, I knew from my previous visit that we could get our bikes in his elevator. We negotiated for a room for two and got the bikes upstairs. Exhausted, I fell asleep with my clothes on.

The next morning, we hurried off to the China Travel Service (CTS) to obtain a visa. In the People's Republic of China, CTS is virtually the only travel agency. The Hong Kong CTS competes with many travel agents, all with different rules and interpretations of how China can be traveled. But the Hong Kong CTS was not encouraging about riding our bikes through China, so we went to see Tony.

We took the ferry to Hong Kong Island and met Tony for lunch. He treated us to a fabulous Chinese meal, which included fried rice, sweet and sour pork, and mushrooms wrapped in bean curd. The mushrooms were huge and flat. The bean curd, made from soybeans, was very similar to tofu. It was great to see a familiar and happy face in Hong Kong. I began to feel more optimistic about our chances.

As plates clattered and Chinese conversation noisily went on all around us, Tony leaned forward and said, "You can, how you say, do it. I know you can. Here is what you must do."

We listened intently as he told us what to expect in China. For example, he told us that we should always expect to hear the word "mei-jo" which means "no". It was easier to say no, Tony explained, than to admit that a request is not understood. He also told us that we would need to be firm but yielding, persistent but passive. He offered us suggestions on how we could accomplish this. He also told us to expect ambiguity in the way the Chinese enforced their interpretation of the law.

Seeing the confused look in our eyes, Tony said, "Rules are different in China. China different from the US. You make one rule there; here there are different rules different areas."

Everything was starting to make sense. It felt right. I knew that we could ride our bikes in the People's' Republic of China. Tony's encouragement was just what we needed; what a wonderful person to meet.

We purchased tickets from Tony for an overnight trip up the Pearl River from Kowloon to Canton. He felt confident that we could get in with our bikes, although he had told us earlier that the Kowloon-Canton train would be out of the question. Officials at that border always turned away foreign travelers with bikes.

We left the Kowloon Hotel during the evening commute hour and headed for the ferry to Canton. Buses and trucks passed us cautiously as we biked two miles through this city full of noise and endless activity. Black soot that billowed from the vehicles left a residue in the creases on my arms and face. Sweat quickly soaked my clothing from the afternoon humidity. But I didn't care; it was a thrill bicycling in downtown Hong Kong.

We stopped at a park next to the ferry building. In what was becoming a ritual, we removed any valuables from our bikes and stuffed them into the day packs that we threw over our shoulders.

Groups of locals in the park stared at us. They said nothing, but watched our every move. A few men came up to my bike, looking curiously at the gears. They pointed to the flags on my panniers, especially the flag of China. Discussions broke out among them. I was sure they were contemplating our travels through China by bike. I enjoyed their interest and just smiled and nodded as they talked.

A line formed at the ferry building. We got in it, and even more people fixed their eyes on us. We stared back. They focused on us even more. Although I was self-conscious about so much attention, I was equally amused that they were all of a height that I could look them in the eye. Back home I'd be facing a forest of armpits.

We waited in line for about an hour and when our turn came, we walked forward. The guards spoke to us, but we couldn't understand what they were saying. Within moments we had caused the line to stop moving. Impatiently people pushed and shoved, inching their way toward the ticket booth. Confused and nervous, we stayed put, not wanting to lose our place in line.

Maybe the attendants wanted to check our bicycles, we reasoned. We offered them our bikes.

They shook their heads.

Maybe they wanted to see proof we had paid for them. We showed them our receipts.

They kept shaking their heads.

The crowd began to push and shout. Finally, an English-speaking man stepped forward to offer his help. As he spoke, the smell of garlic reeked through his broken teeth. This was not an unusual sight. We would see many people with missing teeth and most of them also ate lots of garlic. He told us that the boat attendants wanted more money. He told us that even though we had already paid, we would have to pay some more. We objected to such corrupt methods, but paid anyway. After the crowd pushed us onto the ferry boat, the doors closed and we motored out of the slip.

Suddenly, in a panic, I yelled across to Michelle that we were on the wrong boat. We were supposed to be on an overnight cruise, and since this was a standing-room-only boat, it couldn't be right.

Our faces turned pale as we wondered where we were going and how we could get off. Moments later, we rounded a bend in the river, and there stood a huge boat. 1 let out a sigh of relief as I realized that we were on a shuttle. My heartbeat returned to normal.

Boarding the ship I thanked good fortune for sending Tony our way. Like a luxury ocean liner, this boat offered duty-free shopping, a bar, a restaurant, even a game room. Our stateroom had two beds in it, a private bath, towels, and air conditioning. What comfort, I thought, as I reflected on my California life-style. How easy it would be to slip back into such creature comforts.

We watched with curiosity as workers loaded new motorcycles, washers and dryers, refrigerators and stereos onto our boat. As we would find out later from talking with local students, these luxuries were hard to get in the People's' Republic. They explained that people who had made it big outside the country, usually in Hong Kong, shipped these items to their relatives living in China.

The catch in all of this was the difference in the two currencies that are used in the People's' Republic. In order to buy luxuries like these, the Chinese need a currency called FEC, or Foreign Exchange Currency. The official money used in China is called Renminbi (or RMB). The RMB is not recognized outside of the People's' Republic and therefore has no value. This is why there's a black market. In order to get FEC, the people either had to work in a business that exchanged money with foreigners or exchange the RMB themselves with travelers who knew about the black market.

Although the difference in value between the two currencies hardly mattered to most western travelers, it meant a lot to the Chinese and to those on a shoestring budget (like myself). During my time in China, I could get an extra fifteen cents on the dollar by exchanging FEC for RMB. However, although it was legal for foreigners to possess RMB, it was illegal to buy it. So, I took my chances and traded for it on the black market; (I also needed RMB in villages where foreigners and FEC were uncommon.

After a restful night, we docked in the early morning hours in Canton, also called Guangzhou. It was mass confusion as everyone pushed and shoved toward the exit gate. We decided there was no urgency for us, so we waited until the crowds disembarked. Forty-five entertaining minutes later, we walked down the gangplank. We were the last people off the boat.

We walked our bikes confidently and briskly as Tony had coached past one customs official after another. Nobody bothered us. Fifteen minutes later, we showed our passports and were out on the streets of Canton wondering if all the stories we had heard about the travel restrictions on foreign bicyclists were true. We had even met one cyclist who had tried to take his bike on the same boat five days in a row only to be refused each time.

Maybe the crowds ahead of us had distracted the custom officials. Once again, we didn't know who or what to believe.

We headed for a traveler's hotel. There are three types of

hotels in China: hotels for Westerners, hotels for overseas Chinese and hotels for citizens of the People's' Republic. It's illegal for Westerners to stay in Chinese hotels, so we had to read the confusing symbols and signs very carefully.

The traveler's budget hotel was just across from the famous White Swan Hotel. This incredibly beautiful place was just as impressive as it was five years ago when I had stayed there for two nights. A first-class facility, it offered everything from a shopping mall to a huge lap pool.

Unable to register in our hotel for three hours, we headed for the Temple of Six Bunyans. Known as one of the most significant in Canton, the temple is called Precious Solemnity; it was built in the sixth century. We had hardly started our trek when several teenage boys brushed by us and whispered, "Change money, change money, it's OK."

I was surprised to see the black market working so daringly. We decided to accept their offer and began to negotiate a good price for our FEC. We were the center of attention as everyone on the street stopped and watched what we were doing. Exposed and vulnerable, I felt a little like a crook.

"We better split up", I yelled to Michelle. "Let's get off the main road to do this."

After I counted the RMB and gave the boy my FEC, I returned to the main road. Michelle had disappeared; maybe she was enroute to the temple. I left to go look for her.

I pedaled happily along the two-lane road. I looked very different from the hundreds of riders around me. With my white helmet and red bike bags, I really stood out. In a curious and friendly way, people studied me. When I stopped to look at my map, they stopped, anxious to help me. Even with everyone's assistance I still couldn't find the temple. The sky was darkening and it looked like rain. I gave up my hunt for Michelle and the temple and cycled back to the hotel to register for a room.

Michelle arrived about an hour later, soaked from the rain. I was relieved to see she was OK. We compared the deals we had negotiated. Michelle had been shorted 80 RMB. She was furious for being so trusting and not counting her money.

We then checked into the hotel by going through what would become a familiar ritual. Using the phrases and pointing to the group of symbols or the pictograph in my book, *Southwest China*, I asked if they had a room available. When the answer was yes, I then spoke the Chinese words and showed them that we needed two beds. In Chinese, there are something like 50,000 of these symbols and since the difference between one or the other can be a stray dot or line, we found that showing the pictograph minimized the potential for confusion. They nodded and I asked them, "how much?"

On the other side of this communication game, the Chinese have eight or nine different ways of saying the same word. For example, word *gaai* can mean chicken, street, or prostitute depending upon the way you say it. These differences are called tones because of the way certain parts of the word or syllable rise or fall. It seemed, however, that the phrase for how much was always understood. We paid our money and checked into a room.

We walked our bikes down the cement hallway to the fourth door on the right. Our room had two twin beds, a nightstand with a lamp, and one small window. A dresser stood across the room. We leaned our bikes against the foot of the bed and headed for the showers. At the end of the dark hallway, a picture of a woman denoted the woman's bathroom. There was one flush toilet and one squat toilet. Neither was appealing. The plumbing never worked right while we were there. The showers were concrete and very basic, but I was grateful for a place to bathe.

A friend of a friend had suggested that we contact Barbara, someone who worked in the consulate office in Canton. We rested briefly before we went to her home.

Barbara, her husband and two children lived in a hotel suite the size of a large American apartment. It looked like their entire home had been transplanted from middle-class America.

We sat in the living room discussing our plans.

"Michelle, Sally," Barbara leaned in closer, "you should know that no matter where you go and what you do, you'll be watched. The police will keep tabs on your progress. Since you're traveling alone and on bicycles, you're a real novelty."

The Center of Attention

"Can you give us any information on cycling?" I asked.

"My husband cycles extensively around Canton Province," Barbara replied, "and basically he enjoys it. There are wide bike lanes around town, but it's slow going because of all the riders. Once you get out in the country, there are mostly only narrow roads. According to my husband, the most dangerous part of cycling is oncoming traffic passing one another. The trucks will pass around a bend. They'll head right for you and you'll have to get out of the way."

"That reminds me of driving in Mexico," I said, smiling.

Barbara walked to her desk. "Here's a local map, but it only covers 25 miles. At least it will help you get out of Canton Province."

Handing me the map, Barbara continued. "My husband uses this all the time. This map has Chinese characters so that people on the road can point you in the right direction. I'll get another one for Bill." We finished asking questions and headed for the door.

"Good luck to both of you," Barbara said, shaking our hands.

"Thanks so much for your help, Barbara," I replied. "We'll just have to breathe deep and stay positive."

We took a cab back to our hotel. Michelle and I discussed our meeting with Barbara. We were grateful for her advice and help, but we both felt some anxiety about the conditions that lay ahead. We agreed that we would need to be alert and upbeat no matter how tired or frustrated we got. I was happy for Michelle's company. I knew we would need each other to laugh with when times were tough.

After freshening up at our hotel, we went out for dinner. Using the restaurant-ordering section in the back of *Southwest China*, I selected a vegetarian meal for us. With the help of the book, I even specified that we wanted little oil and no MSG. After dinner, we walked back to the hotel. Next door was an outdoor bar. We sat for hours in the warm evening laughing and giggling while students helped us pronounce selected words and phrases. Warm beer and peanuts contributed to the fun.

Michelle and I pedaled off the next morning for a day of

sightseeing. We headed for the Guangzhou Zoo anxious to see panda bears. But hidden in the back of the zoo, in a dark, barren cage, only one panda begged for attention. Paper cups and plastic wrappers littered the ground in front of its cage. Tufts of hair were missing from its coat. It was disappointing to see the panda living in such conditions.

The monkeys probably had the best playground of all the animals. They countered our depression. I watched as these small brown creatures performed their acrobatics. Swinging from branch to branch, they wrestled with each other and sent the crowd into fits of laughter. After being entertained, we left the zoo and headed for the Dong Fang Hotel.

This spectacular hotel with waterfalls and plush carpeting houses the U.S. consulate. As Barbara had suggested, we picked up a list of "open areas"– those places where foreigners were allowed to travel. I also picked up a brochure about the Trans-Siberian railway just in case I decide to get to Western Europe that way.

We left the comfortable hotel with its English voices and stepped into a rush hour of blasting horns and ringing bicycle bells. At home I probably wouldn't venture out into such chaos, but here it was all part of experiencing China. I watched Michelle pedal through the crowd. Like me, she stood out. Our freckles, light complexions and white helmets confirmed we were foreigners.

We were the center of attention. Barbara warned that we would be watched, but I didn't expect the throngs we attracted everywhere we went. For the most part it was entertaining. But sometimes when we were tired and wanted to get something done quickly, the crowds, the stares, and our inability to communicate frayed our nerves. For me, it was an interesting lesson in patience.

Michelle and I left the next morning enroute to Wuzhou, two days away. We followed the main road southwest toward Foshan and once again confronted truck exhaust and traffic jams. Even though we had a map, we couldn't figure which way to go, so we followed the traffic, hoping that these vehicles were all leaving town. The first major junction we came to, traffic split equally. We pulled out our map and began comparing the characters on the road signs to the map we got from Barbara. Nothing matched.

Every time we stopped, so did bunches of people. It reminded me of the old childhood game "red light green light." They stared at us and studied my 18-speed mountain bike. Before long, a solid wall of onlookers had encircled us. They started playing with the gears on my bike. They pointed and stared at the freckles on our faces. They even pulled at the tiny hairs on my forearm, never meaning harm, just being curious. I enjoyed sharing my "strange" looks with the Chinese people. Their curiosity was innocent. They were not accustomed to a mix of nationalities.

In desperation, I pointed to our destination on the map and shrugged my shoulders to communicate that I didn't know which way to go. Almost immediately they forgot about our bikes and began to point and yell in the direction of traffic. We went through this ritual at each intersection. It took forever to go just a few miles!

We finally found the main road to Sanshui. A few miles out of town, the traffic thinned and we began to pass many local bike riders loaded with goods for market. Several transported cages so full of ducks that the feet and beaks poked out of small openings. Many carried huge baskets of fresh vegetables. At times I saw pigs tied to bike racks. Some of the older men pedaled so slowly I thought they would fall over.

Hungry, hot, and tired, we stopped at a dusty roadside cafe and wheeled our bikes just inside the door. The room fell silent as all eyes turned to watch us. Food and trash covered the cement floor. Michelle and I exchanged glances asking, "You think this place is OK?" We decided to give it a try; it appeared to be the only place in town. A man cleared his throat and suddenly a wad of spit landed at the base of the wall. Everywhere we traveled, it seemed the people spit. Sometimes they would come to a sudden halt while walking on the street, lean over and let the saliva slowly dribble from their mouths. Often they would do just as this man had done. We couldn't believe it. Now I understood why spitting was illegal in Hong Kong.

The waitress avoided our eyes, letting us sit more than 15 minutes. I was sure she was intimidated by our presence and she didn't know how to talk to us. So I walked up to her with my phrase book and pointed to the food section. Smiling, I showed her that we were vegetarian. She nodded. I showed her the kind of rice we wanted. She nodded. I showed her that we wanted tea. Again, she nodded. Then I tried for a vegetable dish and pointed to a selection in my phrase book. She shook her head. I pointed to another choice. She shook her head again. I kept pointing. She kept shaking her head. When I was almost out of choices, I pointed to another vegetable dish and her eyes opened wide. She nodded.

The waitress returned a few minutes later with our meal. Pork covered some overcooked green leaves which swam in a sea of oil. I scooped the meat off and we both stared at what were once green vegetables.

In Australia I had purchased a little bottle of cider vinegar for such occasions. Michelle and I looked at each other as I poured this stomach-protecting agent over the mound of sickly food. We pulled out our porcelain chopsticks and began to eat. We had read about the importance of using porcelain chopsticks in China. Tony had warned us that because of the high humidity and poor hygiene, bacteria flourished on the wooden chopsticks that would be made available to us.

Before leaving I walked through the kitchen to the squat toilets. I almost threw up. A cloud of flies buzzed around the excrement-laden floor. The smell of urine hung thick in the air. Somehow everyone seemed to miss this waterless toilet! Holding my nose, I pulled down my pants, relieved myself and ran out the door as fast as I could.

We continued our journey in the heat of the afternoon. The dirt and grit in the air plastered itself on my face as huge billows of black smoke poured out of trucks. The new T-shirt that I had bought in Hong Kong was already beginning to fade, attacked by the pollution-filled air. Still, even under these conditions,

Michelle and I were excited to be among the few foreigners ever to bicycle through this country.

As we approached Sanshui, we noticed acres of bicycles awaiting their owners' return. They were all one-speed bikes equipped with fenders. A chain guard fully encased the chain to protect it from mud and rain. The bikes all had the same hand brakes. They stood atop their locked center stands like proud servants. We looked across this sea of black bicycles and wondered how their owners could tell them apart.

Once again it was time to begin our hunt for nightly lodging. I pulled out my sheet of paper with the characters for hotel or hostel and we began searching for a match. Once again, we had no luck. So we stopped for help and a crowd began to form. We tried to communicate to the growing assembly with our phrase book. The people just pointed at our helmets and giggled.

When I showed them the symbol for hotel, several hands reached out and grabbed my book. As they passed it around, I pulled out one of my maps and again showed them that we needed somewhere to stay. More hands reached up and grabbed that too.

It dawned on me that we could be in big trouble if they didn't return my map or books. I relaxed: I knew that I would get everything back. Except for episodes on the black market, the Chinese were very honest people. Their curiosity compelled them to always want to touch things. After a few minutes, they returned my books and maps and pointed us in the direction of town.

We pedaled into Sanshui, and were directed to a plush hotel. I walked into the lobby while Michelle watched our bikes. I flipped to the room-ordering page in the back of <u>Southwest China</u>. I showed them that we were two people. They said no. I tried to communicate that one bed would be fine, that Michelle and I could sleep in one bed. That was out of the question, they seemed to be telling me.

I couldn't figure out why, when an English-speaking couple from Singapore stepped forward to tell me that the hotel was full. And because the town only had two hotels for foreigners, they would be happy to take us to the other hotel.

When we got there, it was also full!

Somehow our English-speaking friends talked one of the hotel employees into helping us find a room. She was coming off duty, so, walking our bikes, we followed her in and out of alleys. We thought she must be taking us to the next town! Twenty minutes later, she stopped in front of what looked like somebody's back door. She knocked.

After a long discussion with a woman on the other side, the door finally opened. Our guide left and we used our version of sign language and the phrase book to get a room. For 34 RMB, or about seven US dollars, our night's lodging included air conditioning, a private bathroom and TV. Such luck!

The woman who had answered the door happily helped us carry our gear and bikes up three flights of stairs to our room. She also gave us some laundry soap to wash our grimy clothes. We took a shower and sipped on a cup of hot tea while she drew us a map to a restaurant she recommended.

Carefully following her directions and turning at all the right alleys, we finally found the restaurant. The cooks came over and greeted us. I pointed to the phrase "no meat," and they quickly nodded. Gratefully, we let them decide the rest.

They smiled as they delivered each course to our table. Watching for our approval, they stood next to us throughout each course. Our meal included the ever-present bean curd, mini-corn, bean sprouts, mushroom soup, and plenty of rice. What a treat, and what a great place to land the first day out of Canton!

We returned to the hotel and our first restful night in days! No buzzing mosquitoes bombarded us and we didn't wake up in a sweat from the humidity. It was even quiet. We didn't suffer from bells and horns or loud voices throughout the night.

In the morning we left in pouring rain. Michelle's old five-speed bike, which blended in with all of the other bikes on the road, sported fenders. Mine did not. While I was pedaling along I heard laughter. I turned my head and two men riding behind me were laughing and pointing at my bike. I looked and saw a mud fountain coming off my rear tire. It was spraying a line down my back. I smiled and shrugged my shoulders. There was nothing to do about it now.

We headed west for Zhaoqing, famous for towering limestone pillars. The wet roads, blasting horns, and ringing bells forced me to concentrate on what lay ahead. After a while, I looked back to check on Michelle. I stopped and waited. Still, no Michelle.

I turned around and quickly cycled back. I found her standing on the side of the road glaring at her disabled bike. She had a flat tire. We took cover in what looked like a bus depot, but was a post office, and I began to change the rear tire. Needless to say a crowd quickly formed. I pulled the tube out and held it up to the light. With each of my movements, the crowd pressed closer. Finally, I could not move to finish changing the tire. With a smile, I motioned for them to step back and placed Michelle as a sentinel between our bikes and the crowd. The sun symbolically emerged as I pumped up the tire and we rode off.

Searing heat quickly replaced the rain showers, and we searched for a watermelon stand. Throughout our travels, watermelons were a convenient source of liquid. Besides the boiled and bottled water we got from hotel rooms, we also used melons to fend off dehydration.

Following our watermelon break, we pedaled through the mind-boggling shapes of a mountain ridge that loomed before us. Like children naming cloud formations, we tried to associate different animals with the amazing shapes we were seeing. We saw herds of elephants, a lion, even a camel's back.

The valley floor below us shimmered with its green velvet carpet of rice fields and other crops. The clean air blew across my face keeping me cool. What a place!

Shortly thereafter, another storm moved in and it began to pour, covering us with mud again. We arrived in Zhaoqing late in the afternoon and we spent the next two hours looking for a room. A popular tourist spot, Zhaoqing is noted for the Seven Star Crags. Taking advantage of these fascinating limestone formations, the government built a park featuring lakes, pathways and bridges that offer the visitor tranquility and beauty. This was one of my favorite excursions in China because of its peacefulness. We stopped at a lavish tourist hotel to ask for information regarding other cheaper hotels. The manager took one look at us and asked us to leave.

We tried another hotel, but the receptionist wouldn't even look up at us. Finally, I realized we were in a Chinese hotel and we left.

An English-speaking man offered to lead us to a hotel that had vacancies. We followed him as he slowly paraded his motorcycle up and down streets and through dirt alleyways. He stopped at a hotel. We reserved a room, came back out and gave him some American cigarettes as a thank you. I remembered from my last trip that the Chinese are insulted by monetary tips. Since almost everyone in China smoked, I decided to give away cigarettes in moments like this.

When he left, I realized there was something peculiar about this hotel. It almost looked like one I had stayed in during the vacation part of my business trip to Hong Kong.

No, it couldn't be, I thought.

The clerk showed us to our room. When she opened the door, I nearly fainted. Not only was this the same hotel, it seemed like the same room!

The last time I was here, I drank a lot of cheap beer so I could tolerate the primitive conditions. This time, as I looked around at the cement floors, dinged-up plaster walls, mosquito netting, and the one high window, I thought that I had better not get used to such luxury!

After showering, we washed our bikes in the shower.

The next day we asked an English-speaking man at our hotel about the road to Wuzhou, 60 miles away. We could pick up needed supplies and arrange for other travel much easier in that large town. Our travel books had also mentioned the colorful street markets, the Buddhist temple, and an ancient monastery.

The man suggested that we take a ferry because the route to Wuzhou offered some tough mountain climbing and bad roads.

Uncertain about Michelle's stamina, we decided to take his advice. Neither of us was prepared for what was to come.

Enroute to the ferry, I stopped to write postcards. As I sat on the weathered stairs of the post office, several people gathered around me. They laughed at the way I made letters and words. One boy scolded me for not connecting all my lines when drawing the characters for USA. When I finished writing the Chinese pictographs for "USA" on each of the cards, they cheered.

We rolled our bikes up the gangplank and boarded the ferry. The inside looked like a three-level bus with wooden planks for seats and beds. Michelle and I took another look at our ticket, wondering if we had boarded the wrong boat. We showed our tickets to the officials, and they shook their heads yes, we were on the right boat.

We were directed to the outside deck to lock our bikes. Like fun-loving, curious children, a group of passengers followed us. When we stopped, they quickly surrounded us. A few brave souls even reached over and played with all the strange levers and other gadgets on our bikes.

It was difficult to explain to these innocent onlookers that pulling on the gears was not good for the bikes. Michelle and I sat for almost 30 minutes wondering if we would be spending the night on the deck guarding our bicycles. Finally, a crew member broke them up. We removed our packs and carried all our gear up two flights of stairs. We took turns watching each other's stuff while we slowly made several trips back and forth. The passageways were narrow and the stairs were basically a wooden ladder. Exhausted, we flopped on our combination bed and seat.

Michelle and I looked around. About three hundred sets of eyes were directed at us.

"This is going to be a long night," I joked to Michelle. "I'll be right back, I've got to go down to the bathroom. Can you handle all this attention?"

Thinking I could escape the stares for a while and get a much needed shower, I brought my towel and soap. The showers were coed and consisted of a garden hose that you picked up and sprayed your neighbor with. I began to take off my top. The men stared even more intently. I changed my mind about bathing.

As I walked toward the squat toilets, I noticed that someone had even defecated in a shower. The stench of body odor gave way to the pungent fumes of the filthy squat toilets. Sick to my stomach by now, I relieved myself as I held my hand over my nose to keep from throwing up. I ran out holding my breath.

I climbed back on my bunk and answered any questions Michelle had about the bathroom by hanging my head out the window.

We passed through a fairyland of mounds, towers, cones, and craggy peninsulas. We passed several fishing boats where families lived on board. Commercial liners blew their horns. The activity on the river was a world in itself. I was glad to experience a part of China by boat.

Meanwhile, the mayhem on board continued.

Dinner arrived. We knew it would be best just to watch as we motioned that we were not hungry. As they ate, the passengers spit and threw food on the floor. Spittle, food scraps, watermelon rinds, beer bottles and cigarette butts covered the floor. We were thankful that they put us in the top bunks above all this mess.

I thought about a conversation I'd had with Tony. He had warned us that many young adults were raised with little or no manners. Their parents, mostly Red Guards during the cultural revolution, did not go to school or carry on the culture of the previous generations. Students, on the other hand, would be different, showing more manners. But the average person was not educated.

Thinking back on the book *Life and Death in Shanghai* helped me to understand this reality when I was confronted with it. I had sympathy for these people. As in the US and many countries around the world, a lot was based on a person's background—access to education and other advantages.

At 10:00 pm, the lights went out. As I closed my eyes, I felt something crawl across my face.

"Michelle" I called softly, "What the hell was that?"

"Cockroaches," she replied.

I jumped out of my sleeping bag, put on my flip-flops and went downstairs to buy some beer. Although we had been tempted by the beer all night, we'd avoided drinking anything for fear of the squat toilets. But now the cockroaches changed my thinking. I bought two large bottles of beer and we gulped them down. We didn't sleep all night and I braved the toilets twice.

With a great sense of relief, we disembarked in Wuzhou. Determined to escape the squalid boat, we were the first people off! It was 5:00 am and several street merchants were still sleeping next to their carts as we made our way to a hotel where we could finally take a shower. We checked in, showered in cold water, and then collapsed onto our wooden beds. There were no mattresses, but we didn't care!

Exhausted, Michelle and I slept until we heard a knock on the door. I opened it and there stood a little old man. He introduced himself and said that his name was Ching. Speaking very good English, he quietly and politely told us that he had come to show us around town. From our discussions with Barbara back in Canton, we knew that he had been sent by the police. We were sure that his job was to make certain we bought tickets out of town since we were not allowed to bike on any of the surrounding roads. He was so pleasant, though, that we happily played along.

In his cute and very proper way, he asked to see our passports. He spent a long time reading them before he took us to a bus station where we booked ourselves on a nine-hour trip that would leave the next day.

Our guide then showed us how to get to the Western Bamboo Temple that we had heard so much about. We said good-bye and followed stairs and a steep dusty trail to this Buddhist place of worship. We walked for more than 30 minutes on this dirt path that led around the mountain. Tiny homes sat everywhere along the way. Stairs branched off frequently, leading to even more homes. The view of the river and the town below was fascinating.

At the temple an 80-year-old woman, referred to as a nun, greeted us. She acted as the head teacher for the other 20 nuns who served here. This remarkable woman had a considerable English vocabulary and invited us into their vegetarian restaurant. She joined us for lunch.

As we sat high atop this mountain overlooking the city of Wuzhou and the rich outlying fields of green bamboo and rice paddies, we feasted. We devoured one plate after another of hot steaming fried noodles, bean sprouts and yellow beans. A stir-fry concoction of peanuts, mushrooms and other vegetables came after a savory chickpea soup. The nuns giggled as we motioned with our hands and used words in our phrase book to tell them this was the best meal we had eaten in all of China.

Although I was hardly able to communicate with the younger nuns, I still managed to develop a close bond with them. Looking into their eyes, I could see we were on the same quest. Like myself, they seemed to want a clearer connection to their true inner being. We exchanged addresses and promised to stay in contact.

I was touched by feelings of affection for these nuns. Perhaps this was one example of many to come that my trip was not about pedaling from one place to another, but about the people along the way. It was a very uplifting afternoon.

We woke early the next morning and pedaled to the bus station. As with most stations, it was crowded and confusing. We found the man Ching had introduced us to the day before. He was there to help us with check-in and boarding. After we tagged our bikes and reluctantly handed them over, we sat and waited. I watched my bike like a hawk; I couldn't imagine losing Buddy. When I saw them loading the luggage on top of the bus, I jumped up to show the employees how to load Buddy without hurting his gears. I showed them how to position the bike among the crates and other luggage so that the derailleur would lay up and away from any obstruction. The workers all nodded in agreement. They seemed to understand.

Then I took my seat and every set of eyes on the crowded bus studied us. A short while later, we motored through a dramatic mountain range and then spectacular limestone formations. In this area, big baskets of tomatoes lined the side of the road waiting to be picked up. I felt trapped inside the bus and resented the fact that I wasn't riding my bike through this stunning area.

Later, dust, traffic, and dilapidated roads compounded my agitation. The wheels on the bus bumped and pounded as though they were square, and all I could think of was my bike. Sweat dripped down my face; my bare arms stuck to the seat. The live chickens and ducks on board bounced up, down, and sideways. As the passengers held on, they kept staring at us. My head smashed against the window frame, yet body odor and putrid-smelling animals forced me to breathe outside for fresh air.

Finally, we arrived in Yangshou. While we waited for our bikes to be unloaded, we watched the crowds on the street. Compared to my previous trip to China, not only did people want to interact more, but they seemed to smile and laugh as well.

They also wore more color. We looked through an iron fence at a group of mini-skirted women wearing brightly colored nylons that were intended for use with dressy slacks. Other women, trying to copy American fashion that they had seen in magazines, wore patent leather shoes and pastel-shaded lace blouses.

Five years ago, all that I remembered seeing was Mao blue or gray. This time it seemed that the younger women all tried to dress themselves in anything that had color. They wore bright barrettes and glistening polyester blouses. It appeared the only fashion statement in China was color.

As they were unloading the bus, I heard lots of commotion and realized it was over my bike. I saw Buddy laying on his side, the derailleur down and his pedal wedged into the wooden luggage rack. Everyone backed away as I climbed up to save my friend. I pulled and yanked, finally releasing the pedal. Thankful there was no damage, I hugged my bike and carried him down to safety.

We packed our gear on our bikes and walked to the street. We were greeted by swarms of English-speaking money changers and hotel vendors. We changed money and then headed for a hotel. After we negotiated for a room and took a welcome cold shower, we walked to the main part of town for some food.

Michelle and I felt a touch of culture shock. Signs in English advertised everything from cold drinks to eggs, pancakes and fresh coffee. "Hey Michelle," I turned and said, "do you feel like we have just descended on another planet?"

We heard music playing down the street and walked toward it.

"Now I've seen everything," I said. Up ahead was a Hard Rock Cafe housed in an old wooden building with a boombox playing a scratchy tape of American rock.

We walked up the stairs and joined a group of western travelers sitting outside. This was the first time since Canton we had seen any other foreigners. It seemed strange. Using an English menu, we ordered Americanized fried rice and eggs with tomatoes. We sat and watched this Chinese world go by as we drank another western-style favorite, cold beer. A procession of proud fathers streamed along showing off their infant sons or daughters to friends. Vendors announced their offers of cold drinks in English. Young and old, male or female, everyone here competed for the tourist dollar.

Cormorant fishing caught our attention. We went out the next night as a full moon shone across the river and millions of stars gleamed above the incredible limestone formations. We watched from a covered boat as these domesticated birds prowled the waters. An old fisherman commanded his birds to dive. They plummeted toward the river and then disappeared in its depths. They surfaced again. A fish squirmed in one cormorant's beak as it swam back to its owner's tiny wooden boat. A string had been tied around the bird's neck so that it couldn't swallow its catch. The other three people aboard clapped hands with Michelle and I as the man held up the fish.

The Center of Attention

After a trip to a small village the following day, the axle on Michelle's bike finally gave out. Throughout China it had worked itself loose daily. We would just tighten it and keep on going. This morning, however, we managed to strip the threads. The wheel wobbled against the brake pad.

Happily, there was a bike shop in town! We found it hidden in a back alley. Dust from the dirt floor coated the miscellaneous parts that were stuffed in crates throughout the store. A cigar box served as the cash register. Six or seven new and used bikes leaned on their kickstands awaiting new owners.

A crowd followed us as we walked our bikes up to the entrance. Michelle pointed to the problem and rolled her eyes toward the heavens. She motioned that something was wrong. The man, probably in his late twenties, spun the tire, listened to the grinding sound and nodded that, yes, he could fix it.

He went inside and returned with a pair of pliers, a hammer, and a long screwdriver. We wondered what was next as the crowd grew around us. He took off the wheel and began pounding on the axle. He spun the tire. Not satisfied, he pounded some more. Unable to get the result he wanted, he decided that maybe he could do something with the bearings.

I figured that if the Chinese could maintain some of the bikes I'd seen on the road, maybe this fellow knew what he was doing. As he opened up the race that held the bearings, the shiny beebee-like pellets landed in the dirt all around the bike. The crowd pressed forward, burying many of the silver balls in the dirt. The mechanic scolded the crowd. Michelle yelled at the mechanic. I stood there in a daze.

The man sent a young boy to look for bearings. While the mechanic force-threaded the nut over the stripped part of the axle, Michelle and I discussed our alternatives. Would we be stranded here in Yangshou? Maybe Michelle could just rent a bike in each city. Maybe we could trade the man for another bike. Nothing sounded too good.

About half an hour later, the young boy ran back with both of his little fists tightly clenched. One hand contained a collection of mismatched bearings; the other held a wad of fresh grease. They put the hub back together and spun the wheel. The man nodded that it was fine. I spun the wheel and held my ear close to the axle. A dull, gritty sound came out and I motioned to the man that it was not as fine as he had suggested. He adjusted the axle nuts and returned the wheel to me. Again it was unacceptable. Three tries later, he got it right and Michelle and I breathed a huge sigh of relief. We packed our things and cycled 40 miles from Yangshou to Guilin where we could fly to Xian. Our travel books had suggested that Xian was one of China's oldest and most illustrious cities with a vast array of cultural attractions.

We arrived in town and immediately went to the airline ticket office. Inside, everyone squished together in lines that stretched throughout the lobby. When the manager finally returned from lunch, everyone squeezed in even closer, handing their money to the woman whether it was their turn or not.

Just as Michelle and I reached the window a pair of hands reached around us, trying to buy a ticket. I grabbed one by the wrist and turned to leer at the boy it belonged to. Embarrassed, he managed a weak smile. As we tried to communicate our wishes, the boy pressed forward to the window again. I asked him what he wanted. Speaking English, he told us that he could help us translate. Michelle and I put away our phrasebooks and gladly accepted his offer.

Soon we had our plane tickets in hand, and we left to explore the roads outside this big, smoggy city. Leaving behind the slow bicycle crowds and endless seas of humanity, we managed to escape into the countryside. But, to our disappointment, there was very little to see, just flat farmland. About 20 miles out, we decided that the bicycle riding chaos that ruled Guilin was better than the repetitious fields we were now seeing.

Heading back into town, we stopped along a river where Michelle joined the geese and a water buffalo for a swim. As hot and dirty as I was, I couldn't force myself to jump into the brown mud flow that masqueraded as a river. Instead, I gave myself a rare treat: I cooled off under a tiny tree. In the cities, shade usually can't be found at midday because that's when the Chinese take their daily nap. And because the country as a whole doesn't offer very many shade trees, every one is occupied from noon to about three. Michelle and I giggled as we usually pedaled past these nappers hidden under every tree or available piece of shade. In return, they glared back, certain we were fools to cycle in the heat of the day.

The next morning we packed our bikes and cycled to the airport. After waiting for three hours, we realized that we were not going to leave anytime soon. An English-speaking tour guide told us that the plane had mechanical problems and that an engineer was on his way.

A woman made an announcement over the loudspeaker and everyone stood up and walked out of the lobby. We ran to the English-speaking tour guide who told us we were to go into the restaurant for lunch. In the restaurant, the waitress refused to serve us. Then the tour guide instructed us to go back and get vouchers to pay for the meal. So, we headed back inside.

The security guards demanded our passports and tickets again. They gawked at them for several minutes before they finally let us through. We claimed our vouchers and returned to the restaurant just as the power went out. After another hour, we ate a plate of rice.

After we returned to the waiting area, the security guards once again demanded our passports and tickets. They studied them once more, discussing our passport information with other guards.

Inside the waiting room, we learned that the mechanic couldn't get there due to monsoon weather. We looked out to the runway as other planes came and went. Then the public address system announced that a plane scheduled for Xian, our destination, was arriving. Everyone jumped up, relieved that the long eight-hour wait was probably over. We were certain the airline would give the plane to our exhausted group, and have the group booked for this flight wait for another. Moments later, an announcement requested that passengers holding tickets for this flight board the plane. We were shocked. Everyone scheduled for our flight was furious. Yelling began; people raced up to the gate shaking their tickets.

The tension continued to mount. A fight broke out. People started pushing and yelling. A handful of guards rushed in and quickly quieted things down. We sat some more.

Dinner came and again we were herded into the restaurant. This time, the air conditioner broke. Michelle and I dripped perspiration all over our food as we ate more rice.

On the way back the guards again tried to detain us. This time, however, I shook my finger and shouted, "Mei-jo!" They knew that I meant no. They moved out of the way.

By the time we got back to the waiting area, the air conditioner had quit there too. Then suddenly the lights went out and we sat in darkness. Stories of the airplane's status kept changing. We didn't know what to believe.

Fourteen hours after we had been scheduled to leave, they finally called our flight. I looked around in disbelief to make sure they meant us.

Just as we fastened our seat belts, a group of well-dressed Japanese men and women pranced down the aisle. We looked dirty, sweaty and exhausted; they were clean-shaven and freshly made up. We knew they had not waited like we had.

Soon we realized that the plane had been held all day for them. We later learned that CNAC, China National Aviation Corporation, will hold a scheduled flight for a diplomat or certain groups like this one.

We arrived at the Xian airport at 1:00 am. Although we were certain we had experienced the rudest people in China at the Guilin airport, we suffered even more in Xian.

The baggage workers surrounded us as we reassembled our bikes. They poked and laughed at them. People at the various counters throughout the airport looked down or away from us when we asked them for directions. Because we had refused to heed their advice and take an overpriced taxi, they gave us the wrong directions to town.

Tired, frustrated, and ready to leave China, we found a hotel and passed out on our beds. Four hours later, at 8:00 am, we raced over to the China Travel Service to purchase tickets for Beijing. Not only was it difficult to get to cities in China, we had to make sure we found a way out of them before we did anything else. And at this point, we wanted out of China.

Now, that had become even more difficult. We couldn't get a flight out of China from Xian, but we could in Beijing. So we booked a flight to Beijing and decided to enjoy the sights we had come here for.

The rest of the day we cycled around Xian visiting museums, ancient pagodas, and the enormous bell tower in the middle of town. We couldn't understand why, with all its tourist treasures, the people here stared at us more than anywhere else we had traveled. Then we learned that with so much to see, foreigners rarely venture out of their organized tours to mix with the locals.

The next day, we set off on our bikes to the Museum of Qin, home of the terracotta soldiers. Leaving town was miserable. Black exhaust darkened my lips while the thunder of a million horns and bicycle bells pounded in my ears. In China, Buddy had stopped communicating with me long ago, but this was worse than anything I had encountered. Xian was so noisy I couldn't even hear my chain ripping a huge gash in the aluminum frame that contained it. When I had hurried to reassemble my bike at the airport, I put the chain on wrong. By the time I discovered my mistake, the metal cage had been shredded.

Finally, when we reached the countryside, we stopped in an orchard to empty our bladders. During Michelle's turn, as I stood watching the bikes, I noticed a group of boys running toward us. I yelled to Michelle to hurry up. By the time she returned, however, the young boys had accosted us.

They demanded that we pay them for using their orchard as a bathroom. We both shook our heads and got on our bikes to take off. Then they grabbed our bike racks and tried to stop us. Both of us were yelling and screaming at these teenage boys when I finally exploded. I grabbed one by the wrist and fire burned in my eyes. Then I realized that I was taking all of China's inconveniences out on him. I let him go and we rode away.

After dozens of stops for directions, we eventually made it to the Museum of Qin. We pedaled up the hill into a giant flea market madhouse. Hundreds of wooden booths stood next to each other filled with animal furs, quilts and other items for sale. I had seen very few animals in China, and now I knew why. A display of thousands of furs, many with their feet and heads still on, lay in two-and-three foot piles while the vendors shouted like carnival barkers for the tourists to spend their money.

Our problems continued. The girls inside the coat check area wouldn't take our bags. The security guards wouldn't let us lock our bikes anywhere close by. And they wouldn't accept our RMB for the squat toilets.

Having grown accustomed to such treatment, especially in Xian, we locked our bikes to a tree, forced our RMB on them for the toilets, and carried our bags, water bottles, and pumps with us.

When we finally walked inside the museum and took our first look at one of the world's most spectacular archaeological finds, the terracotta army, all troubles faded. Walking along the railing on a dirt path, I looked down at the rows of life-size clay soldiers, horses, and chariots. Six thousand strong, every figure differed in facial feature and expression. Dating back to 221 BC, the figures sported the armor of that day. The soldiers carried crossbows, spears and dagger-axes in an almost eerie realness.

We left with a better attitude.

After returning to the hotel we parked our bikes and roamed the streets of Xian. We made our way through alleys lined with food stalls. We saw lots of fresh fruit and vegetables. We even bought a Chinese pizza, which was made with pita bread and filled with stir-fried vegetables—a Xian specialty.

The next day, we flew to Beijing. Surprisingly, everything went smoothly. Our flight left only 15 minutes late and we arrived in Beijing an hour and a half later.

From the airport we rode 24 miles along a wide tree-lined boulevard into town. I liked Beijing as soon as we entered the city. Unlike the other cities we had visited, everyone cycled here in an orderly manner. As we pedaled along the wide bike lanes, refreshingly, many neatly dressed people greeted us in English.

We biked to a popular budget hotel for foreigners, the Qiao Hotel. I walked in (using positive self-projection) and I happily greeted the clerk. "Hi, a room for two?" I asked.

"Mei-jo," the receptionist replied, looking back down at her desk.

Being careful with my persistence, I asked, "What time for a room?" I smiled.

She responded in good English, "Two hours or so, after 12:00." She looked down again.

Other travelers had warned us about the difficulty of finding a room in Beijing. They had said to be persistent. So, I smiled, sat down and said, "OK, thank you, I'll wait."

Ten minutes went by and I approached the woman again,

"Excuse me, any rooms?" I asked. "Has anyone left?" My eyes looked into hers. I smiled.

She ignored me.

As I stood there quietly waiting for her to answer, I remained positive. I smiled. I remained cheerful. I let the energy of my request extend outward. Her associate sauntered over and asked me, "Room for how many?"

"A room for two," I replied.

"Sign here and write passport number. And friend, she must sign too," she said.

Excited with my success, I ran outside to Michelle who was waiting with the bikes. I got her passport. I walked back in and paid. As I passed through the lobby, travelers who had spent the previous night on the floor glared at me. I had even secured a private room, no less.

I was learning that in China my needs were never met by force. Back home, I had obtained results in difficult situations by pushing. Here I was learning a whole new way, a more human way. No one likes to lose face or be shown up in a situation, especially the Chinese. So in order to win, I had to make sure that the other side yielded with dignity.

As soon as we had settled in our room, we cycled to the friendship store to indulge ourselves. Major cities in China like Beijing and Shanghai built friendship stores so embassy employees could shop for merchandise from home. Products ranged from washers and dryers to furniture, bicycles, linens, clothes, and groceries. A guard stood at the entrance and allowed only foreigners in. Michelle and I felt like two kids in a candy store. We bought fresh croissants, shredded wheat cereal, M&Ms, Quaker Oats and two ice-cold beers. We shopped at the friendship store almost every day during our two-week stay in Beijing.

While cycling to find a place to eat, we came upon a building that didn't look like a restaurant but we could smell food. I peeked inside and was immediately greeted by three smiling girls. They ran out and grabbed our bikes. Come, they signaled. They led the way to a table.

We couldn't believe they actually parked our bikes.

"Ni Hao," the girls chorused as we settled into our chairs. Seven or eight round tables sat in the center of the tiny room. Two small windows accepted light from the outside. The family members grinned as they chatted among themselves.

Almost immediately I felt a bond with these new friends. They helped us order. Jiao, the manager, spoke some English. We talked about our two countries by using sign language, our phrasebooks and Jiao's English. Then, after they fed us an incredible lunch, the mother went to the local store and bought everyone ice cream bars. We traded stories for hours.

The family quickly became our best friends in China even though we could hardly communicate with words. We ate in the restaurant every day.

Later that evening I met a traveler who could help me get out of Beijing and China. He offered to sell me a train ticket across Russia on the Trans-Siberian railway. Buying a ticket in this way, however, presented problems. Just because you had a ticket did not mean that you had a seat. Nor did it mean that you could get into or out of the countries the train traversed.

He let me borrow the ticket to see if I could make it work. I went to the China Travel Service where they booked a seat for me on a train scheduled to leave in 14 days. Excited about my ensuing journey, I went back and paid the man $150 for his ticket.

I now needed transit visas for Russia, East Germany, and Poland. I cycled to the Russian embassy early the next morning and got in line with several pushy Europeans. The light drizzle soon changed to rain. I shivered as the line slowly inched forward. The transit visa that I was applying for would allow me only 48 hours in Moscow, a transfer stop for passengers heading to various European destinations. I finally made it to the front of the line and dripped all over the counter as I filled out my application. The visa would be ready in five days. As an American, I was charged more than other foreigners for my visa. By contrast, visas for Poland and East Germany were issued on the spot.

Michelle and I next spent a day visiting the Forbidden City which sat opposite Tiananmen Square. Tiananmen means "heavenly peace." The square was created by Chairman Mao, who founded the Chinese Communist party in 1921. Surrounded by wide, almost antiseptically clean boulevards and government buildings, this vast slate-covered city center stretches for blocks. During Mao's reign, crowds of up to a million came to hear him speak. When he died in 1976, another million people came to pay him homage.

We walked across the square, awed by its size, and entered the Forbidden City. For 500 years, a moat and towering walls had isolated those living here from the rest of China. Its 800 buildings housed two dynasties of emperors who had governed the country. We looked upon this fairyland of ancient wooden buildings not believing our eyes. Our view, however, was marred by a trail of lunch containers and other trash which led from one building to another. We competed with the Chinese for a look inside these buildings. Since we were not allowed to go inside, we had to inch along with the crowd to peer through a tiny window.

Giving up on seeing anything, we then stood in line for an ice cream. People pushed and shoved. A fight broke out. We left immediately.

As soon as we started riding, it began to pour. Despite the fact that I had learned after the first rain in China to watch the locals when the skies looked threatening, I didn't notice this time until it was too late. Whenever I saw people pull over and put on their rain ponchos, no matter how tame the clouds looked, it always meant rain. If the sky blackened and they didn't stop, it meant that we could continue riding without problems.

We pedaled back to Jiao's restaurant, ordered lunch, and shared our day's activities with the family. Almost every time we came in for a meal, several neighbors came to watch how we ate. They listened intently to our English. No matter how hard our day was, they always made us laugh.

At two o'clock the next morning I had a rude awakening. When I got up to go to the bathroom, and switched on the light, thousands of cockroaches ran for cover. Cockroaches populated most of the hotels we stayed in, but this was the worst that I had seen.

I went on a rampage and started attacking the little bugs with my shoe. For the next hour, I switched the light on and off, exposing more and more of the crusty crawlers as I screamed and smashed. Michelle begged me to forget about them, insisting that I was not accomplishing anything. Maybe she was right, but I released enough of my frustration to fall back to sleep.

After enduring restless nights of partying travelers, cockroaches, and even bed bugs that gave us both rashes, we decided to check out of the Qiao Hotel and into the Tiantan Sports Hotel. The Sports Hotel cost us twice as much but it was fully carpeted and air conditioned. All of the hotel employees spoke English. It even had a real flush toilet and a cold-drink vending machine.

We celebrated in our room with coffee, French bread and peanut paste that we had bought at the friendship store. The peanut paste almost tasted like real peanut butter. Almost.

I stayed up late to call home. After I told the front desk that I wanted to call the States, it took another hour for them to make the connection. They got through just before midnight and rang my room.

It was great to hear Mom's voice. She told me about what was happening with my brothers and my sister and other members of the family. As always, news from home brought some tears to my eyes. I really missed everybody.

She and I had talked about lots of things when I suddenly realized that people at home did more than just survive from day to day. In this country, I had to be sharp every waking moment. I had to make sure that the food I ate was OK. The language confused me. I couldn't read the street signs or the signs on buildings. I had to stay on top of my own personal hygiene, which, at times was a struggle. This new culture bombarded me with twists and turns from moment to moment. I needed to know how to break liters into quarts, meters into feet and then assign value to this confusing mix using a money system which employed two standards. I realized that I had been fighting to exist on a daily basis.

The next day we took a two-hour bus ride to the Great Wall at Badaling. Fog at first shrouded our view of this 3,700-mile-long wall. As we climbed stairs to the top—25 feet high— the fog slowly yielded a spectacular view of the rugged mountains the wall had sought to divide. Bus loads of picture-taking tourists soon encircled us and we headed off in search of quiet. We walked for the next hour ascending hundreds of stairs and very steep archways.

By this time we were a mile away from the crush of humanity. We sat and rested. The peacefulness of this magnificent wall enveloped us. Constructed at a cost of many lives and resources, the wall was supposed to keep marauding nomads out of the Chinese empire that it protected two thousand years ago. Instead, it mostly operated as an elevated highway over the mountainous terrain it spans. Ancient warriors, silk traders, and even Marco Polo had set foot on it. We walked back feeling we had just emerged from a time warp.

On the way home, we made the mistake of eating at a different restaurant. As we sat waiting for our noodle dish, I watched one of the cooks open the refrigerator door. I caught a glimpse of what looked like internal organs from animals. Somehow, Michelle and I managed to eat without vomiting. Thankfully we ate only vegetables. Michelle was vegetarian and I had decided in China I would not eat any meat. My phrase book helped me communicate that we were vegetarian.

We spent the next few days visiting many sights. We relaxed in the parks as local people played cards and dominoes in the sunshine. In the early morning hours we witnessed groups of men performing their perfectly choreographed Tai Chi routines. Proud parents paraded about with their one child. In an effort to stem the population explosion, the government allows couples only one offspring.

Since parents allowed little children to defecate through the slit in their pants anywhere they pleased, I was careful to watch where I walked. At first I had thought that the little droppings were produced by dogs. But I saw very few domestic animals and quickly learned who the real culprits were.

Michelle's final night in China arrived. Tomorrow we would ride together for the last time when I escorted her to the airport. It was hard to believe that our journey together was over.

We didn't discuss much as Michelle packed. She was happy to be leaving, going back to her homeland, her warm bed, and good cooking. She missed Glen, her horse and dogs. By this time I, too, needed the comforts of home, but I was committed to continuing my travels. So I remained strong and tried not to think about home as Michelle packed her last things.

We ate our farewell dinner at Jiao's and took group photographs. The family gave us each a canister of black tea. We exchanged addresses and hugged. "I'll see you tomorrow," I said to Jiao as I waved good-bye.

At the airport I watched quietly as Michelle boarded the plane. The four weeks we had spent together had almost seemed like four years. In such a short time, the two of us had been through so much. I wondered about what lay ahead for me as she ducked into the airplane. As it lifted off the runway, I began to feel homesick and nervous about the next leg of my journey.

Slowly, I biked the 24 miles back to the hotel. Now that I was really on my own, all decisions were mine. No longer would I be able to discuss a destination, mode of travel, or accommodation with anyone. I had to rely totally on my own inner feelings. Although I felt a tremendous burden, I also felt a massive sense of adventure beginning to unfold.

The person I saw in the mirror told me that I had a big job ahead of me. My inner voice seemed to be telling me that I would have to suppress my femininity. Not only would the physical terrain of the countries after Russia challenge me, but so would the men. To deal with this potential problem, I would need to hide my body with baggy clothes, and cut my hair.

So, I took out my tiny scissors tucked inside my pocket knife and began to cut. A sadness came over me as I wondered how many more sacrifices I would need to make.

I spent the next four days alone in China gathering supplies, ensuring my visas were in order, buying money, and writing letters home.

On the last day in China, I spent most of the afternoon with my restaurant friends. We shared our last meal together.

Jiao helped to translate what I was saying to his two brothers, his wife and three employees. Using sign language, Jiao, and my phrase books, they asked me about work in the States, the people, number of children, and money. The neighbors came in and listened intently, even though they did not understand English.

As we walked out the front door to take photographs, I gave one of the employees my rain poncho. This family had meant so much to me. It almost seemed that they could have been my next door neighbors back home. I knew we had touched each other's lives in an unforgettable way. I wanted to leave them something tangible to keep, learn from, and remember me by. So I gave them my phrasebooks, my last US dollar, and the last two packs of cigarettes. I hugged each of them as hard as I could. True to form, Jiao and his wife said they would see me off at the train station the next evening.

Chapter Six
Russia By Rail

I awakened on my last morning in China full of anticipation. Had I done everything right so that I could just allow the Trans-Siberian train to whisk me away? Did I get enough rubles on the black market? Were my transit visas all in order? Had I bought enough food for the next six days? Did I have enough books to read? Did I have all the necessary papers for my bike? Should I keep some of my Chinese money just in case?

It was hard to believe that only six months ago, New Zealand customs officials were disinfecting me with bug spray. Now I was soon to join some of the world's most seasoned travelers on one of the world's most legendary train rides. Soon, Europe's roads would pass beneath my bike.

Although the train didn't leave until 7:30 pm, customs wanted my bike at the station by 10:00 am. I arrived by nine o'clock and was surprised at how easy check-in was. A customs official helped me fill in all the papers and tag my bike. I paid 103 FEC, about $27.

Leaving the freight building, I headed for the main terminal to check my bags into a storage locker for the day. Placing my tent under one arm, sleeping bag under the other, and clutching my five bike bags, I staggered forward carrying 65 pounds. Ugh!

Every 20 feet I had to stop and reposition my load until I made it to the line for the main gate. Hundreds of people stood in a wide queue that narrowed into a turnstile just big enough to pass through single file. Surveying the crowd, I felt truly alone. There was not another foreigner in sight, just Chinese racing through the gate. Many of them carried a small watermelon under one arm and bags filled with gifts in the other.

As the mob propelled me closer to the gate, it began to rain. Suddenly the crowd surged forward and I was yanked and pulled in different directions. I struggled to keep my balance while several elbows jabbed me in the ribs. At one point, the charging throng hooked my tent and spun me around as I was pushed toward the one revolving metal gate. I began to lose my footing on the rain-slickened concrete. Somehow I managed to keep moving forward.

I finally made it to the turnstile and tried to force my gear through. The crowd began to yell and shout. I thought they would trample me because I slowed down their progress. When I made it through, I collapsed. The crowds barreled past me as I raised myself to my knees. I collected my strength and stumbled out of their way.

As I sat against a small metal pole, I wiped beads of sweat off my forehead. I lifted my shirt and saw a collection of red welts on my body. Crease marks had formed in my hands where I had gripped my bags with all my might. My whole body ached. I tried to calm my nerves before my next task—finding a locker for the belongings I had fought so valiantly to retain.

I hobbled over to what looked like an information booth. The small woman inside shooed me away. I walked to another window and showed the attendant my bags. She shook her finger and said, "Mei jo!" As I stood there wondering what to do next, one of her coworkers came up and told me, in English, that all the storage lockers were full. I nearly passed out.

Feeling discouraged, I made my way to the foreigner's waiting room to spend my final hours in China. There I found someone else with the same predicament, a woman named Kristie. She too, had grown tired of China and couldn't wait to get back to her job in Switzerland.

As a fan noisily rumbled overhead, voices called out destinations and arrivals over the loudspeaker. Workers busily scurried about with luggage carts. Trains came and went. Passengers chatted anxiously in the hallways. Then at 1:00 pm the lights went out. The station lapsed into an eerie quiet. Everything stopped. Kristie and I looked at each other and giggled as we realized what was taking place: nap time. The afternoon dragged on as my anticipation and apprehension about the next six days grew.

Half an hour before my train was ready to leave, Jiao and his wife showed up. My spirits immediately brightened. They brought me gifts. By now, the waiting room was full of other European travelers. They looked on with surprise as my friends and I hugged and carried on.

"You open," said Jiao, who had obviously consulted his phrase book beforehand.

Holding back my tears, I opened the first small package. Inside were two sets of porcelain chopsticks. One pair was for me and the other was labeled "for your mother".

"Thank you Jiao, thank you, I will always remember you," I said, knowing that I would probably never see him again.

"Open," they prodded as they pointed to the other package.

I pulled out a beautiful white silk handkerchief and held it up to the light. They had penned me a message: "For our friend Sally, 7-23-88".

"I will miss you and your family. You are special," I said as my voice cracked.

The loudspeaker announced in English that our train was ready to board. Jiao picked up my bags. I carried my tent and sleeping bag while we made our way onto the train and through its narrow hallways. My cumbersome load blocked the passageway adding to the sense of confusion that plagued everyone. Finally, we found my compartment.

Jiao and his wife stayed on board until the loudspeaker announced that the train was leaving. I hugged both of them one last time before they got off. The train slowly rumbled out of the station; we kept waving at each other until they faded from view.

Sadness overwhelmed me as I sat in my compartment. I looked around at the three men who would share the long journey with me. My focus changed as I prepared for the next leg of my trip.

We began to set up our temporary home. "Boy, we have

some tight quarters here," I joked, not knowing if anybody spoke English. "I hope nobody snores."

Our car, like all the others on the train, had eight very simple compartments just like this one. And in each room, a wide picture window framed the outside world. Small beds sat atop each other like the bunk beds I had known as a child. There was a storage locker under each of the bottom two bunks and a tabletop that we could pull down between us. More picture windows displayed the outside world on the other side of the car.

"Vell, we should know each other for long ride ahead," announced Yop in his very strong Dutch accent.

Quickly we introduced ourselves and became comfortable as a group, before the train made its first stop. I could tell already I was in for a fun time; my roommates were great. Yop and his son-in-law, Peter, who was about my age, had just left their wives in China after completing a month of travel there. Their wives had decided to fly back to Holland, while Yop and Peter opted for the train. The two were alive and ready for some adventure.

Jon, a 70-year-old marathon runner from Denmark, had his own small black market operation: selling excess Russian rubles. He had brought more Russian currency on his trip than he needed, and now he was selling it. Since he spoke many different languages, travelers began to visit and exchange money.

After having spent a full day in the noisy, dirty train station, I couldn't wait any longer for a shower.

"Say, do you know which way the shower is?" I asked.

Peter and Yop looked at each other and shrugged their shoulders.

"OK, what do you call them in Europe, the douche?"

"This train no have douche," Peter replied.

"What! You can't be serious, no douche?"

They shook their heads.

Sitting all day in that hot stuffy station was hard, but knowing a shower awaited me on the train helped me get through it.

Determined to shower, I jumped up and announced, "Well I'm going to create one, then."

I opened the door to the bathroom, and sure enough, there

really was no shower. But there was water, and a hole in the floor that opened down to the tracks. Excited about my new find, I dashed back to my room and retrieved my trusty cooking pot.

Back in the tiny closet-sized bathroom, I peeled off my clothes and filled the pot with water. Holding my breath, I summoned enough courage to pour the cold water all over my body. Then I pressed my head sideways into the tiny sink and ran even more water through my hair. Finished with the first part of my counterfeit shower, I began to soap myself down. My body shivered and my teeth chattered as I dumped more water over myself to rinse off.

The next stage involved the sink. Once again, I pressed my head into the tiny wash basin while the movement of the train vibrated my face against the sink and my head against the faucet. I did not want to think about my face smashed inside this public sink. It was gross, but worth it.

I dried off, brushed my teeth, put on clean clothes, and emerged from the bathroom a new person. As I walked down the hallway, everyone noticed my wet hair and clean, fresh appearance.

Obviously confused, one person asked, "Is there a douche on board?"

I turned and said, "No, but the bathroom sink works fine. But be careful, it's small and the vibration of the train causes your head to hit the faucet."

Soon, other passengers lined up for the bathroom and I went to bed!

We would pass through eight time zones in the days ahead and I would no longer be able to rely on watches to tell me when I was hungry, sleepy or ready for bed. I would sleep a lot as my body recovered from the rigors of China. And as I continually excused myself for more and more slumber throughout our journey, Yop and Peter worried about my health.

I needed this rest, I reasoned. This was the first time in almost six months that I didn't have to concern myself with pure survival.

I didn't have to worry about getting somewhere before dark. The weather, maps, mileage, customs, directions, and mechanical problems no longer placed demands on me. I welcomed the break.

I read books, practiced my Silva techniques, and spent time meditating. The view out the window remained unchanged until we reached a town. Then even it looked the same. Several dozen houses lined the muddy streets. Weeds grew inside the idle, rusted machinery resting in the outlying fields. A cinder block schoolhouse usually stood at the center of town. Little children eagerly pointed and waved at the train.

One of the last towns in China was different and captured my attention. As we pulled into the station, I noted several vending carts. Each appeared to be stocked with fruits, vegetables and flowers. Women stood by each of them. But by the time the train stopped and we got off, the station was deserted. Everyone had disappeared. A large group of us stood there looking at each other. Where did everyone go? Had we seen a mirage?

We would never know; the train pressed on.

Early the next morning we arrived at the Chinese border, the first of two border stops only fifteen minutes apart. Earlier on the train, we had been instructed not to take any photographs of stations, border crossings or guards. Peter and I furtively snapped several photos of the spindly watchtower which looked like a tree house built on metal poles.

Using French and sign language, the Russian steward who had been with us since Beijing sent us to our rooms. There, he instructed us to sit on our own beds, pull out our luggage and passports, and then wait.

Having heard horror stories about this part of the journey, I closed my eyes and visualized a happy, carefree exchange. Moments later, three stern looking Chinese officers walked into our room and asked for our passports. Smiling, I said "hello" and gave them my documents. After reviewing our papers, they handed them back, and gave us all a declaration form to fill out. Then they left.

After completing the forms, the officials let us off the train to exchange our Chinese money. While in line I met Diane, an

English woman who had just finished a backpacking trip through Africa. I had been so entertained by my roommates, that we hadn't crossed paths. Diane had also been distracted: she had been busy teaching our Russian dining car waiter how to speak English. Now that we had met and found we had so much in common, Diane and I would spend much time talking in the days ahead.

Two hours later the whistle blew for us to board the train. It slowly ground through an area called No Man's Land which serves as the buffer between China and Russia. Made up of rolling weed-covered hills and filled with landmines, it had a white fence that formed the dividing line. Crossing into the USSR, we passed a second lookout tower and stopped briefly to pick up more officials. The Russian tower rose solidly from the ground. It was made out of brick, and looked as if it had been built to withstand the ages.

Again we sat on our bunks with everything visible. Four intimidating Soviet officers entered our room. They looked into each person's eyes and asked for passports. Like real pros they studied our photographs, frequently glancing back and forth to confirm the identity of each person. Once satisfied that everything was in order, they returned the documents. When they got to me, I tried not to laugh as the officer's eyes switched back and forth from my photo on the passport to the one on the visa. He kept looking for an answer. My passport photograph had been taken in 1984. In that picture, I wore a suit, makeup and my hair was longer. The visa photo was taken in China within the last month. There was quite a difference! The sun had lightened my hair; my skin was more freckled, dark and weathered. Finally, he grunted and handed my papers back.

The train tracks also differed on this side of the Sino-Soviet border. The Chinese use a special gauge track to discourage outsiders from invading their country. Because the tracks were not compatible, we had a three-hour delay while workers changed the train's heavy iron wheels.

As our train rolled out of the border area, we continued heading northeast. The weather began to change from the hot, muggy, and soot-filled conditions of China to the cool days and much colder nights of Siberia. Soon we would come to Lake Baikal, the deepest lake in the world. According to travel lore, this lake offered rejuvenating properties for those who dared brave its frigid waters. Legend even had it that a dip in Lake Baikal would add years to a person's life.

Since all of us on the train could use a little life extension, we checked the posted schedule. The train made only a nine-minute stop at Baikal; to swim would require careful planning and timing. Not sure if I could pull it off by myself, I went from car to car telling people about the famous lake and the possibility of a quick swim. I reasoned that if enough people joined me, the train would not leave.

Yop would be our timer. He proclaimed that he was too old for such frolic, but he would be happy to call out our time splits for us. We figured that we had two minutes and 30 seconds to run to the lake, and another 30 seconds to jump in and get ourselves wet. We figured that the run back would take no more than three minutes so we'd finish with time to spare.

Yop also agreed to act as our photographer. About 30 of us in bathing suits stood at the doors of the train watching the endless lake. Baikal stretches across 400 miles of Siberia and contains one-fifth of the world's total fresh water. Excitement spread throughout the train as the whistle blew signaling our arrival at the Lake Baikal stop.

When the train finally came to a halt, our steward held up nine fingers and opened the door. Thirty of us screamed and yelled as we bolted out of the station toward the lake. Even the somber Russians who waited at the train station smiled as we whooped and ran right past them.

Throwing my towel on the ground, I charged into the lake. The 46-degree water nearly paralyzed me as I gasped for air. We jumped around splashing each other like kids at the beach. Yop waved his arm and yelled that time was up. I dunked my head one last time, grabbed my towel and raced toward the train. As we sprinted, I flashed back on my marathons and the excitement of crossing the finish line. When we boarded the train shivering and laughing, I threw my fist in the air as I had done in so many races. I had made it just seconds before the whistle blew.

We were still 4,000 miles away from Moscow. The endless green rolling hills, forests of pine and birch and the carpets of purple flowers looked almost like an unchanging wallpaper on our picture window.

After viewing miles of this recurring but beautiful scenery, Diane and I sat down together to discuss our plans for Moscow. I told Diane that I was planning to ride my bike across the city to the Bellaruska Terminal where the trains leave for Berlin.

"But Sally," Diane questioned, "how can you bicycle in Moscow. You don't even know where you're going."

"I picked up a map of Moscow in China," I replied, "and besides, I can figure it out. After all, I survived China."

"Moscow's supposed to have a fabulous subway system," said Diane. "Why don't you just stick with us?"

"How can I?" I protested. "It's a lot easier for me to load all my bags and things on my bike and ride across town. Otherwise I have to lug that 110 pound bike up and down stairs or escalators in the subway."

"We'll help you, Sally," Diane volunteered. "I've got it! I will get my Russian friend, our waiter, to help. I think he's got a crush on me."

"Do not forget, Sally, we have only 48 hours to cross Russia after we arrive Moscow," Peter interjected. He had spent the last few minutes looking at me and shaking his head as he tried to figure out why I was so independent.

"I don't understand you Americans," he said quizzically. "We stick together in Holland. Us train riders, we help you."

"We stick together," said Yop. "We must help each other get seats out of Moscow."

Even though we had all bought tickets that would take us through Russia to various European destinations, it was still necessary to secure seat reservations in Moscow. And rumor had it this might be difficult.

"I read in Theroux's book, *Riding the Iron Rooster*, that Russians don't recognize the individual," said Diane. Looking right at me, she continued, "He took this train as part of a tour group then wrote about it in his railway book. Theroux said something about Russian people disliking solitary travelers. Individuals challenge their group-oriented culture. They feel threatened by such differences. That's why I'm going to follow the group on this one."

I figured that if independent Diane found it necessary to be part of a group, then I would too. I accepted their offer to help me. And perhaps I might really enjoy doing something different. I was anxious to see the famous subway and this was my chance.

Finally, we reached the Yaroslav station on the eastern edge of Moscow. When the train stopped, Peter grabbed my tent. Yop picked up my sleeping bag and a bike pack. Diane carried a bag for me, and we waddled to the freight car at the front of the train to reclaim my bike. I knew the bike was all right because the steward marched me up there several times during the ride to show me that it was still in one piece. I had also used my Silva techniques to visualize its safety.

Peter and Yop took off immediately for the Bellaruska Terminal to book their seats. A few minutes later Diane's Russian friend showed up. Both stood there in awe as I strapped and clipped and tied everything onto my bike.

Three stories beneath us lay Moscow's massive subway system which would take us to the other side of town.

"Well let's go," Diane announced. Looking at her obedient, blue-eyed Russian friend she asked, "Bellaruska?"

He nodded.

We followed him happily as he briskly walked us past several mystifying directional signs. He found security guards to unlock gates for my loaded bicycle and helped me up and down escalators. Once inside the subway, he whisked us past mirror-lined walls and marble statues representing many heroes of the working class.

Diane and I carried on a hurried conversation. "Can you believe how lucky we are?" Diane asked.

We headed down another impressive hallway full of slow-moving Russians. "How much did you pay him anyway?" I joked.

Diane waited for the public address system to finish before she answered. "Nothing, and he's taking me to dinner tonight, can you believe it?"

"I don't know about you, Diane," I said suggestively.

"I told you he had a crush on me," she responded with a smile.

We followed him onto the train bound for Bellaruska Terminal. He cleared a spot for me and my bike. Fifteen minutes later, more stairs and escalators delivered us from the underground subway to our destination. My other Trans-Siberian friends had already arrived in the station.

Worried looks greeted us.

"Hey what's the matter with everyone?" I asked, looking at Peter and Yop.

"We think we go nowhere. Our transit visa expire before we go," Yop answered.

An argument broke out between a member of our group and a train station attendant. Everyone started to grumble.

"Shiste!" a German fellow exclaimed as he mumbled something about the Russians.

A well-dressed man entered the waiting room. He said he was an employee of the railway company. "We heff no trains tonight," he announced. "We just to ask patience now. The trains can no accept seat reserves until tomorrow. You be able to leave tomorrow Moscow then."

"Why not till then?" someone in our party called out.

"Travel restrictions in our country recently, how you say, lifted," the man calmly replied. "Everyone want to travel now. We offer our apologies."

"What happens if all the cars are full? We're only allowed here for two days," Diane asked.

"We add more cars to train. You will no have problem."

He walked off.

Diane looked at me. "Well you heard the man, we're leaving tomorrow. Let's go out on the town tonight."

Some people from our group suggested we go out to eat. I stood there with my bike.

"What about my bike?" I called.

"Put it in one of those storage places," Diane offered. Just then her Russian friend waved good-bye to me and walked off.

"Hey," I beckoned. The handsome young waiter kept walking. Looking at Diane, I continued, "He can't just take off. We've got to give him something for all his help. Call him back here."

"Relax, Sally, he's OK. He doesn't want anything from us,"

"Where is he going?" I asked.

"I told you we had a dinner date. He's going to meet me later tonight, so we can all still go out."

We talked a storage locker attendant into taking my bike. Then we went out on the town looking for something to eat. We saw lots of army personnel directing traffic. Big concrete high-rises bordered bus-filled streets. Automobiles motored about with their lights turned off. But we didn't see any restaurants. In fact, we didn't see anything that looked like a business.

After we walked a few long blocks, a well-dressed man stopped us and asked if we needed help. Unfortunately, what I needed was a bed. The day's efforts in the stifling train station had caused me to feel nauseous and exhausted. I also knew I needed a good meal. I had run out of food by the time we reached Moscow, and besides, I'd grown tired of eating oatmeal, noodles, and goulash for breakfast, lunch, and dinner.

We told our Russian friend we were looking for a place to eat.

"I'll take you to a wonderful restaurant. Come," said Sergei in his excellent English.

We followed him to a gray concrete building. There was no sign on it and just a few windows that faced the street. Except for the faint smell of food, we would never have guessed this was a restaurant.

After sitting down at a table, we discovered that Sergei was educated and very well informed about world issues. He enjoyed sharing information about his job as a computer programmer, life in Moscow, and his opinion of Mikhail Gorbachev. He told us that most Soviets supported their new leader but they wondered how many changes he would actually be able to implement.

Sergei ordered a feast for us. He started with bread baked with sausage and cheese. Considering my oatmeal diet, this tasted wonderful.

I turned to our Russian host and said, "I'm only here for one more day, Sergei. What would you recommend seeing?"

"It's too bad you have so little time," he replied. "There's much to see in Moscow. You must go to the Red Square, of course, and the Kremlin with its domed cathedrals, and Gorky Park. The Bolshoi Ballet is a must, but you probably won't have time."

Diane spoke up. "From what I've seen so far," she said, pausing as the waiter reached between us with a bottle of cherry juice, "Moscow looks like one big government housing project. I mean it looks like they built all these concrete apartment buildings, didn't paint them or do any landscaping, and took off for 15 years. Now they're all coming back to live in them. It's very strange."

Yop asked, "How come no one look happy here? They always look down and they walk like this." Yop hunched his shoulders and moved his arms back and forth.

Before Sergei could respond, a pink-looking chicken dish finally arrived. Diane excused herself to leave. I chuckled inside as I thought about her imminent rendezvous.

Throughout the last course, Sergei talked about the relationship between our two countries. "Most Russians love Americans," he said, "especially the older ones. We've been allies twice. You helped us defeat the Germans. Maybe our governments will begin to cooperate again. Perhaps Gorbachev will help."

After dinner, we trooped back to the train station as the clock passed midnight. I stopped at a soda vending machine looking for something to cool off my throat, which was bothering me.

"I no drink if I were you," counseled Yop.

"Why not?" I asked.

"You have own glass? Machines no dispense cans, Sally," he said.

"Russians use same one." He pointed to a lonely glass on top of the machine.

I continued walking. I was beginning to feel hot and feverish; my joints ached. I wasn't looking forward to a night inside that muggy train station.

When we returned, all the chairs and benches were occupied by traveling Russians. I looked at the heavy creases on their dozing faces. Instead of feeling angry about being displaced by them, I tried to remind myself that train stations aren't a great place to evaluate any country. Under stress, we all act a lot alike.

But I had also heard stories about how roving gangs pickpocketed sleeping foreigners and made off with whatever valuables were unprotected. So, I made a plan. I would sleep in my tent.

I returned to where my bike was stored and asked permission to get my tent and some other belongings. A woman named Chan helped me. I had befriended her after Diane had disappeared.

We found an unoccupied corner inside the station to set up my tent. I was pretty certain that pitching a tent in the train station was not allowed. I figured someone would have to tell me this and I would pretend to not understand. I gave Chan my sleeping bag because I was hot and I wouldn't need it. She had also just completed a trip through China and complained that if you want to lose weight, that's the place to visit. She had lost 12 pounds. Of Indonesian descent, she lived in Holland.

During the night, I awoke several times covered in sweat. My skin stuck to the foam sleeping pad. By this time I was really sick and feverish. We were visited by a guard at one point who was motioning us to leave and yelling. I just threw my hands up in confusion, closed my tent door and hoped he would go away. He finally left us alone.

In the morning, I had to ignore how lousy I felt. We quickly packed my tent and went to the foreigner's ticket window only to find a huge line of pushing, yelling Soviets. We could see Yop at the front of the line. He was trying to hang onto the edge of a small cubicle. His veins bulged, his glasses had fogged up. He looked scared and angry.

Yop had collected our tickets the previous night and was trying to get seat confirmations for as many of us as possible. I stood there in shock as I looked at this violent scene. I recalled some of my Silva techniques and began to visualize getting the best seat reservations. The lady attendant inside the cubicle made a phone call then slipped a few seat vouchers into ticket envelopes. She recorded the transaction, handed out the envelopes, and closed her window. The crowd let out a loud groan.

Yop walked back to us and returned our ticket envelopes. Chan and I anxiously paged through our papers to see if we received a voucher. Nothing. We stood there wondering what to do next. Since the train official who assured us we would get seats had disappeared, we realized we were on our own. So we began to formulate a new strategy. We decided our group would team up with some of the Moscow students who always hung around the train station. They offered to help stranded travelers in exchange for practicing English. Another group would see what they could turn up at the tourist offices. We knew that an organized tour wouldn't have been subjected to such troubles.

A few hours later, we reassembled to compare notes. Nothing had worked. Chan and I threw our arms up in frustration.

Feeling feverish, I needed to get out of the sweltering station. "Well look Chan," I suggested, "I don't know what they can say if our transit visas are no good when we get to Berlin. We can't extend them today, the embassies are all closed. Let's just go and see the city. Are you with me?" She agreed.

Despite my sickness I was determined to see Moscow. Playing tourists instead of embattled travelers, we went to see Red Square. As we gazed upon the onion-domed buildings and acres of concrete that filled this plaza, some teenagers approached us. They asked if we wanted to sell anything. They tried to convince me to sell my Bucci sunglasses and my jeans. There was a nice profit to be made, but I declined because I didn't have anything else to wear.

Long lines stretched around the building that housed Lenin's tomb. The GUM (pronounced goom) department store stood watch over the eastern corner of this sprawling plaza.

I trudged on to the Tomb of the Unknown Soldier. Young brides and grooms posed for pictures. Limousines and taxis dropped off literally hundreds of newlyweds. A student whom we had met earlier told us that though the divorce rate in the USSR was soaring, Russians still married in great numbers. He said that placing a bouquet at the Eternal Flame was part of the ritual.

By this time, I had run out of food, so Chan and I went off in search of supplies that would get us through the next train ride whenever that would be. We finally found a store. Buying something was another challenge and meant more lines. We were getting a good look up close.

While Chan waited in line to make a bread selection, I waited in line to choose a piece of cheese. When I got to the front of the line, I carefully copied down all the Russian characters describing the kind I wanted, and got in another line to pay for it.

Forgetting how big a kilo was, I wrote down that size. When I reached the clerk, I handed her my piece of paper. She started yelling at me. She motioned for me to get out of line.

A man heard all the commotion; he came over and offered to help. He told me that the woman couldn't read and that I had insulted her. He told the cashier what I wanted. She frowned at me as she added up my purchase on an abacus.

Then I got in another line to pick up my cheese. Twenty minutes later the kilo of cheese arrived. My eyes grew when I saw how big a kilo, 2.2 pounds, really was. Chan and I would certainly not run out of cheese in the days ahead!

We returned to the station only to discover that 17 vouchers had been issued to Berlin and we'd missed our chance.

Even though I was exhausted, I had to stay positive. "That's all right Chan," I said, "something better will turn up. Let's just camp here until they close."

By now I had lost track of almost everybody. In desperation, Peter and Yop had bought plane tickets. Jon disappeared long ago. And I would never see Diane again.

I prayed for the best. Chan only grew angrier, especially when she found that they would fine us for over-extending our visas. I was so weak I had to lie down on the dirty lobby floor.

Using my Silva techniques, I kept visualizing the best. Then it happened. Ten minutes before closing, a woman walked in the lobby carrying vouchers for the Berlin train the very next morning. We surrounded her and she handed out the precious vouchers. We had our seats! Although 30 more hours of train travel lay ahead, at least we would cross the Soviet border just before our visas expired.

Then Peter and Yop arrived only to find they'd missed their chance. They were incredibly frustrated-and their plane tickets had left them $900 poorer. Now they would store their belongings at the railway station until their flight left the next afternoon. While they had been out, they traded their Walkman radio to a couple of students for a warm bed and hot shower. They took one look at me and asked me to join them.

Although it was a gamble to leave the station because I had to be back by 6:00 am, I desperately needed a good night's rest. Sweat dripped off me as I hung on for another subway ride 30 agonizing minutes. By the time I got into the shower, I was nearly incoherent. It was wonderful. I had not taken a real shower in eight days!

Yop gave me some cold medicine. I set the alarm for 5:00 am and passed out. Peter and Yop stayed up late. They played cards and drank vodka while I had nightmares about crossing the border with my black market money.

I awakened the following morning feeling almost alive again. Things went well for a change. We made it to the station on time, retrieved my bicycle, and boarded the train by 8:00 am. Just before noon the train arrived at the Russian-Polish border. The crossing went smoothly.

For the next 24 hours I slept as we traversed Poland and East Germany. Early Monday morning the train pulled into East Berlin station. Willie, an office worker from West Berlin whom I met on the trip, helped me carry my bike up the stairs and to the subway for West Berlin. He also invited about six of us to his house, where he could arrange transportation across East Germany.

As we made our way through West Berlin, I reflected on the past 10 days. I was ending a journey across a country I knew little about and had not dreamed of venturing through several months ago. It was my ability to stay flexible and my willingness to try new things that brought me to the USSR. And although I had seen so little of this vast country, I had learned some things and witnessed the hardships the people of Russia faced.

The cheese line revealed some telling things about the Soviet system. And the frantic search for a way out of Moscow forced me to develop a greater understanding of the integral part people play in our lives. Without the help of everyone I met, I don't know how I would have managed. I was thankful for these insights and realized that Russia had been a gift—a helpful preparation for Europe. It had also provided me with another opportunity to look at the US from a different perspective and gain a greater appreciation of freedom and democracy.

On Top of the World
New Zealand

The Underwater World
Great Barrier Reef, Australia

Modern Transportation
China

Road Warriors
China

Michelle ... Fueling Up ... A Watermelon Ritual
China

Beijing's Best: Good Food–Good Friends

Totally Awesome
Yangshou, China

Commuting in Canton

My Friend Yop
Trans-Siberian Train

Sightseeing in Beijing

France's Golden Arches
Arles, France

Monica, Uli and Me

A Tranquil Moment
West Germany

Slim Pickins
Russia

My Adopted Mother
Monte Gordo, Portugal

Neither Rain nor Snow nor Sleet ...
Mackenzie Pass, Oregon

May the Wind Be With You
Canadian Rockies

Technical Difficulties
Kentucky, U.S.A.

Me, Evelyn, Andy and Terry

Almost There...

A Little Farther...

I Made It!! Aptos, California

PART 3
British Isles and Europe

CHAPTER SEVEN:
Family Ties

CHAPTER EIGHT:
Unwinding in the Rhineland

CHAPTER NINE:
Pasta, Problems and Pests

CHAPTER TEN:
Siesta Time

Date: *August 2, 1988-February* 14, 1989
Bike Miles: 5,918
Route: *Cologne, West Germany; The Hague, Holland; York, England; Belfast, Ireland; Pembroke, Wales; London, England; Brussels, Belgium; Munich, West Germany; Rome, Italy; Barcelona, Spain; Lisbon, Portugal.*

Chapter Seven
Family Ties

I spent my first night in Europe in the back of a yellow van that had transported three of us from West Berlin to Cologne, the capital of the Rhineland. After just four hours of sleep, I pedaled off at 7:00 am in a misty rain in search of a map.

The town was quiet as I cycled through the empty narrow streets. It was hard to believe I was now in Western Europe. I wondered what lay ahead as I thought about routing myself through these countries alone learning a new culture, new systems and another way of life.. Although I was a little apprehensive, it felt good to be on my bike again. I needed to get maps and information so I stopped an ADAC office, the AAA of Germany. AAA members can use these services all over the world.

It was early August. I had tried to plan my European route so that I could enjoy the northern countries while it was still reasonably warm. I had already changed my plans, eliminating Denmark and Norway. Some of my friends on the Trans-Siberian train had suggested other places to go without traveling so far north. During our train ride, Yop had insisted I stay with him and his family to rest before crossing Europe. After getting sick in Moscow, I decided to accept his offer. I was three days away from his home in Den Hague.

After exchanging my money, I went grocery shopping. It always took me a long time to shop in a new country, trying to find the food I wanted. Germany took even longer as I struggled to read the ingredients in cereals and other packaged food. I tried to keep sugar, salt, and fat to a minimum, but this would become more difficult as I traveled through Europe. Because of the season, traveling alone, and the higher fat content of foods like dairy in Europe, my diet was about to change even more. It was colder, so I could carry yogurt and cheese for a day or two and it did not spoil. Often I could grap a baguette. I ate heavier foods that helped keep me warm so my body could adjust to the new season.

The mist continued and the sky was dark as I crossed the Rhine River and got my first glimpse of the famous Cologne Cathedral. It took my breath away, towering 514 feet into the sky. A huge plaza surrounded the cathedral and hundreds of tourists gathered around. Vendors sold postcards and other souvenirs. I parked my bike against a massive stone wall near the front entrance.

As I opened the door, my jaw dropped. It was magnificent! The cathedral's grand appearance from the outside gave little clue of the treasures that lay within. Begun in 1248, this Gothic masterpiece took six centuries to complete. When finished in 1880, it was the tallest building in the world. I felt like a lost child as I walked slowly up its aisles, staring at the fabulous paintings on the ceiling and the sculptures and art along its walls. Although I carried about five pounds of reference books on my bike, at times like this, I wanted to know even more about art history and the masterpieces I was viewing.

From Cologne I pedaled west to Aachen, on the far west of the Federal Republic of Germany. This city borders both Belgium and Holland. Aachen, too, had an impressive cathedral. This dome is the oldest north of the Alps. Aachen was once a popular thermal springs resort favored by the Romans.

I made it to a campground outside Aachen just as the sun set. It took more than my usual 30 minutes to set up camp because I was out of practice. I fixed some hot vegetable soup and enjoyed looking at the bright nighttime stars. It was good to be on the road again.

The next morning I awakened to rain, packed up, and crossed the border into southern Holland. I stopped in the town of Herleem to purchase a map of the Netherlands, exchange money, and call Yop. Communicating was often challenging. I had to plan my calls around finding pay phones, having change and hoping for an operator who could speak some English. The map showed thousands of miles of bike paths that were both paved or constructed of brick.

I cycled out of town on the bike path looking for red-and-white directional signs which pointed me toward the towns along my route. Mileage markers kept me informed of my progress. This was great, I thought, as I pedaled along without the problems of traffic and exhaust. This was great, that is, until I started getting lost. Without the sun to give me direction, and because I didn't know what one important sign meant, my progress slowed and my patience wore thin. Getting lost was nothing new to me. My impatience with directions had caused me trouble in the past. For example, as a student pilot I had to learn ground tracking as part of my VFR rating. Flying out of Watsonville CA heading inland over farm country was tricky. From the sky the land was a checkerboard of brown and green patches. It was easy to get off track due to wind correction. Since the ground looked the same, if I missed a small detail I could be off 10 miles or more. I am not sure how I survived those early flights of getting lost. It's not like you can pull over and check your map! Holland felt a bit like the checkerboard. Flat terrain that did not have a lot of variation which meant it was difficult for me to tell if my route was correct or not.

At one intersection, I stopped a man on a three-speed bike. "I'm lost, can you help me?" I asked.

He looked at my bright red bike and my panniers. He looked frightened; he didn't say anything.

Yop had told me that many Dutch speak English because it's a required class in school. Thinking that he was probably embarrassed to speak broken English, I shook my head and pointed at myself. I said, "No good, I only speak one language, no good. You speak many language."

A smile sneaked across his face.

"Where do I go from here?" I asked, pointing at my map.

"You go down road and over highway," he responded shyly, and pedaled off quickly.

In Holland the bike paths are a way of life. Clover leafs and overpasses for bicycle travel are an integral part of this amazing labyrinth. I saw women riding to work in skirts. I saw men in suits. I loved the vehicle-free riding—but I spent most of my time getting lost.

A piece of the puzzle was missing. I was sure the blue-and-white signs that the man didn't explain contained important information. But I didn't take the time to ask other people. Threatening rain clouds blanketed the sky and I wanted to get to Yop's. With hindsight, I probably could have saved myself time and anguish by just figuring out the blue signs. I guess that was too easy; I continued to do it by hit or miss.

Pedaling through Edinhoven, Breda, Rotterdam, and Delft I encountered persistent headwinds and continued to make wrong turns. I was even laughed at for wearing a helmet! But I finally made it to Den Hague and called Yop. Not wanting me to get lost again, he offered to come to the edge of town to pick me up.

As I sat anxiously waiting, I remembered how this wonderful man had nearly gotten crushed by the Russians at the ticket window back in Moscow. That had only been a week ago.

Soon, a station wagon pulled up. "You must be Sally," Yop's wife, Tina, called as she got out of the car.

"And you must be Tina," I said. "I've heard so much about you."

Tina, a strong-looking woman with sandy blonde hair stood next to Yop. Her eyes radiated warmth.

"Was Yop good boy on train?" Tina asked.

"Yes he was good," I smiled, "and he helped many people on the train."

"Sally, this my son, Adolf," Yop said. "I so happy to see you made here all right."

Yop and I hugged, as Adolf looked at me in amazement. No doubt Yop had told his family about the crazy things I had been doing. Adolf, a handsome young teenager, was a windsurfer who spent many hours with his girlfriend, Sandra, who almost seemed like part of the family.

Over the next four days, they treated me like one of their own. Mornings began with fresh gourmet coffee, French bread, and selections of excellent cheeses from all over Holland.

Delicious fattening pastries always followed. I felt so lucky to be with Yop and his family. He was right—I needed to rest and have some fun.

We took family outings and visited such places as the Peace Palace, the Dutch Parliament and the Panorama Mesdag, a mural dating from 1881. Spread over 1,800 square feet, Panorama Mesdag offers a fascinating view of the old fishing village of Scheveningen. Yop, Tina and I drove north to Amsterdam to watch the flower parade. Merchants and auto dealers sponsored this annual event. New automobiles were promenaded around the downtown area with bouquets of flowers strapped on fenders, hoods and windshields. A small brass band blew their horns from a horse-drawn carriage decorated with even more flowers. The innocence of it all pleased me.

On the return trip we stopped at an outdoor cafe to have a soda and watch boats motoring on the canal. Many Dutch people live on boats; canals and other waterways make up a major part of the country.

We often ended our excursions with Holland's version of Italian ice cream. This wonderful concoction was served in a large glass goblet with ice cream, a pineapple slice, whipped cream, orange juice and generous offerings of vodka. It always upset my equilibrium.

Yop ended our special weekend with what he called a California Barbecue. He served us chicken marinated in a peanut sauce followed by an excellent German wine and ice cream cake.

The cake read "China 1988! China 1989?"

We laughed, knowing that one trip to China was enough to last a lifetime.

The next evening, Tina drove me to Europort, a departure point for northern England. I wept as the ferry motored out of Holland. I thought about what the last four days had meant to me. Yop, Tina, Adolf and Sandra had allowed me to see traveling in a whole new way. Seeing the world through a family's eyes helped me catch a glimpse of what I needed from my personal quest. This experience reminded me again about the importance of life's simple pleasures. And the value people play in making life more meaningful. Striving to achieve goals as a measure of success lacks a deeper understanding of our purpose. Without this balance, it's easy to get caught up in chasing goals instead of living them.

Suddenly, the focus of my trip began to change. It was no longer about reaching certain places at certain times or even getting there on a bike. Somewhere inside a voice was telling me that I did not have to push myself so hard, that it was OK to be more relaxed—that there was no price for simple joy.

The luxurious liner I sailed on spent the whole night powering through the North Sea. I justified the exorbitant cost (175 Dutch Gildas or $87) by the fact that a cheaper crossing would have meant an additional week of cycling. It was costing me about $20 per day to ride my bike. Taking this route on the this liner made sense.

Just before the boat was ready to dock, I decided to splurge again. Lonely for music, I went into the small gift store and bought a portable AM/FM radio. For $25, I acquired a new friend. I plugged in the earphones and rolled down the gangplank in Kingston Upon Hull. I quickly tuned to the BBC to catch up on world news. Enroute to York I took a wrong turn, but I didn't feel very anxious now that I was among English-speaking people. Here it was just as easy to get found as it was to get lost.

Cobblestone streets and gingerbread houses greeted me as I rolled into York. Tourists crowded the sidewalks and small alleyways. But, like New Zealand, they drove on the wrong side of the road. I switched my mirror and pedaled on.

On my way out of town, heading north in the general direction of Scotland, I stopped at the AAA office for a map of the region. This AAA was just like the ones back home and, of course, they spoke English. I spent my first night at a trailer park outside a quaint village.

The next morning I cycled to Studley Park where I visited the Fountain Abbeys—ruins of a monastery built by monks in 1200 AD. I spent a few hours walking through the surrounding park. Miles of picture-perfect velvet grass covered the rolling hills. Canals and lakes added to the fairy tale atmosphere.

From the Abbeys I cycled through charming hamlets all built from stone and brick. Stone walls lined the narrow roadway as I pedaled up and down the undulating hills that separated one town from the next. In between, cattle grazed behind the stone fences that also divided one farm from the next.

As I approached Richmond, a busy tourist town, I began to notice that these communities followed a pattern. A large castle often stood at the center of town. It towered over the small shops and eateries. The cobblestone streets usually began at the base of a hill and weaved through the narrow alleys and roadways that led to the top. The villages always sat on a hilltop.

I had a hard time pedaling. My bike rattled and pounded as I concentrated on keeping my tires out of the cobblestone grooves.

Getting myself around the English countryside both challenged and frustrated me. Since many of the rural signposts had been taken down during World War II in anticipation of a German invasion, I had to count side roads and watch for curves to determine where I was. My map-reading skills improved greatly in England; this proved to be invaluable throughout the rest of my journey. It gave me confidence that I would utilize to escape from the beaten path.

I camped at a few farms along the way. Many people walk and bicycle in the beautiful English countryside, so farmers often welcome campers looking for a place to pitch their tent.

Unfortunately, the weather turned on me. One day, as the winds howled and the skies roared, I turned off the main road and followed the signs to a chateau. Nobody was there, so I took cover on the porch and made myself a cup of coffee. Raindrops splashed in the bird bath which sat in the middle of a carefully manicured lawn. Rose bushes and fruit trees bordered the grass. While I enjoyed this serene picture, it stopped raining.

I jumped back on my bike and headed for Durham, a popular

tourist town which sits above a crazy loop in the River Wear. I found a bike shop that would install a set of fenders on my bicycle. The recent rain reminded me that I had to prepare for winter.

I sat on the steps of the shop and talked about my trip with the owner as he mounted my rain guards. Looking over the top of his glasses, he asked me why I had waited so long to prepare my bike in this way.

"Well, I'll tell you," I said. "When I started on this trip, I didn't know the first thing about cycle touring. I bicycled for ten days under summer skies in Washington State where I met an experienced cyclist. We began this trip together and he didn't feel it was necessary to install fenders. He also said they would add extra weight and cost a lot. Thinking I would be following summer seasons around the world, I took his advice."

"Is that right?" he said and changed his attention to a screw he had dropped.

"Summer season, right!" I exclaimed. "I've been looking for a pair since I got to Europe."

I thought about our conversation as I pedaled toward Allenford. Mark had always complained that things cost too much. Now I realized I had adopted that attitude to justify missing many travel opportunities. That philosophy had caused me to endure substantial discomfort when the weather grew colder.

I was also beginning to recognize my own false economies. I was too thrifty in some ways and extravagant in others. I felt five dollars every night was too much to pay for camping, but renting a small Cessna to fly in New Zealand and chartering a trip to scuba dive was not. It was easier to blame Mark for some of my choices versus taking responsibility for them myself. This made me think of past relationships and the twisted logic I used then too. It's hard to keep clear on what's one's own baggage and what's not. In the months I'd been traveling alone, I reflected on how powerful it was that all my thoughts, attitudes and decisions lied solely on my shoulders. Up ahead, I could see groups of walkers hiking up and down wooden stairs which traversed farms and fields that comprised the rolling countryside. I consulted my *Europe by Bike* book and discovered that I was seeing Hadrian's Wall. The wall dates back almost 2000 years to the days of the Roman Empire. It was built to protect England from invading marauders. I cycled beside the wall until I made it to Carlisle where I sought shelter from the rain clouds that began to fill the sky.

I stopped a man walking his dog and asked for directions to the campground. He introduced himself. His name was Tom.

"Oh, you don't want to go there," Tom insisted. "It's too far away."

"According to my book, it's only four miles," I replied.

"That's right, it's too far. Listen if all you need is a place to camp and water then I have the perfect place for you. Follow me."

Tom set me up in a quiet field just behind the complex he lived in.

"My house is the third one on the right. There's a water faucet by the door. If you need anything else, come see me."

As I assembled my tent in the field, a woman walking her dog stopped by. Her name was Anita. Soon after, she invited me for dinner and to stay in her home. I gladly accepted.

We sat up until midnight talking. Since her two children were both leaving for school in the fall, Anita was planning a hike through the Himalayas and was curious about my expedition.

Glad to be indoors in a warm bed, I slept through a powerful rainstorm. Tom's field would have been miserable and I was sure to have gotten wet.

I awakened late in the morning and drove with Anita to her boyfriend's gas station where I could get some screws for my broken toe clips. As the wipers groaned and squawked, Anita asked me, "Sally what are your travel plans here in Great Britain?"

"Well, right now I'm headed for Northern Ireland," I said, "even though everybody back home thinks I'm crazy. Then I'm going to cycle Southern Ireland and take the ferry back to Wales and see what that looks like."

"What have you heard about Ireland?"

"Well, my father, when I called him from Holland, said that they're still having problems. He said that cars are getting bombed and that I'd be a fool to travel there. I know I've been hearing a lot about it on the news but I'm not going to be anywhere near the big cities. Besides, my Irish friends I met in China said most of the trouble is overdone by the media anyway. I've experienced many situations on my trip where people have been negative about a place and I have seen it in a whole different way. I don't pose a threat as a woman cycling alone. I seem to get more support with my choice of travel. I realize most people would not considered traveling this way and many feel it is unsafe for a woman alone. I listen to the advice I am given and then make the decision I think is best for me".

"Some friends of mine just got back from Ireland and they didn't get bothered," Anita volunteered. "They said most of the trouble happens at night. You should be fine."

"That's what I've heard," I replied. "I don't plan to be anywhere near Belfast at night. I've come so far and Ireland is so close. And after all, I'm part Irish."

When we returned to Anita's house, I called Mary and Margaret, my Irish friends, to let them know my plans to arrive by the weekend. They assured me that nobody would bother me, especially in the daytime. I left the next morning-- destination Ireland.

Shortly after leaving Carlisle, the rain started and continued all night. I cycled 88 miles in unrelenting torrents. Even though I blessed my fenders, the steady downpour tested my determination to stay on schedule. The freezing wind stiffened my joints. With my hood pulled tightly over my helmet, I saw very little of Scotland. My eyes looked one way—straight ahead. Surprisingly I was upbeat. I pretended to be competing against the conditions and I was determined to win. Having a radio now helped to distract me from the cold rain. I heard a news report about more bloodshed in Northern Ireland. It seemed car bombings were now making the news on a daily basis.

That night, while camping in the mud and rain, I had a

nightmare about Ireland. Wondering if it was still a wise decision to go there, I took a few minutes to meditate on it. My answer was still yes, so I continued on.

I made it to the ferry dock by nine o'clock Friday morning only to find that the ferry was delayed. Instead of leaving at 10:00 am as scheduled, the ferry wasn't leaving until 1:30 pm. And even though it was not going to arrive in Larne, Ireland, until 4:00 pm, I figured it was still possible for me to cycle at least 50 miles before dark. That would leave me 25 miles short of my destination to Dundalk. From that point maybe Mary and Margaret could pick me up by car.

A major rainstorm sabotaged my plans. No sooner had I rolled off the ferry and cleared Irish customs than the sky unloaded on me and didn't let up for the rest of the day. At times it poured so hard that I couldn't open my eyes. Black dye from my cycling gloves ran down my handlebars. Cars and trucks splashed me with more water. I thought about pedalling in Cyclone Bola in Auckland New Zealand and how the tailwind pushed me so fast that I thought I would hydroplane my bike. Now I was dealing with such a strong headwind that all my pedaling left me averaging less than 8 miles per hour. The miles went by very slowly. I couldn't distract myself from the wet conditions with music because the road required so much concentration. I had to just pedal on.

Three cold, wet, and miserable hours later, I arrived in Belfast. It was now 7:00 pm and everyone I stopped to ask directions smelled of alcohol. It was Friday night and happy hour. A couple of businesswomen warned me of the danger of continuing south with darkness approaching. Although I figured I still had three hours, I took their advice, borrowed some coins, and called Mary and Margaret.

"Hello, Mary, this is Sally," I said with relief, "I've had a lot of problems I'll tell you about later. I'm in Belfast right now."

"Oh, Sally, it's so good to hear from you," replied Mary. "We've been worried about you. We expected to see you this afternoon. There has been more trouble and plenty of bloodshed. We would feel better just to have you inside right now."

I paused while an army truck rumbled by. I wondered what was brewing on this wet Friday night.

"Mary, I don't think it's such a good idea for me to ride anymore," I said. "Can you pick me up?"

"Sally, we can't drive to Belfast, especially tonight. With southern license plates, the army has been known to commandeer cars for their own use."

In the background, I could hear Margaret saying something.

The operator interrupted and asked me to put in more money.

"Operator, can you reverse the charges?" asked Mary. "Sally, Margaret just said take a train or bus as close to Dundalk as you can, and then we'll come get you."

My body shivered and my teeth chattered as I pedaled off to the train station. When I got there, the last train had just left. I began to get scared as my body became colder. I could do nothing to warm myself as I pedaled to the bus station. Fearing hypothermia, I fired up my stove for some hot coffee. It did little to stop the shivering. After waiting an hour outside in the cold, I boarded the last bus to Newry, 15 miles north of Dundalk.

My clothes were soaked and plastered to my skin. My whole body was shaking out of control, but finally I was safely en route toward Dundalk. Exhausted, I fell asleep.

An hour and a half later, the bus jerked me awake. I looked around and saw I was the only passenger.

"Hello, where am I?" I asked the driver.

"Ma'am, this is the last stop. You're in Newry."

I looked outside at the darkened streets. A light shone on a corner. "Where's the bus station?" I asked. "That's where my friends are picking me up." "This is it. There is no bus station; your friends should know that."

I walked my bike to the only lighted corner and waited. Standing alone in the late evening was scary. It was 11:30 pm and I knew being out like this was not safe. A small group of British soldiers marched back and forth across the street. They held machine guns against their chests.

Suddenly I heard a door swing open. Startled, I turned around.

A man leaned out from his office and yelled, "Hey, you want to wait inside?"

"Yes, thank you!" I exclaimed. Relieved, I walked quickly indoors.

I tried calling my friends, but there was no answer—they were probably out looking for me.

Finally, a pair of headlights illuminated the darkened street. Mary and Margaret!

"Oh, am I glad you found me! What a night!" I exclaimed.

"We've been looking for you all over town," said Margaret. "We forgot there was no depot here."

We set off in their car. Just before we crossed the border into the Irish Republic, Mary pointed to the side of the road, "You see that gas station there? It just got bombed a few weeks ago."

I could see that windows had been boarded up, but they were still open for business.

"Why would anyone bomb a gas station?" I asked.

"That's where the southerners go for gas," Margaret answered in her sing-song dialect. "Everything's about 50 percent cheaper in the north. We take our chances and drive over the border just to buy cheaper gas. Things have really gotten a lot worse since we talked to you in China, Sally."

As we crossed the border, Mary and Margaret pointed out a hilltop watchtower and special cameras that shoot photos of drivers and license plates well before the border checkpoint.

We drove to their home in Dundalk, a large town just two miles inside the border on the east coast, about 50 miles north of Dublin. We sat up until two-thirty exchanging stories. Mary and Margaret told me that with violence and bombings on the increase, the hills around their house were crawling with IRA soldiers. They apologized for the mess they had brought me into.

Early the next morning, the radio reported that the IRA had blown up two busloads of British military personnel near Belfast. I was relieved to be in Southern Ireland and indoors.

Mary and Margaret, who were sisters in their late 30's, lived with their mother. They were a comical study in contrasts. Mary was petite; Margaret had a much larger frame. While Mary's style was formal—she wore carefully pressed blouses and slacks—Margaret's clothes always looked more casual.

The sisters also had a lot in common. They both had bright, rosy cheeks and smiled with their eyes closed. They were teachers and went to church every day. Each enjoyed good food and cigarettes and they both loved to talk a lot. They kept me laughing the whole time I was there.

On Sunday we drove into Northern Ireland to tour the countryside. The British army and IRA call a truce for the holy day. What a contradiction, I thought. We stopped at a lake to watch wind surfers.

A military boat patrolled the waters; boundary lines were strictly enforced because of an ambush that happened nearly 10 years ago. The wind surfers all went to a certain point on the lake, and just when they started to pick up speed, they had to turn around. I felt sorry for them.

We visited Newcastle, a busy little resort town. Everywhere we stopped during the day, we backed into parking spaces to hide our Southern Ireland license plates.

We didn't stop talking until we went to sleep each night. We shared philosophies about children, marriage, and work.

On Monday I decided to press on. Even though Mary and Margaret, who were on summer break, doted over me, I knew that it was time again to move on. In the miles ahead I would reflect on this experience and think about its influence on my life.

"Why don't you wait until tomorrow, Sally? It might stop raining by then," Margaret suggested as I wheeled my bike toward the front door.

"You know it's not going to quit," I laughed. "That's why Ireland's so beautiful. And besides, remember Michelle from China? I committed to being at her uncle's home by nightfall."

"Well how about if you stay today and we can drive you there later?" she asked.

"Oh no," I shook my head. "I want to ride, but thank you for offering."

Margaret dropped her head. She understood. I needed to go and I needed to pedal to my next destination.

"You both have been great to me," I said. "I've never laughed so much, but I've got to move on. You know what it's like, you've traveled. But you'll hear from me."

We hugged.

"God bless you Sally," Mary said.

"Yes, God bless." A tear formed in Margaret's eye.

The rained barrelled down hard on my face forcing me to squint my eyes tightly just to keep going. As I pedaled along, my mind wandered. Now so far into my trip I had come to realize that people I met played an important role beyond just a place to stay or a chance encounter. I thought about how Mary and Margaret fit into this trip and what meeting them first in China and then again in Ireland meant. I had just observed first hand the powerful influence family and religion had over the Irish people. I was also raised Catholic and in a traditional way; I could see why I was having such a hard time breaking free from my family's expectations.

For the next 70 miles I replayed our conversations in my head, looking for clues about how my mother's Irish background has shaped my life. In order to be truly free, I needed to know what belief systems I had inherited. But just then, I turned down the driveway to Michelle's uncle's home.

Joe greeted me as I crunched through the gravel that led up to the small stone house.

"Greetings, Sally," he said. "We've heard so much about you. Now come inside and sit by the warm fire. I want you to meet Babs." Joe, a big, strapping man in his 70's, took my bike and rolled it into the house.

These people immediately felt like old friends. Even though I had never met them before, we had someone in common, Michelle. This was a treat for me since I often spent a lot of time looking for common ground in such meetings.

"Let me pour you a shot of some good Irish whiskey," Joe said as he went to the kitchen.

Babs, who could hardly walk anymore, smiled as she said, "We understand that you spent a lot of time in Australia with Michelle's family. Michelle's father is Joe's brother, you know."

"Yes; they really were good to me," I nodded.

"Drink up, me folks. To Sally and her bike," Joe said as he returned.

Handing each of us a full glass, he exclaimed, "To health, God, and the people of Ireland. May we live in his name."

Like my grandfather, who had passed away when I was a teenager, Joe had a different saying for each toast. They always said something about God and health and may the wind be at your back.

The next day, Joe took me to see the castles and cathedrals around Mullinger. We met Babs for lunch at a restaurant named after the Irish novelist James Joyce. We then toured an old whiskey distillery. At the end of the day, Joe took me to Bord na Mona, a large peat company.

According to Joe, peat is an important part of the Irish economy. Because coal and wood are scarce, the Irish heat their homes with a dried version of this decaying plant matter. Joe explained that companies like these were gearing up to supply more of the world's energy needs when the supply of fossil fuels runs low.

The next day as I began to pack my bike, Joe interrupted. "You don't leave an Irish home without food. You just hold on and let us pack some good ole Irish hospitality."

I watched as Joe began to stuff my bags full of cheeses, fruits, and French bread.

"Babs, Joe," I said, " I am so glad to have met you. Keep me in your prayers; I've got a lot of riding left to do."

"Sally, we're happy Michelle gave you our address. We'll write her immediately to tell her you were here," Joe replied.

We hugged. Sadness crossed our faces.

I wondered when these good-byes would get any easier as I pedaled off toward the famous Cliffs of Mohr on the southwest tip of Ireland. Joe had taught me a lot about the importance of tradition. He remained loyal to the Irish government even though it teetered on the brink of collapse. Joe believed that things always work out for the best. He saw the world as a bright and cheery place.

All I saw for the next five days was rain, rain, and rain. I went to sleep each night to the sound of water falling on my tent. I awakened each morning to the same noise. Fortunately, few cars competed with me for space on the road. I never saw the Cliffs of Mohr because rain and mist persisted, reducing my visibility to just a few feet. Trying Joe's outlook, I kept expecting a better tomorrow. I kept on cycling.

But the rain continued when I rolled off the ferry at 3:00 am in Pembroke, South Wales. As buckets of rain poured down, I asked myself if this was really happening. I was certain a campground lay just around the corner where I could dry out and take a hot shower. Like a fool, I left the ferry building.

The rain was falling so hard and the streets were so dark and desolate I couldn't read my map nor the street signs. In desperation I pitched my tent in a field.

What a disaster! The rain kept flattening my tent as I tromped around in the sludge trying to set it up. By the time I got inside, mud coated everything. When I tried to push out the puddles that had accumulated, even more mud oozed across the floor.

I watched my bike, which I had leaned against a fence, sink into the muddy bog. I pushed my gear to one side, took off my shoes, and climbed inside my now muck-encrusted sleeping bag. Why was I making travel so difficult, I wondered? Why was I so tough on myself? Why did I leave the ferry building? I could have slept in a chair for the night. Somehow, I cried myself to sleep.

A passing truck signaled morning for me just a few hours later. Looking outside, I could see the horrible muddy field that now held me prisoner. I couldn't have picked a worse place to camp. It was still raining.

I packed my messy gear back on my bike and set off. Frustrated, angry and teary-eyed, I just couldn't imagine another day of wet.

I wondered what I was really doing on this trip. I could be home, curled up by a fireplace with a good book and my dog Toshia.

Was I really cut out for this type of traveling? How much more rain could I take? I wanted to quit, but David, who I had met on the train to East Berlin, lived in Swansea, only 60 miles away. I pushed myself to continue, knowing that tonight would surely bring a hot shower.

I finally found cover along the way. At a large bus shelter, I setup my tent to air it out. I fired up my stove and cooked a bowl of oatmeal. And as I sat there drinking a cup of coffee, the sky began to turn blue! I couldn't believe my eyes.

I ran around draping the fences, poles, and branches with my wet gear. Before long, my sleeping bag, ground tarp, tennis shoes, bike clothes and other wet things decorated the area. The bus stop came alive with all the color of a campground. People on their way to work drove by in their cars. Some looked entertained, others shocked. I was encouraged by the blue sky and happy to know my things could dry. It was only temporary, but it helped my morale.

I spent the rest of the day in intermittent rain. I tried calling David's house all day, but there was no answer.

I finally made it to the town of Swansea, and when I did find David's house, I caught his mother as she walked up to the front door.

"Hello," I called.

The woman turned and smiled. Her eyes were warm.

"I met David on the Trans-Siberian train," I continued, "he gave me his address here to visit."

"Oh, my name is Norma," she replied. "David has left on a bicycle for France to pick grapes. But he did mention you, and told us about your travels. Are you Sally?"

I nodded.

"Well, you encouraged him to buy a bike and travel," she said. "He purchased a mountain bike and decided to cycle to the south of France."

"That's great, but why couldn't he wait until I got here?" I joked. Then I became serious. "You know, I was really looking forward to seeing a familiar face. He really helped me get through all those tunnels and subways that separated East Berlin from West Berlin."

"Don't you dare think of leaving," said Norma. "You're staying with us. Now why don't you get out of those muddy clothes of yours and let me wash them for you."

Norma was a small woman with tightly curled hair who bubbled with energy. She asked me to come inside and meet her sister, Beth, who had never seen a long-distance bicyclist before.

Beth stood no taller than four feet and had Down syndrome. She asked me what school I went to.

"Well, well, what have we here? You must be the girl who encouraged David to travel on his bike," Norma's husband, Allen, said as he walked in the front door.

"Honey, this is Sally," said Norma, introducing us.

"My, we've heard all about you. You are staying, aren't you?" he asked.

After dinner we talked about my trip, England, the problems in Ireland, and about Beth.

"Beth has been a real blessing for Allen and I," Norma said, "since Mom died what, about 18 months ago?" she continued as she looked at Allen.

"That's right, it'll be two years in February."

"Well, since then, Beth's been with us. At first it was hard. It's still hard. Beth will fly off on these unpredictable temper tantrums and she's constant work. But she has taught Allen and I a new meaning of love."

"And patience," Allen smiled. "But she's such a special person, we just never knew we could love someone so much."

"Despite all of her problems, when she's happy, and she usually is," continued Norma, "we can feel her excitement. It's nice to be around."

The next night I got a chance to see for myself. Beth kept coming into the front room to ask us what we thought of the clothes she had on. She asked Norma what she thought of her makeup. She kept asking us what time it was. When she heard a noise, she came in to see if her friends had arrived.

Just as Norma had said, I could feel the excitement of Beth's upcoming night out with other adults with disabilities. I was thankful to be a part of this special moment as Beth gave me a hug when her bus finally arrived.

The next day I fought back tears as I gave Norma, Beth and Allen hugs and pedaled out to the main road. I didn't make it very far before the tears I was holding in streamed down my cheeks. Just two days ago I had questioned myself and this trip. Now, a very intuitive, developmentally disabled woman had given me a lesson in the joy of life's simple pleasures. I would remember Beth for years to come. I could not imagine giving up my quest now.

As I rolled down the road, I thought about my need to push myself to try new things. Setting goals, achieving them and then wanting more. I reasoned it was my sense of adventure and need to live a full and rewarding life. I believe this was true, but did I think the simple things in life were not enough? Did winning a title, a certificate, and other awards validate me? Goals give direction. Achieving them is an important part growing. But equally important is how we recognize the value of simplicity, family and love. My trip continued showing me why.

Pressing on for London, I rode through rolling terrain and had lunch with a group of rock climbers who were in between ascents. Susan, a friend from home, had given me her brother David's name to call if I was in London. David made a living taking photographs of rock bands.

"You're not going to believe this, Sally, but Susan's going to be here in two days," said David on the phone.

"How'd she know I was going to be here?" I asked.

"She didn't," he replied. "It's just luck. By the way, we can only guarantee you a place to stay until Susan arrives. Our place is real small."

"I'll call you tomorrow afternoon," I said.

"Well, I've got to be out of here by 2:30, can you be here before then?"

"Let's see, I'll need to make 140 miles. I'll call you at noon tomorrow," I replied.

Adrenaline fueled my legs as I set my sights on London. I would have to get in some big miles today and hit it early tomorrow to catch David before he left. The challenge excited me. When something seemed impossible or someone said, "no you can't," then I was damn sure going to do it! I covered 50 miles before darkness forced me into a campground.

At the first hint of sunrise, I focused on making London by noon—90 miles straight ahead! The weather finally cooperated as a tail wind helped push me along. The rhythm of my breathing kept pace with my effort. Blood engorged the muscles in my legs. My arms welded themselves to the handlebars. My bike and I connected as one machine. Nothing could stop us.

Triumphantly, I called David at noon.

He was surprised to hear that I was already in London. He gave me directions and I weaved through the bustling city, depositing myself on his doorstep an hour later.

A short, quick-witted man, David helped me get my bike and gear up the narrow staircase that led to his flat. Inside, a small living room sat adjacent to a bedroom. There was a tiny bathroom and small kitchen. Several of the album covers he had photographed occupied space on the walls.

David took me on a tour through London as he ran errands. Looking at him from behind, I could hardly tell him and Susan apart. They both had long hair that hid their small bodylines.

We took the subway to Portabella, a section of London, and walked around the streets. They resembled Telegraph Avenue back home in Berkeley, California. Second-hand clothing and music stores dominated the area. Tables with jewelry, candles, and fruits and vegetables lined many of the sidewalks.

And everyone wore leather. David fit in perfectly, with his black painted boots, matching black leather jacket, and tight blue jeans. A heavy silver chain functioned as his belt. I stood there in my tennis shoes and bike shorts. I felt out of place.

We took a double-decker bus back to his house so that I could see more of London. All that I really saw was traffic and choked streets. Black soot stained many building facades.

By the time we got back to his flat, his wife Penny had returned from work. She was petite and soft spoken. Her responsible position as a supervisor/engineer for British Airways' 747 fleet intrigued me. Penny announced that we were going to a rock concert tomorrow night.

"Are you ready to rock out tomorrow, Sally?" she inquired. "I've got tickets for the three of us. But I don't think you'll feel comfortable in bike clothes."

I got the hint. The next day while I picked up mail and did other errands, I bought a pair of jeans. And yet, when I returned that evening, Penny thought I still needed some help.

"Those jeans are nice, Sally, but I think you'll fit in better tonight if you let me dress you," said Penny.

Before long, I would hardly recognize myself.

Penny gave me some makeup and I did my face. It seemed awkward just putting makeup on. Before this trip it was a morning routine. She talked me into wearing a 1940s-style black dress of hers. And as I stood there looking at the black stockings and brown boots that were supposed to round out my costume, David offered, "Sally, you look smashing, but you need something else. I got it," he said as he reached for his ear, "you need one of these. Don't you think she needs my bat earring, Penny?"

"I was thinking of something different, but I guess that will do," said Penny.

We went to a pub; I felt pretty uncomfortable in my costume. I tried to numb myself with a few beers, but they just made me go to the bathroom more. And each time in the ladies' room, the mirrors reminded me of how ridiculous I looked. I kept telling myself that this was just a different kind of adventure.

The concert began with clouds of cigarette smoke and a band named Dammed. They were terrible. The concert finished with cigarette smoke and a band named The Volcanoes. They were terrible too. My head pounded; my eyes burned. But I sat there and smiled. I didn't want to offend David and Penny.

Susan arrived the next day. Tears filled my eyes as we talked about home. It seemed so strange to see a familiar face and to hear about all the changes my friends were making. We talked about Mark, China, Russia and all the rain. My mood lightened when I began to talk about all the wonderful families and how they kept me going. By talking about it all, I felt relieved.

It was time to go—and just as well, really. Although I would have enjoyed spending more time with Susan, I wanted her to have a chance to visit with her brother.

Everything worked out for the best. I could still make the final day of an international air show I thought I had missed. Penny checked the dates and found out that this was the final weekend. So, on Saturday afternoon, I decided to head for the show. After my 90-mile push to London the week before, this 40-mile sprint was pretty easy.

The traffic leaving the air show slowed me down as I approached the area. The sun began to set as I came upon a huge field with hundreds of camper trailers.

"Are you part of the air show?" I asked as I cycled up to the closest group.

"Yeah, we're going to it," a man with a goatee answered. "What do you need?" He held a beer in one hand. His shirt read, NO BOZOS. I started to feel funny about this group.

"I was just wondering if I could pitch my tent over there," I said.

"How does 'no' sound?" he said gruffly.

Going with my feelings, I sat back on my bike and pedaled out of there. By now, cars could barely see me in the darkness. After five miles of headlights and near misses, I spotted a garden that I knew would be fine for me and my tent. A small hedge and trees shielded it from the road. A gray house with a red roof sat next to the garden.

Nervously, I walked up to the door and knocked.

It opened a crack. A white-haired women in her 60s peered out.

"Can I help you?" she asked.

"Hello," I replied. "I cycled here from London this afternoon to see the final day of the air show. It's dark now, and dangerous. The cars are coming very close to me, and I don't have a bike light." I was rambling. "Do you mind if I put my little tent up in your yard just for tonight?"

"Well, let me go see what my husband says."

Closing my eyes, I visualized a positive outcome. The woman returned. "My name's Barbara," she said. "James says he wants to meet you first. Please come in."

We sat down in their living room. I introduced myself and pretty soon the discussion centered on my journey and how I was traveling alone. Barbara's eyes grew wider as I talked about the challenges of doing it as a woman.

"You know, Sally, let me give you a book that I read a while ago," said Barbara. "It might help you. It's about this lady; I think her name is Christina Dodwell, who travels through Africa by herself. I think you and she have a lot in common." She left the room.

"Forget about the tent," said James. "You can stay in our trailer tonight. It has nice soft beds and electricity." He shifted his glasses on his nose. Laugh lines carved deep grooves next to his happy eyes.

"Yes, Sally," Barbara said as she walked back into the room. "Christina Dodwell, that was her name. She says that she ate lots of garlic so men wouldn't bother her. That fascinated me."

"Well, I'll tell 'ya, I'm doing everything I can think of," I laughed. "In China, I cut my hair. I forgot what makeup was. And I'm usually so wet and muddy I don't think any man would want to get near me."

"Well, yes, come to think of it," Barbara said, "when I first peeked through the window, I thought you were a little boy until you started talking. Of course, I could barely see you."

"Sometimes, I even wonder myself," I cracked. "I rarely get to see what I look like anymore. And the last thing I even care about is what I look like. It probably would be different if there were mirrors on the side of the road. But there are just so many other things that I have to worry about, what I look like is very low on the list."

"How have men been for you so far? Any problems?" asked James.

"No problems yet. It's been raining so much, I think they just don't care to bother with me."

I didn't want to get into some of the Silva techniques I was using, such as surrounding me and my bike with light. They probably wouldn't understand.

I stayed in their trailer that night. Barbara brought me a chicken pie with potatoes and green beans for dinner. For dessert, she spoiled me with a piece of apple pie and a candy bar. I dozed off reading my new book.

The next morning, over a breakfast of eggs and bacon, we talked about dinner.

"Sally, why don't you plan on having dinner with us tonight?" James offered. "What do you like?"

"Only if I get to stay in your trailer again," I joked.

"You can stay with us as long as you want. You're welcome here anytime," said James.

I pedaled off to the air show, wondering why the trailer campers had refused me—and why Barbara and James had opened their home and hearts to me.

Up above, fighter planes roared across the sky. An aerobatic team flew in magnificent patterns and swirls. The sky was alive with the excitement of the latest in aeronautic technology from around the world. As I cycled home, the planes departed into the sunset. It was spectacular—what a way to end the day.

I had dinner with Barbara and James again that night.

"Was that air show worth traveling around the world for?" James teased as Barbara served me a plate of salad.

"It was a wonderful distraction," I answered. "But really, I feel so blessed to have met both of you. I cannot believe all the wonderful people there are in this world. This trip is not about air shows or castles or pretty countryside anymore. It's about the people along the way. People like you. I don't even know you, but I know you have touched my heart, and tomorrow it will be difficult to say good-bye."

And sure enough, I left the next day saddened. I knew that a part of my future had been shaped by these wonderful people. They had shared themselves and their home without condition.

And they didn't expect anything in return.

As I pushed off toward the Canterbury ferry, I began to sense a pattern beginning to unfold. A song that I had heard back in my Silva classes seemed to describe it. The lyric played over and over again in my mind:

"*Change your attitude and you will change your life!*"

This idea was working for me. I knew I got the best train out of Moscow for that reason. It was also becoming clear to me that the trailer campers had refused me so that I could meet Barbara and James. I could have it hard or I could have it easy. It was all my choice! And I could have it any way I wanted as long as I remained pure in my thoughts—as long as I did not cloud my thinking. This would be tested several times during the coming months.

Chapter Eight
Unwinding in the Rhineland

After a ferry ride across the English Channel and a three-day dash through Belgium and Luxembourg, I crossed the Saar River into West Germany. The first place I visited was Trier, a wonderful medieval town founded by the Roman Emperor Augustus. People were dancing in the streets, celebrating the year's wine crop. In the town square, in front of ancient Roman baths, temporary booths were set up displaying a festival of food and drink. Everybody in town seemed to be there, singing and celebrating.

Enjoying this wonderful collection of happy people, I stood there and watched for a few minutes. Then they motioned for me to join them.

"Come, you are welcome. Enjoy our food and drink," a man called to me.

Excitedly, I parked my bike. Soon, I found myself caught up in their merriment as I raced from booth to booth sampling the many different wines and cheeses. Delicious sausages, breads, pastas and pastries begged to be eaten. I indulged. The sounds of a brass band filled the air.

I left the festivities and pedaled through quiet neighborhood streets toward the Moselle River. I crossed the Moselle and headed east along a bike path. Glancing back toward town, I watched as the green vegetation framed the river and Trier's old buildings and cathedral stood perched in the background. I thought about the rich history here. Not only is Trier the oldest city in Germany, but it's also the birthplace of Karl Marx. What an introduction to Germany's Rhineland!

Pedaling east along the Moselle River, I encountered one picturesque town after another. Though each had its own unique setting, all the towns had central plazas featuring cobblestone with homes and stores built side by side.

Celebration of the wine harvest along with intermittent rain was the theme for three fun days as I made my way down the Moselle toward the Rhine River. Each town competed with the others to attract wine lovers. It almost seemed as if I was participating in a progressive dinner party as each vintner provided plenty of wine and fantastic food.

Emerald vineyards climbed the steep hillsides between towns. In the distance, I could see an occasional worker picking some of the last remaining grapes. The thousands of endless vertical and horizontal rows hypnotized me as I pedaled by.

I took one last look at the Moselle before leaving the river's edge and entering the busy city of Koblenz, named after the Roman fort Confluentes. This strategic fortress stood on top of a hill and looked down on the confluence of the Rhine and Moselle. In a certain sense, not much has changed. Today, one-fifth of Koblenz's residents are involved in some way with the West German Armed Forces.

After numerous wrong turns and several efforts to get on the right bridge, I pedaled south from the city along the Rhine. In this area the river flows through a dramatic gorge between Koblenz and Bingen which features rock cliffs 400 feet high. It was truly spectacular and many regard it as the most beautiful river landscape in central Europe. Fairy tale castles stood high above the towns and villages. Freight barges plowed along the river next to me. At night it was fun to watch all this commerce on the river. The barges' lights danced on the water and I thought about how this same scene had occurred for centuries.

The Rhine continued south and I veered east to Heidelberg, one of Germany's most famous tourist towns. An old stone bridge carried me across the Neckar River. Although Heidelberg features renaissance architecture and other treasures, I had no desire to savor its charms. The wind and rain I had encountered over the past week had finally taken its toll. By now, I had only one thing in mind—getting to Munich where I could stay at Monika and Uli's house. They were the honeymoon couple Mark and I met in New Zealand. I was excited to reconnect with them. New Zealand seemed like a lifetime ago!

Following more rivers through the tranquil Tauber Valley, I finally stopped at a farm, hoping I could get permission to camp from the people I saw there.

An old man in coveralls and a little gray-haired lady stood before me as I walked down their gravel driveway. The closer I came, the stiffer they got. The woman held the man's arm tighter with each step I took.

Using some Silva techniques, I rehearsed what I was going to say as I approached them. I smiled. I smiled with my eyes.

"Guten Tag" I exclaimed.

A grin started to sneak across the man's face.

Continuing to smile, I pointed to my bike and then to the patches which were sewn on my bags. They represented the countries I had visited. Pointing to Germany, I smiled as broadly as I could.

"Die ganze welt—all the world," I spoke in my broken German.

The two looked at each other. Their eyes began to gleam.

Next, I pointed to my map and traced out my day's ride for them. I motioned with my legs that I had pedaled that far. I said, "heute—today."

They shook their heads in disbelief.

I felt a connection building.

I patted my sleeping bag and held my hands together against my head as I pantomimed sleep.

They looked confused.

Then I patted my tent and formed my hands in a cone shape. "Campingplatz?" I asked, grinning.

Now my German friends knew what I wanted.

They shook their heads as if to say nein-no, and pointed at the threatening sky. They exchanged words. The man signaled for me to follow them.

We walked into a barn where they led me to a carpeted room with a punching bag. A light hung from the ceiling. They motioned that I could stay here.

"Willkommen-welcome," the man said.

I held out my hand and said, "Danke schon."

We sat outside at a picnic table talking and eating. They told me that they would have to leave in half an hour and wouldn't be back until late. They insisted I stay for breakfast in the morning. After some sign language, picture drawing, and use of my broken German, I finally understood. It was also time for them to go.

When they left, I decided to pitch my tent inside the room because I noticed rat or mice droppings on the floor. Next it was time to find a way to shower. There was a hose next to the watering trough around back so I started to undress. Just as I proceeded to wet myself down, a farm tractor sounded a friendly toot. Embarrassed, I waved. By the time that I was ready to rinse the soap off, another tractor appeared. Damn, where are these guys coming from, I wondered? He honked; I waved.

Shortly after I climbed inside my sleeping bag and turned off the light, the rodents went to work. I thought I heard one scamper across the floor. I flashed back on the movie, *Willard*, and recalled the grisly scene where huge, long-fanged rats attacked people. Terrified, I prayed that they would not eat through my tent. I prayed myself to sleep.

In the middle of the night my bladder awakened me. I heard rodent noises. I dug my cooking pot out of my pack and starting banging on it with the back of my flashlight. I shouted. The noise stopped. I zipped open my tent, being careful to close it behind me, and ran outside clutching my noisemakers. Quickly, I relieved myself. By the time I got back in my tent, the scratching rodents had returned. I banged some more. They stopped. I heard more scratching. I banged. They stopped. They made noise. I made noise back. I finally fell asleep.

I awakened to a rainy morning. The farmer's wife came out to get me. I wanted to laugh with them about the night I had just survived, but I knew that would be impossible – they'd be insulted.

On the way to the kitchen, they showed me pictures of their children and grandchildren. I realized that their needs, wants, and desires were a lot like mine. We were separated only by language. It was becoming clear to me that regardless of our culture, country, language and other differences that we just wanted our life to matter.

Reflecting on home, I knew Mom and Dad were worried about me and I knew I was important to my friends. Parents love their children; it's unconditional. But what about friends? What had I done to deserve their love? For that matter, what had I done to deserve the attention of this farm couple and all the other families who invited me to their homes? Maybe these connections were deeper. These feelings that could not be explained were definitely real and mutual.

We sat down to a mouth-watering breakfast of boiled eggs, toast, bacon and grapefruit. Possessing an incredible appetite from all of my bicycling, I enjoyed two helpings of everything. Afterwards I patted my stomach and nodded that the meal was very good. As we sipped our coffee, I could see in their eyes that they wanted so much to be able to communicate with me. We felt close, but the language barrier was frustrating. How much more rewarding would these encounters be if I spoke the local language? Could I have done more to prepare?

Before I left, the farmer took me back to the barn. He proudly unlocked the door next to my room. Dozens of white and black rabbits played in cages. I thought about the rats I had heard last night in my room. Maybe most of the noise was from rabbits. I wanted to scream. I wondered if any of my other fears existed only in my imagination.

It didn't seem so long ago that even staying with English-speaking strangers had frightened me. And now, as I pedaled back to the main road, I thought about how much I had gained from people whom I couldn't even talk with. The farming couple and I had certainly touched each other's lives.

"Hooray!" I exclaimed, joyful about these revelations. I threw my fist into the air. I felt victorious. "Go ahead, rain," I taunted. "It's OK!"

As the puddles engulfed my wheels and rain dripped off my uncovered arms, I began to reflect again on where I had been.

More than taking me to places, this ride was taking me deeper and deeper into an understanding of myself. People along the way were there to show me my fears, my limitations, and myself.

Rain continued throughout the day and I just kept pedaling. I wanted to make it to the Munich area in time for the final weekend of Oktoberfest. Monika and Uli were also expecting my arrival.

The wind grew more ferocious and the rain pounded harder as I passed through towns like Rothenberg and Creglingen. I endured three more days of water, camping and wet clothing before I made it to the outskirts of Munich. I called Monika.

"Sally? From the States? Monika shrieked when I announced myself.

"Monika, I am north of Munchen," I said. "How do I get to your house from the Olympic Stadium?" I tried to choose simple words and be as specific as possible. Monika spoke English, but it was very limited.

I couldn't find any of the roads she told me about on the map I was using. We decided to give up. I told her to expect me sometime before nightfall.

I made it to other side of Munich and as I crested a big hill, I saw Holtzhausen, where Monika and Uli lived. It was a small village clustered around an onion-domed church in the middle of open farm land. Off in the distance, I could see the edge of a forest. The yellow and red, colors of autumn completed this almost perfect setting.

Wow! I thought. Monika and Uli had bragged about this place back in New Zealand, but I never imagined it could be this picturesque. I took a deep breath and excitedly pedaled on.

A short while later I rang their doorbell. I heard footsteps running on the hardwood floors above. Monika came down the stairs as she exclaimed, "Sally? I no believe."

We hugged each other very tightly.

"Sally, you made here," Monika looked at me in disbelief. Her blue eyes sparkled. "Uli, he at work, he be . . . home soon. Come."

I followed Monika up the stairs to their apartment.

"I finish," she said, as she nodded for my approval.

I looked out the window as she poured batter into a muffin tray and put it in the oven. I still couldn't believe I was here.

An hour later Uli returned from his job as a computer programmer in Furstenfeldbruck, nine miles away. A tall, blonde-haired man with a beard, Uli squeezed me so tightly I could hardly breathe.

"Sally, you sit down," he commanded. Compared to Monika, he spoke very good English. "I will explain ground rules to you only one time. And you must obey as guest of mine."

He pointed his finger at me. "Number one," he said as I prepared myself for the worst, "you must stay here at least two weeks."

A feeling of relief overwhelmed me.

"Number two, Sally, anything we have here is yours. If we no have something, please tell us and we get for you."

Monika, whose English would improve dramatically over the course of my stay, listened intently as Uli finished. "You must pretend you are at home while you are here. And you can stay as long as you want."

Did this mean I could let my guard down just a little? Would such an invitation soften me? How far could I indulge myself above pure survival, I wondered, and not lose the edge I had developed? Would the memory of a soft bed cause me to weaken when the cold of winter began to really hit?

Overwhelmed by these questions and concerns, I paused before responding. "Uli, Monika, you both are so kind but I must make it over the Alps before it snows."

"Sally, you no worry about snow. You are here and warm. You stay, see Germany. We take you," Uli said.

"But Uli, don't you see? I must cross the Alps before the snow starts otherwise I can't get over the roads."

"If must go, you can take train, Sally. You have nothing to prove. I no can make it to Munich on bicycle and we met you what, seven months ago and you still riding bike. And all that rain in New Zealand. Sally, we no here to suffer, we here to make good life." Damn, I muttered to myself. He was speaking right to the issues that I was still trying to reconcile. Was I still living in the world of shoulds and have to's? I thought I had broken that pattern when I cashed out of my old life style. And yet here it was coming back to haunt me. When would I let myself just relax without feeling that undertone of "you should be farther down the road, push yourself?"

"Let me think about that one, Uli," I said. "You are so kind."

That evening we went to Holtzhausen's version of the famous Munich Oktoberfest. Only 60 people lived in this storybook village and most attended. They made me feel like one of them, even though we couldn't converse with words. But we talked with our eyes and the laughter that many pitchers of beer brought.

Everyone seemed to have a beer mug in one hand while juggling garlic bread, German sausage, or a huge freshly baked pretzel coated with salt crystals in the other hand. I ate, drank and laughed myself into oblivion.

The next morning I awakened in a real bed to the sound of bells. My head felt like it was inside a music box. When Uli told me how much beer I had drunk, the chords struck even louder. My poor head!

After two very strong cups of coffee, I was ready for the breakfast Monika had laid before us. I didn't know where to begin as I looked at the table full of juices, muffins, cheeses, bread rolls, nut butters and muesli. Muesli, a popular European cereal, is made from corn or wheat flakes and includes raisins, nuts, dates and rolled oats. Muesli would become a staple as I traveled through Europe. This was a welcome change from my daily breakfast of oatmeal.

Afterwards, we piled into Uli's old BMW and drove to Neuschwanstein Castle, about 50 miles away. Built by King Ludwig II, this stone masterpiece with sheer rock walls and limestone facades is one of the most popular castles in Europe. It stands in front of a lake in the Bavarian Alps and receives over 6000 visitors per day in the summer. Nothing I had seen prepared me for Neuschwanstein. The castle has turrets and arches and towers. It looked like Disneyland's most outrageous fantasy. It was breathtaking.

At the castle, several large tour groups full of US travelers milled around. I suddenly began to feel uncomfortable. They talked so fast. Even though they were from my homeland, I didn't feel that they belonged here. This scene reminded me of the tour groups in China. They were making no attempt to mix with the people or get any real feel for the country.

Over the last year, I had grown accustomed to talking very slowly and using only the most basic words whenever I encountered non-English speaking people. I had found this necessary since so many of our words have several different meanings. Out of respect, I made attempts to speak the native language. I almost resented English-speaking people who weren't sensitive about this.

At the end of our day of visiting castles, we took the train into Munich for the last hours of the famous Oktoberfest. Thousands of Germans and foreigners filled the huge circus tents that lined city streets. There were carnival rides and games. Robust, big-chested women ambled about holding as many as five heavy beer mugs in each hand. Drunken men stuffed tips into their brassieres. Loud voices and hearty laughter competed with the band that noisily played for our enjoyment.

"Prost," I toasted, as Uli and I touched our beer mugs together. Like everyone else, we laughed as a lot of the sudsy drink spilled to the floor.

Once again, I drank a lot of coffee the next morning.

During my stay in Holtzhausen, I usually ran in the nearby forest before I spent the day in Munich visiting museums, cathedrals, the Olympic Village, and neat little parks. One morning, however, I took a side trip that would affect me like no other. I went to Dachau, a former Nazi concentration camp.

I pedaled through 25 miles of rolling, green countryside not knowing quite what to expect. The rooftops of quaint villages rose up to the road from the little valleys below. Sheep grazed in the fields.

I came upon a small cluster of buildings surrounded by a simple wire fence. It was Dachau. Hundreds of thousands of Jews and other war prisoners had been slaughtered here by Hitler's Nazi regime. A chill ran down my spine as I thought about the suffering that took place here.

Inside the museum I watched a film which portrayed the actual killings. It shocked me to see the firing squads, the medical experiments, and the gas furnaces as they exterminated one life after another. Tension and apprehension spread through my body as I read the news articles and looked at the photographs and other displays that retold the history of this grisly human slaughterhouse.

Seeing this rekindled an appreciation for the freedom I enjoyed as an American especially after having observed the oppressive Chinese and Soviet cultures. My safe and comfortable life back home had made me take freedom for granted.

Before leaving the museum, I signed my name and wrote, "God please forgive them."

And as I walked out, I turned back for one more look. I saw the foundations where the rows of barracks once stood. A concrete building concealed the furnaces which had ended countless lives. I thought about the senselessness of this hideous tragedy. I wondered how human beings could do this to one another, how anyone's very existence could be so cheapened. Standing on the very soil where so much loss occurred was deeply upsetting. My legs wobbled and my heart throbbed.

Making the sign of the cross, I pedaled off.

As much as I tried to fight it, Dachau played over and over again in my mind as I cycled back to Holtzhausen.

When I returned, Monika bubbled about the musical she had just gotten tickets for. "Sally," she said, "we have so much fun tonight, I dress you for very special show."

Oh no, not again, I thought, as I recalled London. David and Penny had figured I looked great as a punk rocker. But surely Monika was different.

And she was. When she finished with me, I looked like a Bavarian princess.

"I like it, Monika," I said as I looked in the mirror. "I've got a body again. All I've been wearing is baggy clothes. And how did you know I would look good in navy blue?"

"Come in here, let me see," Uli called from the kitchen.

"Let me blow-dry my hair and put on some makeup and I'll be there," I responded.

After a few moments, I started out for the kitchen, ready for final approval. I stopped in disbelief and looked at myself again. I had forgotten that I could look like something besides a bicycle traveler.

"Sally, is that you?" Uli exclaimed.

Monika and I laughed. I pranced to one end of the kitchen. I stopped and pranced back. And before leaving the room, I did a curtsy.

And even though I didn't understand any of the words, I enjoyed the play.

I had been with Monika and Uli now for three weeks. And for the last few days, the road had begun calling to me. I felt strong and able. But with the dead of winter just ahead, I didn't feel ready for the Alps.

So, while Monika and Uli were at work, I called up an organized hitchhiking service and arranged for a ride into Florence, Italy, on the warm side of the Alps.

Monika sensed something when she returned from work that day.

"Sally," she came closer, "what is wrong?"

I looked into her beautiful, warm eyes and tears ran down my cheeks. "It's time to go," I informed her.

Saddened, she bowed her head and said, "Uli will be disappointed to not say good-bye. When is your ride?"

"Tomorrow at 10:00 am," I answered. "Where will Uli be?"

"He call me today. He to be out of Munich for computer class for oh, two extra day. You will call him?"

I said good-bye to Uli on the phone. Monika and I were sad as we packed my things that evening. After a quiet breakfast and my last cup of fresh-ground coffee, my ride came. Monika and I hugged and said good-bye. Tears streamed down our faces as we embraced for the last time.

When I headed off, I prayed that our paths would cross again. Monika and Uli had claimed a very large part of my heart—and all from a chance meeting in New Zealand. It tore me up to leave them and yet I knew that so much still lay ahead. There were many more people who I would meet and learn from. It was time to move on to my next adventure.

Chapter Nine
Pasta, Problems and Pests

Twelve hours after leaving Munich, the driver let me off at a campground on the edge of Florence. The Arno River stood between me and the city's now dimming skyline. Even without the sun, it was still wonderfully warm!

Standing there with my bike, I was stunned by the vision before me. A huge campground crowded with tents and trailers sat atop a steep hillside! Florence spread out across the Arno, its lights glittering like a spray of diamonds. The Piazzale Michelangelo, with its famous statue, David, was a stone's throw away.

The dense, stagnant air was permeated with cooking smells as campers busily prepared evening meals. Italian rock and roll flowed from many stereos. Everyone laughed, drank and partied—like a scene from a gypsy carnival. And the Italians, whose language dominated most of this revelry, talked very loudly.

Turning away from the activities, I approached the office to register.

"We musta have you passaporta," the man at the counter told me.

"My passport?" I asked. "You need to keep it?"

"Law of country. We musta have for youra stay," he replied.

"What happens if I have to go to the bank or buy an airplane ticket or something?"

"Then wea let youa, how youa say, borrow."

"Is that in writing, is that really a rule?" I was suspicious. "Can you show me a book or paper that says that?" I tried to be diplomatic.

"Behinda you is sign."

Sure enough, that was the policy in Italy for all overnight guests, even hotel patrons.

After registering, I began my search for a level spot to pitch my tent. My first impression of this dramatic campground—so different from others I'd seen because it was perched on such premium land—was, "This is awesome." However, my excitement wore off after walking unsuccessfully up and down every aisle. No one had a flat spot. And anything left would surely be tilted. Finally, I found a place that would work, but it was next to a smelly garbage enclosure. Tired of wandering back and forth, I reluctantly settled for this spot. Then I joined other travelers in an outdoor cabana while I fixed my dinner and wrote in my journal. When I returned to my tent, I watched the lights of Florence illuminate the sky, exposing the all too familiar rain clouds.

During the night, thunder exploded across the sky and rain literally pounded my tent. I grinned as I thought of my hillside garbage site and that water couldn't puddle here. Maybe this is a great spot after all, I thought.

In the morning my mood changed quickly as I crawled out of my tent. On my way to the bathroom, I slipped on the mud-slickened surface. Pulling myself to my feet, I assessed the damage. Muddy clay covered over half my body. Angrily, I stomped to the bathroom, only to be greeted by squat toilets. Welcome to Italy, I thought.

After washing up, I left for town—and encountered more culture shock. I had grown accustomed to the fast-moving Germans and their incredible sense of order. Italy required another way of seeing things. Mopeds putted up and down the wrong side of the road. Three-wheeled cars resembling golf carts noisily darted in and out of mysterious alleyways.

In contrast to the wrong-way drivers, honking horns, and the frantic, high-pitched motor vehicles that scurried about, the people themselves had slowed down to a crawl. It seemed as if everyone was trying to be slow. I first encountered this when I walked into a cafe.

"Buon Jiorno," I greeted the waiter. "Coffee, please."

He nodded and returned five minutes later with a small cup the size of a shot glass, and a bill.

Looking at the cup and again at the waiter, I shrugged my shoulders. I motioned that I wanted a bigger cup.

He smiled. He understood.

Ten minutes later he returned with a large cup and a new bill. I took a sip. My eyes began to burn. The waiter, who by now was standing near the back of the cafe, started to laugh. And by the time I finished my cup of what I thought was coffee, I knew why the Italians drove the way they did. I found out later that I had just drunk a triple shot of espresso. I was wired!

In Italy, when you ask for coffee you get a concentrated form called espresso. They call the version of coffee I wanted cappuccino. During my stay in Italy, I made sure to specify cappuccino.

I began to wander through Florence's ancient, winding streets. Some were so narrow, that two cars couldn't pass; it was like being in a wonderful maze. Founded by the Romans in 59 B.C., Florence presents an earth-tone tapestry of weathered sandstone buildings. The Arno bisects the city, and several beautiful bridges, including the famous Ponte Vecchio, connecting the east and west. With its cathedrals, palaces, and galleries, Florence provided a wonderful introduction to Italian history and culture.

Almost four weeks had gone by since I had done any actual bike touring. Anxious for the road again, I packed up, paid 25,000 lire for three nights' camping, and headed south for Rome.

After a couple of days of challenging mountain climbs through Siena and the Lake Bolsena area, I made a wrong turn. It took me into a small hillside village where I stopped and asked directions from two men standing by the road.

They looked at me curiously as I pointed to the map indicating I was lost. One man showed me how to get back to the main road. I thanked him and pedaled off.

Since there were no cars, I took my helmet off to let the warm air blow through my hair. Then I heard a car slow down behind me. I turned around and saw the man who had helped me. I stopped. Maybe there was something he had forgotten to tell me.

He motioned for me to get in the car with him.

I acted like I did not understand. I kept smiling and showed him where I was going on the map.

All of a sudden, he reached out and grabbed my arm. He began to pull me toward his car.

My eyes began to narrow. My body stiffened. "No," I shouted.

With all of my might, I jerked my arm away from him. I pointed at the sun. Shaking my head, I pretended that he was not the problem but that the limited amount of sunlight was. He looked at me as if I was crazy.

I jumped back on my bike. "Come, on Buddy, let's get out of here," I yelled. We raced down the hill. I kept checking my mirror for several miles. Happily, I never saw him again.

Late one Saturday evening I pulled into Bolsena just after sunset. For an hour I had been looking for a campground, but they all had closed for the winter. It was cold and windy, and I leaned on Buddy thinking what to do next.

Moments later, a car drove up and a young couple got out.

"Are you OK?" they asked in perfect English.

"Well, yes," I answered, "but I'm looking for a campground and they all seem to be closed."

The couple jumped back in their car and signaled me to follow them. For a mile and a half I pedaled behind their car. Then we turned down a long driveway and stopped in front of a huge multistory building. The man went inside and brought out an employee.

"This is hostel. You stay here for night," said the woman. I thanked the couple for their help, and they drove off. I followed the woman inside. She knew some English but I had to choose my words carefully.

Within an hour all the employees had taken a personal

interest in me their only guest for the night. The chef, Lido, a tall, bald man, walked to my table and proudly presented me with his specialty, pizza. What a treat! I looked in his eyes, thanked him, and shook his hand. Wow, I had planned on eating what was my daily staple, white rice. But now I was devouring a homemade pizza in Italy. Yeah!

Within minutes the staff joined me and we sat around drinking wine and talking. The group included a handsome actor who spoke English well. He had lived in Los Angeles while acting and was back in Italy as a computer programmer. He translated most of the conversation for the others.

During my two days in Bolsena, I became friends with two women named Vanne and Antuanea. They offered to put me up during the month of December if I taught English to a group of their friends. I was excited at the possibility of living indoors and with a fun group like these folks, yet my heart was in traveling. I had a month to think about it.

On the way to Rome the next day, many truck drivers honked their horns and whistled at me. I just smiled and waved. I didn't want to offend them out of fear they might run me into a ditch. So I tried to ignore their motives while being receptive to their attention.

On this stretch of road, a man in a car stopped and waited for me. I stopped, I said hello and pedaled off.

He passed me again and honked. He stopped again.

Trying not to anger him, I also stopped.

He put his hands on my shoulders and said something I could not understand.

Pointing to the sun, I exclaimed, "No!" I jumped back on my bike and pedaled off again.

He stopped again. Only this time, I rode right by him. A confused look crossed his face as I kept pointing at the sun.

He gave up. Lunacy has its rewards!

I camped on the outskirts of Rome in a shepherd's field. As his flock grazed around my tent and his dogs barked and played, I looked at the nearby lights of Rome. I had actually arrived!

Almost.

It took me three hours to go five miles into Rome the next morning. The cars and trucks which slowly inched along sandwiched me between them and the curb. Mopeds were suicidal as they dodged the oncoming traffic. The exhaust caused my stomach to knot and my head to spin. Horns blared, assaulting my ears.

I tried to escape this mobile, noisy parking lot by joining the mobs of people who walked on the sidewalk. It was worse there, so I gave up and went back to the street.

By the time I made it to St. Peter's Square, however, the morning commute seemed like a small price to pay for all the treasures around me. I visited the Vatican, the Coliseum, and the ancient ruins of a once-proud empire that were everywhere in this city. I decided to come back the next day.

But before I could think about the next day, I had to focus on how to safely navigate cycling out of the city. I would have to ride aggressively and stay on high alert. In my imagination once again, I would have to call up my protective light that had shielded me so far. With my loaded mountain bike, white helmet, and droopy clothes, I made one gutsy move after another. Everyone seemed to be looking at me as I cut in front of cars and darted in and out of traffic at the intersections and roundabouts. Finally I was moving through traffic like the locals! This reminded me of the bike messengers back in San Francisco.

It suddenly became a game to see who would make it to the next available open space first. My head was spinning and I felt as if I was inside a pinball machine. My heart raced, yet I felt invincible as I glided by every obstacle that jumped in front of me.

By the time I made it to the campground eight miles outside of the city, I felt a sense of accomplishment. Not wanting to press my luck, however, I took a bus into town the next day. By sheer luck I happened to arrive at St. Peter's Square and heard the Pope speak. I toured the Piazza Venezia (the Capitol), the Roman Forum (a political and social forum), and the Colosseum, Rome's best-known monument. (Its real name is the Flavian Amphitheater.) To visit such historic beauty and to stand in the middle of the ancient ruins, the basilicas, and the churches, sent chills up my spine. Yet it was difficult to grasp such history because our nation is so young and modern.

When I returned to my tent that night, I thought about how far I had come since New Zealand. Rome would have totally frightened and intimidated me then. I recalled the first roundabout that I had cycled through with Mark. And now, here in Rome, I had handled my bike like a real pro. We were a great team.

I also thought about how, back home, I didn't want to be bothered by public transportation schedules. And yet, my travels had forced me to develop this skill—especially if I wanted to see anything at night.

In Munich, Uli had shown me the basics of getting around on buses and subways. I now felt proud that I had toured Rome using public transportation on my own. My confidence soared with my new skill. Getting around this great city became fun and rewarding.

After escaping Rome for the fresh air and cool breezes of the Italian coast, I stopped at an old harbor and walked into the water. Being on the beach and in the ocean was a bit like returning home to a familiar place. It had been several months since I had enjoyed rejuvenating salt water and the calming and peacefulness it brought me.

By the time I reached Montallo di Castro, something felt strange. The people appeared less than friendly. I had asked to stay at two separate farms along the way, and all I got were doors that hardly opened. At the third farm, the man understood my request and pointed to an abandoned house across the way. Something inside me said no. Even though the sun had just slipped below the horizon, I thanked him and pedaled off in the growing darkness.

A police car inched by and the men inside studied me. Even though they were policemen, they were leering at me and I felt uneasy. OK, Sally, don't worry, I thought. This road is plenty wide and you'll be fine. As I thought about the danger of being a woman alone in the darkness, I worked with my Silva techniques. I prayed.

The police car drove off.

I struck gold at the fourth farm I tried. As I pedaled down the gravel driveway, a nice-looking man in his 20's greeted me.

"You needa help?" he asked.

He spoke English!

"It is dark," I said as I pointed to the sky, "and I need a place to pitch my tent. Can I camp in your garden?" I patted my tent.

"Si, yes, yes, of course, you camp here tonight." He nodded his head excitedly.

By now his younger sister and brother had come out into the yard and had begun touching all the gear and interesting levers on my bike. Paul, my handsome host, directed me to a spot near their flower garden where all three of them helped me put up my tent.

"You eat, we eat," Paul said as he motioned for me to come inside. He didn't know the word for shower, so he pantomimed taking one and asked, "You want?"

"Yes, thank you," I excitedly replied.

"After we eat," he said as their mother busily worked at finishing the meal. He introduced me to her.

As we waited for our meal, we talked about their farm. He told me about the animals on the farm. "We havea . . . ." he held up three fingers. A flustered look came across his face. He didn't know the English word. He made an oinking noise.

"Pig," I laughed.

Paul laughed. The kids laughed. Their mom smiled.

"And we havea . . ." he held up four fingers and mooed.

"Cow!"

And as the laughter grew even louder, Giovanni, the father, walked in. The room quieted. He had finished his day's work in the fields. A tall, good-looking man with pronounced features, he said something to Paul as he looked at me.

Paul introduced me. Giovanni smiled. He bowed his head and led us in a prayer. He began serving.

He piled my plate high with spaghetti and lasagna. Paul poured me a glass of red wine. The mother, Amneris, served me some salad. They finished in minutes while I sat there with almost a full plate.

Paul cracked a joke about how much food I had left, and everyone laughed. They waited for me to finish before Amneris served a dessert of sliced pears, apples and cheese. We topped off our wonderful meal with an excellent Italian cappuccino.

After dinner Paul served as an interpreter while we talked about the US and my trip. Paul, who took some night classes in Rome, retrieved his English dictionary and phrasebooks to help us along. We laughed and shouted as we tried to guess the words Paul was using.

My stomach was full. A warm breeze blew in from the window. The evening could not have been more perfect

Later, as I lay in my tent, I thanked God for bringing me to this very loving family. I knew that I had been turned down three times for a reason. I was learning that if I could let go of my need for things to happen only in certain ways, then a bounty of new adventure and new experience awaited.

Prior to taking this trip, I had little faith in using meditation and energy to help me meet my goals. I had not taken time to listen to my inner voice. Nor did I believe that I could alter outcomes by taking control of my thoughts. Putting myself in vulnerable situations tested this power over and over again. Choosing to travel alone by bicycle was the ultimate challenge. It was so beyond my abilities and comfort. I guess for me to learn, I had to make the circumstances difficult. Although I knew what was happening, change was difficult. Quiet messages were missed leaving the frightening and extreme situations to contemplate. These experiences taught me how powerful a mind is and made me a true believer in the universal forces.

Breakfast with my Italian friends consisted of biscuits the size of a slice of bread that we dunked in our cappuccino. Amneris insisted on packing me a lunch. I looked inside the paper bag and saw a large roll stuffed with cheese and scrambled eggs. Paul strapped a huge jug of wine onto my bike.

"Thank you all so much," I said as I as I fought back tears. "You have been so good to me."

They lined up and hugged me one at a time. Paul was last. He looked at me with his deep brown eyes and said, "Sally, you make good trip. You make us all so happy. Thank you."

I climbed back on my bike, waved and said good-bye.

After cycling for half a day, I stopped at the first campground I saw. Immediately I headed off to a nearby beach with a book in one hand and my jug of wine in the other. A gentle breeze rustled through the pine trees that lined the sleepy roadway.

This is the life, I thought. I'm finally relaxing. And yet, as I dozed off, the inner battles continued.

One voice scolded me for getting too comfortable. Another voice replied, "You don't have to do anything; you can hang out here for weeks if you want."

Then the first voice taunted, "But what if you get too lazy and you don't even make it to Spain? Or worse yet, if you totally cop out and don't cross the States, how will you be able to live with yourself?"

"OK, OK, leave me alone," I said as I woke up.

I took a swim in the ocean to cleanse my body and my mind. I enjoyed my afternoon on the beach and congratulated myself for trying to relax. I felt better about the diminished role that all of my have to's and shoulds were beginning to play in my life. In order to be truly free, I needed to let them go completely.

I followed the coast north toward Genoa which reminded me of the Big Sur area near home. En route, climbing began to challenge me more and more. One of my travel books had warned me about the difficulty of the roads in this area and had even recommended a train or an alternate route to circumvent them.

"No way," I said to myself, "if I can handle rain and if I can handle Rome and if I can come as far as I've come, I can handle these mountains."

They were steep! And the downhills were fast. Along the way, a man selling food tried to tell me that they would only get steeper. He used his hand to form the shape of the mountains that I was riding. He pointed to the left toward Pisa and made a gentle rolling motion. He pointed to the right toward Genoa and his hand went straight up. He made the sound of a train and made a thumbs up sign. He pointed at my bike and pointed his thumb down. And then he held his hands in prayer.

But I needed this challenge to see how far I had come. I wanted to see what my limits were.

As I cycled along what seemed like an edge of the world, I was captivated by the scenery around me. Emerald vineyards climbed a steep mountain on one side of the road, while cliffs dropped hundreds of feet to the ocean on the other. I could hear the surf pounding on rocks far below. I listened to the wind in the trellises above me. Ahead stood a nearly vertical wall.

"Come on," I told myself, "no walking." I began to feel adrenaline pumping through my veins. The muscles in my arms began to bulge as I braced against the handlebars. I used strength in my back to pull my legs through each laborious revolution of the pedals. My speedometer read two miles per hour.

The cars that passed me weren't doing much better. Their engines strained as they, too, tried to conquer this mountain. As they crept by, the drivers beeped their horns and shouted encouragement.

I passed a group of bike riders who were having a difficult time walking their bicycles up the steep grade. They looked at me and the camping gear strapped to my bike in disbelief. Sweat covered my body; I felt like I was conquering the world as I assaulted the summit. Nothing was going to stop me.

After six miles and three hours of this exhilarating ascent, I reached the top. I yelled. I celebrated. I jumped up and down. But not for long.

Four more miles of up-and-down gravel road awaited me. As I wound around one switchback after the next nobody passed me. I had this deserted world all to myself.

On the rewarding descent into Levanto, I realized that I had not eaten for hours. As the wind cooled my body, I began to shake and quiver. I knew that I needed food—fuel. But it was 1:30 pm. Because the smaller towns in southern Europe closed from noon to three for their lunch break, finding a market could be a problem.

Thankfully a small bar was open so I bought a couple of candy bars. That was my best option. Generally, I kept extra food with me. But anticipating all the climbing, I decided to keep my load light thinking there would be something along the way. I didn't expect the area to be so remote.

Another eight-mile climb beyond Levanto awaited me before I stopped to camp in a hillside vineyard. And as I lay awake, gazing at the moon shining over the miles and miles of mountainous terrain, I congratulated myself for not giving up.

Early next morning I set off for Bracca Pass. Although it was extremely cold, I enjoyed the peaceful feeling of this serene place. Birds serenaded us as Buddy and I rolled along in solitary splendor. Beginning the descent, I waved at some fashionable male cyclists going the other way. The only women I saw were in cars, and they stared at me as if I was crazy.

There did not seem to be any female cyclists in Italy, or Italian women participating much in athletics. However, they were always very beautiful, and now in this part of Italy they were very well dressed.

By the time I pedaled into Trigoso, the beginning of the fashionable Italian Riviera, dried sweat made a white mask on my face. Walking along the beachfront shops, tourists stared at me. A layer of dirt covered my legs. My socks drooped over my shoes. My T-shirt hung sloppily. Buddy didn't look much better. Laundry hung off his rear and he, too, was looking weathered. His paint was chipping and the panniers were fading. At times, several of the shop owners hesitated before taking money from my hands.

More climbing stood between me and the next town on the way to Genoa. As I came around the corner of one ascent, I spotted an obese man on the side of the road with his pants down. Thinking he was urinating, I looked the other way as I cycled by.

A few minutes later he passed me on his motor scooter. As I slowly ground around another corner, he had stopped again. Only this time, determined to be noticed, he turned toward me as he furiously masturbated.

I looked the other way.

As I rode on, I considered my situation. If he caused me any trouble, I could turn around and easily outrace him down the hill to a town where I could get help. In the background, I could hear his motor scooter as he slowly made his way toward me again. The closer he got, the more my body tightened. I gripped Buddy's handlebars firmly. I watched him in my little mirror as he edged closer. I took deep breaths. He came up alongside me.

He tooted his horn and kept going.

I held my breath as I rounded each bend, but I never saw him again.

The challenging yet beautiful quiet mountains finally gave way just before Genoa where the traffic, horns, and car exhaust made me want to turn around. But I couldn't just power through Genoa because this was a prearranged mail stop.

When I arrived at the American Express office, the door was locked. Oh no! Now what's today, I wondered? In the cafe next door, a man explained: "National Holiday".

So I camped 10 miles out of town and returned the next day. After reading my mail, changing money, and picking up some supplies for the road, I found a public phone and called home.

My mother and I arranged to meet between Christmas and New Year's in Portugal. After we worked out the details of that exciting new development, we talked about the rest of the family. My younger brother who had successfully battled cancer was now a proud father of a little girl. My younger sister was pregnant with her fourth child, and my older brother who recently married was expecting twins. Between my discussion with Mom and the letters from my friends, I realized that my old world was changing drastically without me. So much would be different when I returned. It made me wonder how I would fit in and relate to the people I cared about. There was a sense of loneliness as I contemplated these changes.

My route continued through several tunnels just beyond Genoa. These tunnels were barely wide enough for two cars and some stretched for miles. The only light inside the tunnels came from vehicles that passed me. These long, dark passageways terrified me because I was not visible and did not carry any lighting. Taking the routes with tunnels saved a whole lot more climbing, so it seemed the best option.

As I emerged from a tunnel and viewed a straight stretch of road that bordered the ocean, I noticed a red sedan approaching from behind. The driver, a wild-eyed man in his 20s, stared at me as he passed.

Up ahead, he pulled over and waited. I didn't know what to expect. He watched me in his mirror as I approached. When I reached him, he flung open his door and exposed his penis.

I looked away and kept pedaling. He passed me again, stopped his car and waited. OK, I told myself, this guy is mistaken if he thinks he can frighten me.

So, this time when he opened his door and exposed himself, I laughed out loud. He sunk lower and lower into his seat. I kept laughing while pedaling down the road. Thankfully, I never saw him again.

This kind of episode was becoming uncomfortably common. It became necessary to diffuse their power by embarrassing them without making them angry. Thinking about my options, I recalled back home the water bottle trick. I'd squirt them with my bottle. It works for dogs, I reasoned, and these men were acting like animals—and certainly within my target range.

Laughing about my new discovery, I shouted, "Come on, you bastards, just try it once! I have my weapon!"

I couldn't wait for my next victim. Unfortunately, he would probably not be an Italian.

My odometer turned ten thousand miles as I passed into the new language, new culture and different money of France. Along the Riviera, miles and miles of mansions skirted the cliffs. They overlooked harbors full of tarpaulin-covered pleasure craft.

The nights grew colder as I made my way beyond Monte

Carlo and the other French resort towns. I stopped at a snack bar to stock up on portable food. The owner spoke English. I told him a little about my trip, and he asked me about the nights. When I mentioned they were starting to get cold, he offered me a spot inside his food storage room in the back. After agreeing that could work, I changed my mind. After spending more time talking with him, something didn't feel right.

As I pedaled away, I recalled stories people shared about certain areas along the coast. It was easy access to kidnap someone. Did this man plan to lock me up? Were the stories about sex slaves true? Back home, no one really knew where I was. It would have been the perfect crime. Even though a warm room was tempting, I just couldn't take such chances.

Coincidently, the next day some travelers told me about a black market slavery ring that still operated somewhere near the area I had just been. Who knows if that was true or if that was why the snack bar man got on the telephone when he thought I was going to stay.

With winter fast approaching, I had to be more careful about who wanted to take advantage of my situation. Throughout the day I had to remain attuned to everything, every suspicious quirk in conversation, every wandering eye. It was exhausting to always be alert. As nightfall approached, it was hard to refuse a warm place under a roof, especially after a long day of exhausting cycling. Days were shorter and my gear was minimal. But just as the Italian drivers had toughened me up to "friendly" roadside conversation, I could not afford to let my guard down when it became time to find a place to sleep. A hasty decision could cost me dearly!

After a few more days of cycling northward in cold wind, I couldn't get warm. My chest began to ache. I started to cough. I began to look for places to camp where I could enjoy a fireplace and something warm before I crawled inside my cold tent for the night.

I stopped at a small bar to ask permission to camp in the adjoining field. I pitched my tent and returned to the bar for a glass of wine.

A good-looking Frenchman in his late 30s insisted that he pay for my drink. He also kept filling it as he told me about his life. He told me about all of the places he had visited and people he had met while working as the chauffeur for a wealthy widow who lived nearby.

He kept telling me how beautiful I was. He stroked the back of my arm.

Falling for his flirtatiousness, I accepted his offer to walk me to my tent. I missed male companionship. I was also beginning to question my femininity that I was working so hard to disguise. But when he showed that he wanted more than companionship, I began to cry. I felt embarrassed and foolish for getting myself into this situation. I ordered him out of my tent and he left.

In Arles, inland from the coast, I visited the Allycamps. Vincent Van Gogh had made this cemetery famous because he painted here during his periods of insanity.

I sat among the old tombstones reflecting on the shortness of life. Already my trip was more than half over and I felt so much was still unanswered in my mind. Although I was gaining insights to my experiences on the road, it was not clear how it would direct me once home.

I put my head down on my knees, sat quietly, and prayed. At times like this I would surrender to God hoping for an answer or clue that I could understand. It was hard to stay positive when I felt so vulnerable and confused. And yet it was times like this that would remind me that there was a higher power in charge. I needed to have the faith to accept the unknown and the courage to keep on going.

A deeper sense of peace filled my body, as I stood up to leave.

Over the next few days I pedaled through small towns and villages heading for the famous Pyrenees Mountains dividing France from Spain. It was raining lightly as I rolled into a campground seven miles east of Narbonne. Just as I put up my tent it began to pour. Throughout the night the rain pounded down and water seeped into my tent. With cold wet temperatures, it would be difficult to dry my gear out. Unfortunately, there was nowhere to escape to except a small building used for an outdoor bathroom.

Without much choice, I packed up in the morning and pedaled off to find a room in Narbonne. The rain worsened. I took cover on the porch of a closed restaurant, fired up my stove, and enjoyed a hot cup of coffee.

Sipping on my coffee, I thought about alternatives. My experiences over the past few months were causing me to question my safety as a woman traveling alone. With winter approaching and fewer campers around, I found myself more exposed to problems. I began to avoid cities especial late in the day even if it meant giving up a warm bed—because I felt more vulnerable there. I had become tired of all the harassment and having to constantly watch my backside. I was becoming paranoid!

The storm didn't look like it was going to let up, so I packed my stove and cycled on toward Narbonne.

I stopped at the first hotel I saw, but it was too expensive. They suggested I try the hostel down the road. But when I arrived, it was closed. Discouraged and cold, I stood there looking for an answer. The streets were deserted and many places were closed for the lunch hour.

I stopped at a tiny newsstand to ask the attendant what she knew about the hostel. She spoke very little English and didn't know anything about the hostel. But she could see that I was cold and miserable and needed a place to stay—Pointing to the time, she said, "You go."

I studied her as she spoke. A petite, fair-skinned woman a little older than I, she seemed very friendly. But what did she mean, "you go"?

Then pointing to the number "1" on her watch, she said, "You go, come back." Struggling with the words, she continued, "my house." She smiled.

I came back an hour later hoping, that was what she meant. I helped her close the newsstand. As I carried one of the racks inside, ice-cold water spilled all over me. Already so cold and numb from head to toe, I didn't even feel it.

She got in her car and led me to her home which was not far away. There I met her husband, Gaby, her nephew, Michael, and her two angel-like daughters, Carrine and Marie. They all greeted me as I stood there dripping on the floor.

My savior, Monica, asked Michael something in French.

He turned to me and asked, "Monica say, you want douche?"

I felt relieved that one of them knew a little more English.

"Yes, thank you," I replied, " tell Monica that I have been cold all day and that a shower would be great."

As I savored the hot water, I suddenly felt my heart stop. Yikes, I left my money, passport, and other important papers on my bike. Although my first impression of this family felt good, my growing paranoia caused me to think twice. Had they brought me home to take advantage of me? Well, Sally, I told myself, it's already done. I finished showering and got dressed while Monica put my wet clothes in the washer. Gaby, a short, rough-looking man, prepared dinner.

After checking my bike and seeing that everything was fine, I felt embarrassed and guilty for even thinking suspicious thoughts. Had I judged Gaby and Michael by their appearance because they were rock singers? I thought I had left those judgments at home. However, with all the recent episodes, maybe it was not possible and regressing was normal.

It felt good to be dry and warm by the time that we sat down to eat. The family all looked at me with warm, caring eyes as Gaby, who couldn't speak any English, said something to Michael, our interpreter.

"Gaby say to tell you what he make for us," said Michael. "It is called Les Basque."

Monica said something to him in French.

"Oh, Monica want me to tell you that it is name of state in France and Spain."

When Gaby served the dish, it consisted of chicken with a red spaghetti sauce on top of a bed of noodles smothered in cheese. It tasted great and was a welcome change from my diet.

With Michael as our interpreter, we talked. Gaby and Michael, who were originally from Spain, had formed their own rock and roll band and were about ready to release their first record. Monica frowned as we talked about the strain that such a life style had put on her and Gaby's marriage over the last 10 years. Their daughters continued quietly to do homework as we adjourned to the TV. We watched "Beauty and the Beast" and a documentary about EI Salvador. The French language had been dubbed in.

During my three-day stay, Carrine, the older of the two girls, spent a lot of time with me. She took English classes at her school and used samples of my writing for show and tell. My affection for this family grew as I took advantage of the respite to clean my bike and dry out my water-logged gear.

The family included me in everything they did. Their friends came over to visit with me. We enjoyed hot rum and card games. Monica took me shopping. I played games with the kids. I wrote in my journal. My strength returned.

Sadness crossed our faces as I packed my bike for the road again. Even Gaby's eyes watered as we hugged for the last time.

As always, I pedaled off feeling both happy and sad—happy returning to the road and sad for saying one more goodbye. My heart ached.

I remembered my sudden fear while taking a shower. How had I allowed such paranoia to influence my thoughts? This family didn't have to invite me home. At the newsstand, I didn't tell Monica that I needed a place to stay where I could regroup. And yet, on some level, she determined that I needed the support and warmth that her family could give.

I reflected on goodbyes back home. Pursuing my careers required me to move around. Each time I moved it became more difficult to leave new friendships and communities. This made me question my choices. Yet with every, there were new experiences, cultures and people to meet. It seemed like each time these experiences were more meaningful, which made leaving even harder. This taught me the importance of detaching from the past to create the future.

Two days later I stopped for the night at Port Baracares, an interesting fishing village where I bought a bottle of wine and set up my tent in a deserted campground. The owner, a woman, had offered me a little bungalow, but I decided to enjoy the beautiful day outdoors. A vicious windstorm in the afternoon altered my plan.

As I ran around trying to scoop up my tarps, maps, books and water bottles, the woman insisted that I relocate to the bungalow. Grateful, I took the offer and stayed for the next two days.

It was interesting that I was indoors and alone. The pressure of constantly being around people was amazing but also very tiring. All of a sudden in this bungalow, I did not have to entertain. For the first time in months, I could let my guard down. I could just relax.

As I waited for the windstorm to pass, I lay on the bed and read. I drank wine. Later, I spent time running on the deserted beach and visiting with the fishermen as they worked on their boats. My campground host was so kind and brought me fresh apples and walnuts every day for lunch.

Resting in the bungalow gave me time to think about my trip. It was easier when I was taking rest days to contemplate my experiences and the situations I encountered. I often wondered why me? Why would someone like me take such risks, give up so much to pedal around the world and live in a tent? How could someone who lacked the experience I did, be successful? And yet here I was, day after day getting on my bike and pedalling. Trying to answer my questions, or too much detail about the scope of my trip was overwhelming. I wonder if I was successful because I did not worry about the future, but stayed focused on the present. To get through just one more day. I looked forward to the road again.

Chapter Ten
Siesta Time

For the next few days I cycled up and down the barren terrain of the Pyrenees Mountains. Rocks, many in fascinating mounds and shapes, were the only things that sprouted from the crimson soil. Little seaside villages, about 10 or 15 miles apart, sat at the bottom of cliffs where bleached white houses lined the coves in perfectly arranged rows.

The wind persisted as I continued to make my way through the Pyrenees and on to Barcelona—it blew the cold right through me. Although the November wind was brutal, at least there were not many cars to contend with.

However, siesta time would be a detail to pay attention to. Business hours were different in Spain than in most European countries. The Spanish take a five-hour rest in the middle of the day, called siesta. Beginning at noon, everything closes, including shops, restaurants, post offices and banks. This unique break in the action gave me freedom from traffic but little opportunity to shop during afternoon hours. Now that winter had arrived, with cold weather and short days, I wanted to set up camp by 5:00 pm—before dark. This change would require even more planning.

Seventy miles north of Barcelona, I had to leave quiet country roads and take the main highway. This put all my knowledge, skill, and road sense to the test. Trucks raced by in convoy fashion, each blowing a layer of soot on me. Horns honked and cars nearly sideswiped me. My head began to pound. Exhausted and cold, I arrived in the city limits and urgently began to look for a hostel.

Along Barcelona's great tree-lined boulevard, called Las Rambles, I found a tourist center. A woman there gave me directions to a hostel. As I pedaled down wide streets, I watched curiously as well-dressed men and women busily hurried along.

Off in the distance, the unfinished spires of a cathedral designed and built by Gaudi (a great Catalonian architect), rose high above a patchwork of new old buildings. Parks full of noisy children added to this lovely city. Narrow cobblestone streets led through the historic district. Something was different about Barcelona; there was a connection of sorts. It was almost as if I had been here before. Spain had called to me in my dreams it seemed for a lifetime. These unexplained feelings can have a strange way of bringing a sense of familiarity inward even when it is not clear why.

After I checked in at the hostel, I called home. It was Thanksgiving. Mom and I talked for awhile about my trip. Then I asked her about home.

"Sally," my mother responded, "Mrs. Rowe isn't doing so well. Her health has taken a turn for the worse." Mrs. Rowe was part of our family. She had spent 10 years of her life as our nanny during a time that was mother was pulled away to handle her father's estate.

"What an amazing 92 years she has lived," I said. It saddened me to know that I wouldn't be there to say goodbye. I was grateful to have loved her as our nanny and to have cared for her later when she retired. But regardless, losing loved ones is difficult, as it is another goodbye.

Mom continued, "And I hate to share more bad news, Sally, but your cousin Cheri was recently involved in a car accident."

"Was it bad? What happened to her?" I stammered.

"I don't know the details," Mom replied. "Her brother tells me that Cheri is totally paralyzed and that she may have brain damage. Nobody knows if she's even going to make it." Mom's voice began to crack.

"No! Not Cheri! That's impossible," I lost my composure. "Mom . . . I'll . . . call you in . . . a few days."

I hung up and headed straight for the Barcelona Cathedral where I knelt and began to pray for my two dear friends. Saddened by this news, my mind again raced around searching for answers. Based on my own experiences, I believed that we can create good and bad situations in our life. That we can direct thoughts subconsciously that become real. Maybe this is why it's easier to look back to understand the why's. This triggered thoughts around my dear cousin's life and I wondered what chain of events could have caused such a life-threatening outcome.

During the next five days in Barcelona, I spent a lot of time walking back and forth between the cathedral and the hostel. Because of Cheri's misfortune, I began to call upon the tools that my religious upbringing had provided me that I had discarded in my teens. I looked for answers in the Bible. I bought a necklace with Jesus on the Cross and wore it daily to remind me to send healing energy to her. And I stopped in a religious store and bought a new candle so that Cheri could have a bright and powerful light in the house of God.

Cheri's accident was also causing me to blend my Silva meditation techniques with the religion I had been taught. Having grown tired of the guilt associated with Catholicism, and not always abiding by its rules and structures, I had allowed traditional religion to leave my life. And yet now I began to see it as a tool that I could use in a way that was meaningful to me.

The cathedral setting seemed to supercharge my meditations. In them I began to talk to my cousin. I was close to Cheri. My summer time trips cast brought us closer.

Imagining sitting next to my cousin I began to talk. "Cheri," I asked, "what happened with your life? Why was this change needed? And why so drastic?"

She seemed to be telling me that I shouldn't worry about her. That she would be okay.

"You will live, Cheri," I said from thousands miles away. "Cheri, you are a strong and resilient person, you can beat this"

This conversation felt real. I know she heard me.

Seeing Barcelona, a grand city full museums, open markets and little cafes was a needed distraction but my mind was still preoccupied. With Cheri as a catalyst, I examined all parts of my life. Trying to understand my new appreciation for religion, I questioned politics, history, and geography—really any subject I had not taken the time to learn about.

Just as much of the ceremony surrounding religion was starting to make sense to me, a lot of the values and structures that I had identified with my country suddenly began to take on new meaning as well. When I had left home almost a year ago, I was questioning my relationship with my homeland. I felt powerless to help make it a better place. And yet what I really lacked was knowledge.

Instead of learning about my country and getting involved, I had expended most of my energy reaching one goal after the other. This pattern was distracting and ultimately not fulfilling. This trip was demonstrating the importance of developing my inner self first. For me, this meant a return to basic values. Through the simplicity of bicycle travel, I began seeing that there were many paths to fulfillment. The families that invited me home were showing me many different ways to live, thus reminding me that my choices were infinite. If I were guided by my inner self rather than the external pressures, then my direction would be more true.

Returning to the US would surely test me. Could I apply my learnings and new perspective in the world I once knew and left behind? Would the temptation of old habits and behaviors weaken me?

I was becoming anxious to return to the US, to a familiar place with a new mindset.

I pedaled away from Barcelona, hoping to spend time with my thoughts. Instead, traffic on the main highway nearly killed me. Bundled up in mittens, wind pants, and a hooded jacket, I fought with the cars and trucks for a sliver of the white line that separated me from the dirt shoulder. At times, all I saw was the road's edge. I summoned all my nerve to face the grueling up and down terrain of the Spanish coast. Many truckers applauded my efforts. When I could look up to acknowledge their friendly honks, I saw them wave at me. Some even stopped and offered me rides.

As I headed south toward Malaga where campgrounds were abundant, I began to meet many retired northern Europeans who traveled south to Spain and Portugal for the winter. The moderately priced camping facilities here all offered restaurants and bars which gave me a place to escape from my tent. Many of my evenings were spent next to the warm cozy fireplace while writing in my journal. It was a delightful and needed change of pace.

Three days of hectic highway cycling brought me to the lovely town of Orpesa. A long, narrow dirt road led me to a beachside campground. The management, eager to have an American be part of their upcoming fiesta, reduced my rate to almost nothing. I decided to stay for the fiesta.

The special dinner that night was baked chicken, a salad, vegetables, potatoes and garlic bread. Afterwards, the band played and everyone danced, laughed and celebrated. I kept up with them until the wee hours of the morning. I slept well that night.

During my stay in Orpesa, my stove finally quit. So, on my last night, I went into town and treated myself to a restaurant dinner. As I watched the couples come in, sharing each other's company, I began to feel lonely and uncomfortable. I rarely spent time in cities, especially at night. And I rarely ate out. Partly the money but it was difficult to be so far from home, watching couples, families and friends socializing. The holidays were approaching and that was a reminder that I would not be home celebrating our traditions.

The last few days of travel from Barcelona exaggerated my loneliness. The constant traffic, road construction and fumes took a toll on my health and my morale. This was a particularly tough time.

As I continued down the coast, many Europeans opened their motor homes to me. Since my stove was now broken, and I could not replace it yet, they frequently offered me breakfast and dinner. Others gave me places to sleep. Still others offered me whiskey after a cold day's ride. Back home, I didn't consume much alcohol. I was finding now, however, that strong drink allowed me to numb my mind and body from the pain of winter. People along the way helped me with my arduous quest to be in Portugal by Christmas.

Outside Almeria, a tall teenage boy followed me on his bicycle for more than 25 miles. I tried not to let him bother me; locals along the way would often try to keep up. I thought that he was using my interference to shield him from the headwind.

After a while, however, something about him began to feel strange. Even when I waved him to pass me, he stayed where he was. Finally, I couldn't take it anymore. I slammed on my brakes. The boy swerved. He almost hit me and stopped.

"You get the hell out of here," I shouted. Pointing with my finger, I continued, "Just leave me alone. Go on, split."

He laughed not knowing what I was saying, but he knew what I meant. I took off.

A few minutes later he caught up to me and kept on following an inch or two behind my back wheel. I stopped again. He missed me again. I yelled. He laughed.

And we went on.

Finally, after the third time, he gave up.

Near Algeciras, an eight-mile climb offered breathtaking views of the Rock of Gibraltar and Morocco. As I looked across the Mediterranean, I wondered if my travels would take me to Africa. I thought I might like to see its northern tip, but many people had warned me of the danger a woman alone on a bike might encounter. I would stay open and flexible.

After an absolutely freezing night near St. Marie, I could hardly pedal the mile to town for a cup of coffee. My body still shivered, my teeth chattered, and it hurt to breathe. I had just spent the night inside my sleeping bag with all my clothes on. All could find in town was tepid espresso. Three cups didn't warm me up. I pedaled off, cursing my stove for breaking. Thankfully in two weeks I would have a new one. It was expensive to ship and extremely difficult to plan a mail drop, so I decided to wait the month out until my mother's arrival in Portugal.

I left the coast and headed inland toward Seville. The nights became even colder. After nearly freezing and awakening to a frost covered tent, I decided that I would tax my budget and spend my last night in Spain in a pensione—a Spanish version of a bed and breakfast.

Arriving in Huelva just as nightfall approached, I knocked on the door of the first pensione I saw. Trash littered the streets outside. Oil stains blackened the asphalt. An old man holding a cigarette greeted me.

"Hello, speak Englaise?" I asked.

He nodded his head excitedly.

"Do you have any rooms?"

"Yes, yes!" he replied, "and bicileta, too, come. Hot douche also."

We talked price. I followed him.

He led me and my bike up three flights of rickety wooden stairs. The air was stale. He opened the door to my room. A sagging mattress spoke of its many years of use. A battered radio sat on the shelf above it. A small light with a torn lamp shade occupied the top of the nightstand.

"Room grandee for you!" he said as he held out his hand. I rolled my eyes. In the States this dormitory-like building would surely be condemned.

"Where is douche?" I asked.

"Come."

I followed him back down a flight of stairs and through the kitchen where a group of men smoked cigars and played poker. We stopped at the bathroom.

"Douche grandee!" he exclaimed as he held out his hand.

A black hose with a nozzle on it hung from one of the linoleum walls. The man pointed to it and said that it was my hot shower. A yellowish stain from where it leaked flowed down to the floor. Cigarette butts floated in the leaky toilet. The mirror on the medicine chest was cracked. An altogether charming place!

He told me about a restaurant where the locals went for dinner. So after my garden hose shower (reminiscent of Hong Kong), I ambled down to the main part of town in search of a meal. When I walked into the restaurant that my pensione host had recommended, everybody stopped talking. They all stared at me.

I looked around and realized that I was the only woman in the place. During the days when I had stopped for lunch at the bars along the way, I rarely saw women. And yet, I had fit in more readily because the road had left me sweaty and grimy. I usually sat at the bar. Generally, I wore blue knee socks to cover my legs, and no one bothered me. A lot of the time, the men wouldn't let me pay for my food. But this was different. My hair was clean and I wore my one change of street clothes. The men kept staring as I ordered chicken and potatoes.

My diet had changed drastically in Spain. Without a stove, I was forced to eat what I could find in local bars. Breakfast usually included corn flakes and whole milk. For lunch, I often ate French bread and cheese. And for dinner, I found myself eating heavy meals like this one right before I went to bed.

I couldn't imagine eating a salad or fruit—it wouldn't be enough to keep me warm. And between meals, I had begun eating candy bars because that was all I could find. Combined with the wine and other liquor I was drinking to numb myself from the cold, I'd added 15 pounds to my small frame.

I accepted the additional weight, just as I was learning to accept other things about myself. Even though I had battled weight all my life, I knew that I needed it now to insulate me from the cold. Besides, this journey was not about what I looked like. It was about what went on beneath the surface.

The locals kept watching me as I devoured every last scrap from my heaping plate. Nobody said anything. They just stared. I kept smiling. I got up and went back to my "delightful" room.

The next day I left Spain and crossed the Rio Guadiana by boat. Arriving in Vila Real de St. Antonio, I took my first steps on Portuguese soil.

After a quick jaunt around this bustling resort town, I pedaled three miles to Monte Gordo, a small town known for its gambling casino. I turned off the beach front road and headed down a driveway that led me to the registration office.

This place was huge! A Mercado the size of a US supermarket was conveniently located in the center of camp. Hundreds of tent/

trailer sites surrounded it. Tall pine trees shaded the area. With rolling terrain on one side of the road and miles of beautiful open beach on the other, it reminded me of home, Aptos, near Santa Cruz, California. It was a perfect place for me: attractive, clean and only a $1.50 per night.

From Monte Gordo I had a choice to take the mountainous route north that would be quiet, but cold, or take the coastal road which promised to be busy and commercialized like the coast of Spain. I opted for the mountainous route even though I knew it was a gamble. The weeks of traffic, road construction, and whistling, leering Spanish men had worn me out.

The Portuguese men seemed different. At the town squares, a popular gathering spot for the afternoon siesta, they clapped as I pedaled by.

Heading north from Monte Gordo, through the Portuguese countryside, I saw women washing their clothes in a river. Their muscular arms showed the years of such manual labor. Narrow, pot-holed roads leading me over gently rolling hills offered spectacular views of the valleys below. These long bumpy stretches left both Buddy and me in a state of numbness.

Portuguese villages were very similar to those in Spain. Homes with red tile roofs and white stucco walls sat clustered together. From a distance they looked like alabaster mirages floating on the barren terrain. Narrow cobblestone streets generally led to a central plaza with a town clock and church. I felt like I was back in time as I wandered through the narrow alleys, looking at the buildings with their worn and weathered exteriors.

Enroute to Mertola, I came around a hill and spotted a tall, bearded man walking along with a duffle bag. We stopped and talked. In his broken English, he told me that he was from Austria and had started his walk on the coast of Portugal, now almost 400 miles away.

"Where is your tent?" I asked.

"Not necessary," he replied.

I persisted. "Do you have a stove?"

"No, no, not necessary," he shook his head.

"Aren't you cold at night?"

"No," he answered. He told me that he was headed for a small town in Spain to stay with some relatives. The whole time we talked, he smiled. He spoke confidently. He was a proud man.

After our short talk, I picked up my pace. He had inspired me. I had been complaining about the cold and that my stove was broken. Now every time the road ahead challenged me, I would recall my conversation with this man.

The following day, on Christmas Eve, I settled down for the night in a campground in Beja. I walked through town watching last-minute shoppers as they hurried from one store to the next. Children laughed. Couples hugged each other. It seemed that all the townspeople were with their families or the ones they loved.

Here I stood all alone, worn and tired. The last few months had proved difficult, and Spain had drained the last of my reserves. The combination of language and winter isolated me from people. My loneliness was so profound that it hurt to move my body. I slowly walked to my tent.

A Dutch couple spotted me and invited me into their trailer. We laughed and watched comedy on their VCR.

We said our good-byes and I headed for the campground office to call home.

My entire family had gathered at my mother's house for Christmas—this was the first year I was absent. Tears I had been holding back streamed down my cheeks as they told me how much they loved me and missed me. Then my six year-old niece got on the phone, "Aunt Sally," she said, "I love you. When are you coming home? I miss you, Aunt Sally." It was heartbreaking to hear her innocent little voice.

I swallowed hard. "Soon," I said.

I spent Christmas Day biking to Evora where I met Eric and Ada, another Dutch couple, in a campground. Since I was slightly ahead of schedule, I went sightseeing with them. We spent the day after Christmas touring a medieval town, visiting a winery and touring a marble quarry.

Eric and Ada were great company. Ada had fought and won a battle with cancer, and Eric taught people how to practice self hypnosis. Ada even read my palm and told me I would have one child and live a long life.

I biked to Lisbon feeling refreshed and set up camp. Mom's flight was due tomorrow. That night I felt excited yet nervous.

The next morning I rented a car, put my bike in it, and drove to the Lisbon airport. At the designated hour, I watched as a petite blonde-haired woman stepped off the plane. I could hardly believe my eyes! Mom's really here, I thought. Yeah! Mom's in Portugal! Thank you, God!

I raced to the arrival doors and greeted my mother as she walked through. We hugged each other tightly as tears of joy and relief ran down my cheeks. It was great to see her, yet something seemed different. There was a distance between us.

What was wrong, I wondered? Why did this encounter suddenly feel so awkward? What had happened to us? Was this the same person I had loved so dearly and yet had left 12 months ago to find myself? She was so quiet. Was she overwhelmed by the moment or just tired from traveling? I think we both knew that working together had strained our relationship. Yet I knew that our love for each other was never questioned. I could only hope that my phone conversations and letters home were helping Mom understand my need to make this trip.

We spent our short time together touring medieval cities, museums, castles, and other sights of Portugal. We enjoyed excellent Portuguese meals including plenty of potato bread, fresh fish and good port. It was really fun to share travel eating, shopping, and sightseeing with someone I loved.

We drove several hours each day and stayed in special places called posadas—a network of historic castles, palaces and monasteries converted to hotels by the government. Since Mom's business specialized in restoring unique and historic hotels, she had a particular interest in posadas.

The rooms were simple but elegant, and they all included a welcome hot shower and a cozy bed with freshly starched sheets. Small monastery windows offered views of the town below.

In the public areas, courtyards flanked the central dining room where we usually ate our dinners. These great halls had majestic vaulted ceilings and chandeliers. Handsome oil paintings and tapestries graced the walls in the corridors.

Living like this for a week—in warmth and comfort—tempted me to quit my trip. Mom also made me an offer.

"Sally," Mom said to me as she paged through our dinner menu, "you know, when I was putting that stove you wanted in my suitcase, I was thinking that I could at least offer to bring you home,"

I looked across the table. Her eyes reflected the wisdom of her words. She knew better than to try to convince me to come home, but she also felt compelled to give me the choice, letting me know it was perfectly OK to end the trip.

"I can't give up, Mom. All I have left is the US,"

"Well, I didn't mean quit," she said. "I don't want you to think that I want you to give up. I thought that maybe you could rest up for the winter in Aptos and then finish your ride next summer."

"I just can't do it, Mom, If I return home now, I don't think I will return," I replied.

"So where are you going to go from here?" she asked, "You're in the dead of winter."

"I've got a lot of different things that I'm considering. I met a man who worked his way back to America on a freighter. I'm going to look into that. I don't know, I've always wanted to see Africa and I hear that Morocco is pretty cheap."

Mom's eyes widened. "Morocco! Sally, I hear that's not such a safe place to travel alone."

"I've heard that too," I replied, "but if you can hook up with a group, then it's not supposed to be so bad. And if I can get down near where the boats cross the Strait of Gibraltar, maybe I can find a group of travelers going that way."

"Sounds like you're not coming home for a while," she said.

"Next summer, Mom. I'll be home then."

The week raced by, and before I knew it, Mom and I were hugging at the airport, wiping tears from our eyes. Was she really going? Was I really staying? This whole experience didn't seem real. My stomach knotted up.

My mother's plane left. Once again, I was all alone.

Siesta Time

It's not time to return home, I assured myself. My stomach was unsettled and my mind confused like it was when I first decided to make this trip. Yet like before, I felt something more powerful pushing me forward. Somehow it felt right to continue on and so that is what I did.

I packed my bike into our rental car and drove back to Faro on the south coast of Portugal. There I formed a plan. I would return to Monte Gordo. That way I could still keep my options open for either a Morocco excursion or a freighter trip home (or both). For $1.50 a night, I figured that I could buy enough time to consider any other possibilities that might pop up.

Spoiled by my mothers visit and hotel living, I mistakenly drank from a local spigot and became violently sick. What a way to start my first week back on the road. This reminded me how easy it was to get distracted and lose focus.

Ultimately, I would spend five weeks in the Monte Gordo campground. My camping neighbors were all northern Europeans trying to escape the winter cold. Between flash flooding and bad orientation to the sun I was cold and wet. My neighbors helped me move my tent three times before I finally had it pitched correctly for the conditions.

Since it was bitter cold at night, they also loaned me candles, wool blankets, and hot water bottles. I adopted a mother, father, uncle and big brother from this fun group of interesting people.

I collected dried pine needles to make a walkway into my tent. This kept the sand out. I dug a ditch around my portable home to keep the rain water from forming a pool. I salvaged a wooden fruit crate from a nearby garbage dump. It served as a shelf for my food while a smaller one became my desk. A plastic bag hung in the trees. It kept my perishables in the shade during the warm afternoons. A large clay vase that I found abandoned on the beach stored the water I drew from a nearby well. I added color to this picture with large sea shells that I placed around my camp.

Unwilling to brave the cold, I hibernated in my tent sometimes as late as noon. I read several books, meditated, and practiced my Silva techniques. I wrote many letters home and even started compiling journal entries documenting patterns of my past.

Over the last several weeks, we had turned into a community of campers—a village in-and-of-itself. Everyone was courteous and friendly. If I stayed in my tent past noon, a neighbor would come by to check on me.

Each day I went into Monte Gordo to pick up supplies, check on mail and send telexes to the various ocean freight companies in Spain and Portugal. At the newsstand I always stopped and read a copy of *USA Today*.

During my stay I met a Portuguese man who spoke English well. He jogged and owned a bike shop. Here was a friend to spend time with, I thought.

No sooner had he gotten me over to his house, however, than he turned into an animal. All he wanted was sex. He became violent when I tried to explain to him that I was not interested in accommodating him. I needed time, I explained. He didn't have any. He was mad. I knew I had lost a friend.

All I wanted was male companionship. I thought he understood that. I had explained to him my disillusionment with Mark, and my disgust with the harassment I'd experienced along the way. I left, never to return.

How much more could I let my appearance go before men would leave me alone? My skin was rough and my face weathered. I packed an extra 15 pounds into my raggy, sweat-stained clothes and they still saw me as a sex object. My hair was short, brittle and dry and I even ate a clove of garlic each day. Still they bothered me.

My boat never came. Morocco never materialized. And after five weeks of introspection and unhurried times, I finally felt called to the States. I was ready to finish my journey.

As the 747 lifted off the runway in Lisbon, apprehension and excitement filled my mind. I was going home. It didn't matter that many more miles of pedaling still stood between New York and Aptos, my home town. What mattered was I was returning to a familiar people, folks that I shared history with. In the US, people spoke English. I would surely find traveling cyclists again, and I could read the road signs.

But was I ready? Would I be any safer traveling there? I had left the States feeling disgusted with its crime, its drug problems, and its violence. What had changed? Me? Perhaps.

I watched until I could no longer see European soil. Europe, a continent I had only dreamed of visiting, was now behind me. I had pedaled six thousand miles, forming a huge Z, as I crossed its lands three times.

Now, after 14 months and over 12,000 miles on three continents, I was leaving behind a feat that I could hardly comprehend. How did I make it this far? Surely there was a reason for this— but I didn't know what. It seemed certain, however, that I would survive the rest of this trip. My eyes closed as I sank further into my seat, saying goodbye one more time to Europe.

PART 4
United States

CHAPTER ELEVEN:
Back in the USA

CHAPTER TWELVE:
Only My Body Not My Soul

CHAPTER THIRTEEN:
The Rhythm of Cycling

CHAPTER FOURTEEN:
Coming Home

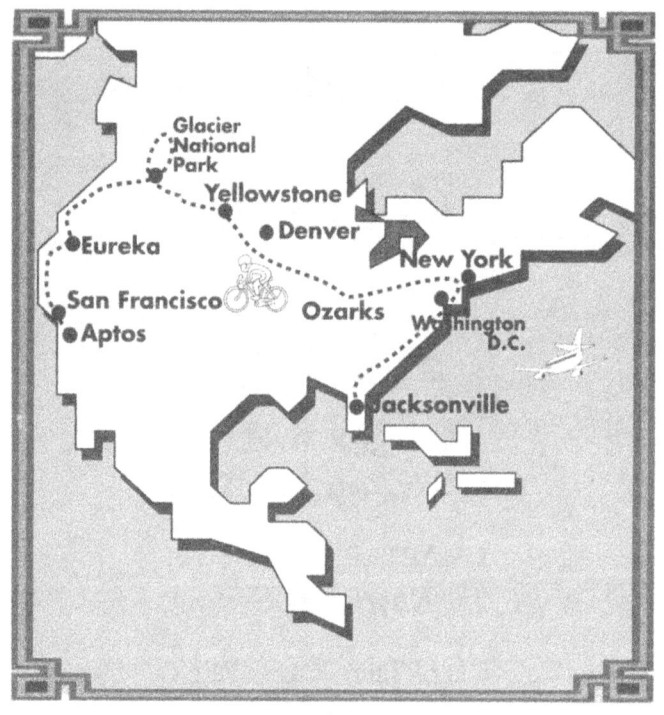

Date: *February 14, 1989-July 29, 1989*
Bike Miles: 8199
Route: *Florida, Georgia, Carolina's, Virginia, Kentucky, Illinois, Kansas, Colorado, Wyoming, Montana, Canada, Idaho, Oregon, California.*

Chapter Eleven
Back in the U.S.A.

As the plane droned across the Atlantic, I reflected on my past year and how far I had come, not only as a traveler and cyclist, but also as a person. Pushing my boundaries every day just to survive made me realize how strong my mind really was. That I could alter my outcomes through positive thinking and positive visualization. My ability to attract so many loving people who helped me along the way was truly amazing. It was like angels showing up when I needed them most. The love and support from people all over the world inspired me during my darkest moments.

Living on the road toughened me as a survivor but softened me as a person. I learned to be more patient and accepting of other cultures and lifestyles. Forcing my way to a solution through old habits rarely worked. But connecting with people through kind and gentle energy always worked.

My only job was to get from one place to the next each day. That in itself was daunting at times, but life on the road did not compare to life at home. My trip allowed me time to reflect on events that occurred that day and pondered why. At home these subtleties would go unnoticed.

The cultures that I had worked so hard to adapt to faded from my consciousness as New York began to fill my every thought. Had I chosen the right destination? Would the culture shock of the State's biggest city be too much for me? Where could I stay? Would I find a cheap airplane ticket to the warmer weather of Florida, until I could cross the US?

After seven hours the plane landed at John F. Kennedy airport. A chill ran down my spine as a voice announced that we could unfasten our seat belts. I was really back in the U.S.A.!

A short while later I stood in the lobby watching others hug and kiss as they reclaimed their loved ones. I was alone and felt like an alien.

Noisy video games and popcorn, bagel, and ice cream stands lined the hallways. Travelers with carts and suitcases hurried about. American voices called out departures and arrivals. A feeling of urgency filled the air. It dizzied me to watch. It felt foreign to me.

After I reclaimed Buddy, I made my way to the ticket windows. Everyone stared at me. My weathered skin, dirty shoes, and worn clothes communicated that I was different. My road-scarred bike, faded packs, and tattered gear explained why.

Now that language was no longer a barrier, it became easier to figure things out. Within an hour I had tickets for a flight to Florida, a storage locker for my bike, and room reservations in New York.

By the time I left the terminal, the sky had blackened and it was raining. A temperature gauge at the bus stop read 30 degrees.

The speed with which people spoke English intimidated me. I listened intently. My English had become so broken and slow from living in Europe that it embarrassed me to talk. I couldn't distinguish the various accents that I heard around me. All I knew was that people spoke English and they spoke it fast.

"Excuse," I called to a short, gray-haired lady, "what time for next bus?"

I had grown so accustomed to economizing on basic sentence structure that people thought I was from another country.

The woman studied me. She tried to hide her fear.

"Where are you from, dear?" she asked.

"California," I replied.

"California?" Her eyes shifted to my bike, then to my grimy clothes.

"I'm returning to the US after a 14-month trip around the world on a bicycle," I said. "Now I'm heading for California."

Several others joined in and asked me questions about my journey. These inquiries would become a familiar pattern during the next five days in New York. I welcomed this interest; it gave me an opportunity to practice speaking English again.

I stayed at a hostel in the Chelsea district and spent each day touring the city on foot. Although the storefronts and street signs served as a sort of welcoming committee (everything was in English!), the crowds of people and noisy streets unnerved me.

On my second day, as I looked across the harbor to the Statue of Liberty, a new understanding of freedom began to overwhelm me. I thought about my Chinese friends. I wondered if my phrase books were helping them attract new foreigners to their restaurant. Would they ever be able to travel, to leave their country? I thought about Dachau. I thought about the Russian people. I remembered the repression I had seen in Ireland, where Mary and Margaret used alcohol to numb the daily fear that gripped their lives. And I realized that as Americans, we had the freedom to live our lives any way we wanted to. A few tears ran down my face as I thought about how far I had traveled and how much I had seen.

When I returned to the hostel, I called my father.

"Dad, guess where I am?" I bubbled.

"California," he replied.

"No, Dad, I'm in New York. I've tried to call you the past couple of days. Hey, but since we last talked, I made it. I'm back in the states now."

Dad and I talked about the family and how everyone was doing. He bubbled about the grandchildren and updated me on his daily jogging progress. "Sally, you've still got a long way to go," he said, "please be careful. It's so great to hear your voice. Your mother was telling us that you were doing just great when she came to see you."

Dad and Barbara gave me some tips on places to go in New York.

"Listen," my Dad continued, "Barb and I are going to be in the Kentucky area for a business convention in about two months. Would you like to meet us in Atlanta?"

"Sure! It would be a great side trip. I'd love to see you both."

We worked out the details. I hung up feeling excited that I would get to see Dad and Barbara in the not too distant future.

When it came time to leave New York, I flew out of JFK and arrived at the Jacksonville airport at 11:00 pm. I planned to spend the night on one of the chairs in the lobby. I pulled my partly assembled bike out of the box which New York officials had made me use, and walked it across the floor to the escalator.

"Hey, lady!" a portly security guard called. "Where do you think you're going with that thing?"

"Upstairs, sir," I replied.

Pointing his finger, he bellowed, "The only place you're going with that bike is outside!" A scowl crossed his face.

OK, Sally, be careful with this man, I reminded myself. Don't let your ego get in the way. Remember what you learned in China. He's just trying to make a show for the others and you've got to honor that.

I lowered my voice. "Sir," I looked into his eyes, "I have nowhere to go tonight. I don't have my bike together to ride, and if I did, it's illegal to ride at night without a light. What do you suggest I do? I just flew in from Portugal and tomorrow I begin my journey across the US."

He began to soften.

"Leave it there while you go upstairs," he said as he pointed to a corner near the bathrooms. "I'll be here all night. It'll be fine."

I never told him that I needed to be upstairs so I could sleep. He never asked.

Not completely convinced he would let me stay all night, I hid myself from his view and feverishly put my bike back together. I wanted transportation in case he kicked me out. At two in the morning, I walked back out into the main area. Grease covered my hands. My eyes were half closed from exhaustion.

"Excuse me," I called to him. "It's all back together. Can I just lock it up right here?"

"Isn't that what I told you?" he responded, trying to brush me off.

"Say," I said, "do you know much about Florida?"

His eyes lit up. "What do you want to know about it?"

I quickly pulled out my maps and asked, "If you could take a month to travel here, where would you go?"

He forgot all about his uniform and how he was supposed to act. His arms and facial expressions described his fishing excursions throughout the state. He motioned excitedly as he talked about the fish he and his buddies had caught, where they caught them, and how much beer they drank in between. He told me about all the wonderful national parks in Florida and circled places of interest on my map. By the time he was done, I had won over a friend.

"You go off and get some rest," he said. "I'll guard this bike with my life."

All that he had wanted was someone to notice him and make him feel appreciated. I realized that adversity during my trip had taught me to deal with difficult people.

Six hours later I opened the door and walked my bike outside to inhale my first breath of warm, humid Florida air. I straddled my bike and began to pedal south toward town.

Cycling in my shorts and tank top, I couldn't wipe the grin off my face. It was hot! I inhaled wonderfully warm fresh air and pedaled along miles of flat, tree-lined roads. I stopped often to talk with locals. By now, English was no longer much of a problem.

Along the way, I saw a campground that I couldn't pass up. Judging by the number of huge RVs that filled this quaint river hideaway, I knew that I could probably buy a hot shower. And, I reasoned, if the price was right, I would stay the night. I walked into the office.

"You can spend the night on us," the campground owner said when I told him that I was on the last leg of an around-the-world journey.

It took me two hours to set up my tent as one camper after another came over to talk with me. One middle-aged couple invited me to dinner in their huge RV. Even though it was the largest in the complex, they still didn't think it was big enough. We held hands, said grace, and enjoyed a wonderful meal. We talked for hours.

Larry, a trim, balding man, had just retired from 36 years as a pilot for Continental Airlines. "You know, Sally, women pilots are in great demand," he said. "Once you get this trip behind you, with your business background and education, you'll have good offers. Don't worry about your lack of flying hours. You have a lot going for you."

He was right. During my trip, the issues of surviving from day to day, of finding food, good roads, and a place to stay had distracted me from evaluating my past accomplishments— and future opportunities.

I pedaled off into headwinds the next morning. Although the going was slow, the gently rolling terrain was tolerable and I made it to Ocala National Park well before dusk.

While I was sitting at a picnic table watching the squirrels play, a middle-aged couple walked up to me. They introduced themselves as Polly and Willy from Vermont. Like many of these travelers, called "snow birds" by the locals, they were retired and living in Florida for the winter. Willy was bald and wore glasses; deep laugh lines marked the edges of his eyes. Polly wore loose-fitting clothes and sunglasses.

"You know, we see lots of bike riders out on the road," said Willy, "and we always feel so sorry for them when they're pedaling into the wind. Why, I told Polly just the other day that if we ever met one who needed a place to camp, we'd share our campsite."

Happily, I accepted their offer.

Polly and Willy had recently married. It was the second time for each of them. At home they both worked part-time. Polly taught school and Willy was a fix-it man. During their travels, Polly spent most of her days carving wood birds while Willy enjoyed cooking and helping other campers repair things.

A threatening sky terminated our conversation.

"Do you guys see that out there?" I said as I pointed to the sky. "Those clouds are moving our way and they're pretty dark. One thing I know is rain. I've been on the road so long that I've developed a good sense for what the weather is going to do. I've got to pitch my tent."

"Is there anything we can do to help?" Polly asked.

"Not really, but thanks," I said as I walked out of their trailer. As I untied my tent from my bike, another camping neighbor introduced herself. "How would you like to see yourself on film?" she asked.

"That might be nice," I said, " but right now I've got to put my tent up."

"Well, that's what I meant," she replied. "Do you mind if I ask you questions and put you on video while you go through your routine?"

"No, I don't mind. But do I get a copy?" I joked.

"You bet."

But when she played the tape for me in her trailer, I was so disgusted with what I saw that I wouldn't take the copy she had made for me. In fact, I was so shocked at what I saw; I had to force myself to sit through it.

Did I really look this bad? I had gained at least 15 pounds. My face looked red, pudgy and weathered. My eyes were puffy. My short hair lay plastered against my head. And as I viewed myself explaining my various tasks, I saw a boastful woman who had lost her femininity.

I had created a monster, I thought to myself as I climbed into my sleeping bag. Then I remembered how extra weight had been needed to insulate me from the cold. I thought about the absence of mirrors to keep an eye on my complexion, and the problems that men could make for me if I had appeared any other way. I forgave myself.

But I couldn't get that boastful image out of my head. I resolved to keep my trip in proper perspective. It's not about me and what I've accomplished, I reasoned, but about what's taking place on the inside, where others can't see.

The next morning the news reported a major freeze heading our way. Polly and Willy decided to drive to the west coast of Florida where the weather might be a few degrees warmer. They invited me to go with them.

I was torn. I couldn't wait to get back on the road and work off some of that fat I had seen the previous night. But I thought about what 25 degrees felt like on a bicycle. I reflected on some of the miserably cold nights in France, Spain and Portugal.

"Yes, I would love to go," I answered.

We piled into their motorhome and drove most of the day. The wind blew us all over the road. The cold worked itself deep into my bones during our brief stops for gas and food. I knew that my tent wouldn't hold up to any of this. Biking in this weather would surely have been a nightmare. I had made the right decision.

We arrived at Polly's sister's house during a hurricane warning. Oh swell, I thought, this may be worse than the cold weather.

The house, located in Bradenton Beach on Anna Maria Island, faced a bay that separated it from Florida. A block behind the house, whitecaps raged on the Gulf of Mexico. Polly and Willy told me that during bad storms, the homes on this thin strip of land were flooded by waves which hit from both sides.

News bulletins reported that this storm was headed north, away from us. Feeling better, Willy and Polly retired to their motor home while I spent the night in a real bed. During the next four days I went fishing, jogging and exploring on my bicycle. Every night Willy cooked us a feast.

The more I ate, the more anxious I was to get back on the open road. So when Polly's sister returned from her three-day vacation, I thanked my new friends from Vermont, promised that I would write, and headed for the Everglades.

I welcomed everything about the warm weather that now engulfed me. I no longer had to bundle myself up, and it didn't hurt to breathe. And because Florida was filled with salad bars, fruit stands, and health food stores, I could eat lightly again.

The Tamiami Trail, which was the only road connecting Miami with the west coast of southern Florida, tested my cycling skills. I glued my eyes on the faded white line at the road's edge as cars and trucks rumbled past me. A canal bordered the road; it was full of alligators (and no doubt poisonous snakes). The only barrier between me and the gators was a strip of saw grass that grew along the edge of the canal.

As the sun began to set, I pulled into Collier Seminole State Park. In Florida, during tourist season, the state parks charge everyone the same $25 to camp, whether the visitor travels by bicycle or in a huge air-conditioned RV. Willy and Polly had shared their campsite with me, so I thought others would do the same. I asked a man who was waiting in line at the ranger booth if I could use a small corner of his campsite.

"If I can pay, why can't you?" he snarled. "I'm not gonna be a part of any freeloaders."

When I got back on my bike, hoping to explore the park, a ranger called out to me, "Excuse me, lady, unless you're willing to pay $25, we can't let you in."

"I can't see paying $25 for one night's camping," I replied. "I was hoping to find someone to share a site with." Across the way, the selfish man who had refused my request climbed inside his RV.

As we watched him pull away, the ranger said, "There's a rest area down the road where you might camp."

"I don't think it's very safe out there," I replied.

"I'm really sorry," apologized the ranger. "If you hadn't asked that man, I could have let you in."

Damn! That man had no sense of anything beyond the comforts of his oversized RV.

The rest area was the size of a postage stamp. On one edge sat the canal. A spot had been cleared inside the brownish, spindly saw grass. I sat behind a picnic table waiting for darkness so I could pitch my tent, but a mosquito attack forced me to set it up in the twilight. As I raced around, I brought everything inside, even my bike. I didn't want anyone to know that a female was camping here alone.

I fell asleep as cars stopped and doors opened and closed throughout the night. At about one in the morning a man's voice on a loudspeaker awakened me.

"Put the money in the bag or I will kill you!" it demanded.

Startled, I sat up. Did the robber mean me?

I peeked outside into the darkness and didn't see anything. I hid my passport, charge card, and traveler's checks in different parts of the tent. I put $50 into my money pouch and left it in plain sight, hoping the thief would not search me or my portable home. Somehow, I fell asleep. Maybe the voice was intended for someone else, or maybe it was a prank. I would never know, because nobody bothered me.

I left early the next morning and beat most of the traffic into Everglade City. There I inquired at the tourist center about canoe trips through the Everglades. They gave me the telephone number of a man named David who owned North American Canoe Tours. When I called, he asked if I could handle six days of paddling. Satisfied that I would fit in, he told me he was looking for a fourth person to join a tour that was leaving the next day. Then he told me the price.

"I charge $600," he said.

I swallowed hard. "Do you have any cheaper tours? That's a lot of money for me."

Earlier in the conversation I had described my trip. David had been intrigued by my journey.

"Well, I don't usually do this," he said, " but if you want to work, and it sounds like you've done a lot of it on your bike ride, maybe you can come along for nothing. I think you earned it."

"Yeow!" I exclaimed.

I rode to David's house. He was a short, husky man with a big stomach and an even bigger cigar. He lived in the Everglades in the winter months and at his home in Connecticut during the rest of the year. We visited for a long time and he told me more about the canoe trip.

The next day we loaded the canoes with 20 gallons of fresh water and four huge ice chests full of food. We added four waterproof duffle bags for our clothes and other personal belongings. We stored our cameras, wallets, keys, and navigation maps in metal boxes. I helped David file a float plan with the park service so we could reserve camping space on the tiny islands and wooden docks (called chickies) that were usually three or four hours of paddling apart.

During the next six days, Al and Jenny, the middle-aged couple that paid for the trip, and David and I paddled through a fascinating ecosystem. Al and Jenny occupied one canoe while David and I navigated the other. Before we left, David spent an hour instructing them on how to steer, stop, and climb out of the boat safely.

Throughout our adventure, Al and Jenny, both businesspeople from New York, kept the mood light. They seemed to make physical activity harder than it was, but they always maintained a good attitude and brought much humor to our time together.

As we paddled through this beautiful watery maze, David frequently guided us into small creeks that forked off the main river. Often, vine-covered mangrove trees shielded us from the brilliant sun. In these narrow, dark passageways we watched carefully as we brushed under the branches of trees. David told us they were a popular hiding spot for snakes just waiting to drop into the canoe.

We passed alligators, their beady eyes bulging just above the water line. They were very secretive, careful not to expose their long, gnarly bodies. Turtles startled us by diving off rocks. My senses became keen as I tuned in to the life of the everglades.

On the main river, manatees and dolphins joined us. Fish jumped high out of the water. Pelicans, wood storks, and great white herons roosted on distant treetops.

We completed our journey in the little town of Flamingo, at the southern tip of Florida. This special trip to a different world had really touched me. During the last six days, I had not seen a car, a boat or hardly anyone besides David, Al and Jenny. Our only company had been the wildlife that lived quietly in this natural world.

We drove back to David's home in Everglade City where I picked up my bike and returned to the road.

I pedaled along flat highways to Orlando, where I stayed with family friends in a beautiful home on the Arnold Palmer golf course. While I was there, my hosts Tom and Sherrie took me on evening sailboat rides. I played golf with them and their sons, Carter and Matt. They loaned me their car to visit Epcot Center.

A sprawling Walt Disney production, Epcot Center covers many acres featuring man-made lakes, eclectic architecture, and perfectly manicured gardens. It showcases current exhibits (like World Expo in Australia) and representations of future worlds. I spent three days enjoying energy and auto displays as well as castles, pagodas and other buildings that housed exhibits from other countries.

From Orlando I headed east to Satellite Beach, where I spent Easter with Evelyn's friends, Ken and Ruth. Evelyn, my close friend from back home, had gone to college with Ruth, who was now a lieutenant colonel in the Air Force. Ken, her husband, was a flight engineer with Northwest Airlines.

For the next five days the theme of my visit was aeronautics. I went on trips to the Kennedy Space Center and returned to discuss what I had seen with Ken and Ruth. We also talked about their careers in air-related fields.

From their house, I left busy route A1A and followed a scenic road along the Indian River north toward Daytona Beach. Produce stands filled with oranges and grapefruit lined the road. There were signs everywhere encouraging tourists to send fresh fruit home.

I returned to route A1A just out of Daytona, where traffic worsened. It was a narrow two-lane road, barely wide enough for two cars let alone me and my pregnant bicycle. My eyes were riveted to the white line when all of a sudden a sharp object hit me in the back. It sent a stinging pain up my spine. I stopped and watched as a car full of laughing teenagers zoomed by. Stunned, I looked down to the ground to see what they had thrown. It was a metal bolt, three inches long.

Cyclist are vulnerable to poor road manners by some pissed off drivers. Considering how many miles I had cycled so far, I had been lucky. Perhaps my white light shield helped protect me this far. I reminded myself to keep using these tools to keep me safe.

Just because I was in the United States did not mean I could let my guard down.

During the next several days of pedaling up the east coast of Florida, I enjoyed hot weather, tailwinds, and the comforts of home as people took me in for hot showers, good food and great conversation.

Finally, after six weeks of easy living, I said good-bye to Florida as I crossed the state line into Georgia. Despite all the rumors I had heard about the Sunshine State, and some of the adversity I had encountered, I will always hold Florida close to my heart because of the people I had met. The folks who lived there and the snowbirds who had come south for the winter all made Florida the right place for me to re-acclimate myself to the states. I was glad to be back on US soil.

Chapter Twelve
Only My Body Not My Soul

I focused my sights on Atlanta. Georgia's hilly terrain and lush countryside confirmed that I had left the flatness of Florida. Compared to the Sunshine State, southern Georgia looked run-down. Paper, Styrofoam, broken bottles and aluminum cans littered the edges of the roadway. Many people lived in trailers that dotted the hillsides. Dozens of vicious dogs roamed freely.

In the small towns along the way, fast food establishments lined the streets. After a while I began to stop and enjoy the deep-fried cooking that was a staple of Georgia cuisine. An affordable meal usually included deep fried catfish, hush puppies (fried cornbread balls), and, of course, French fries and Coleslaw.

As I headed inland, toward Atlanta, the weather turned cold again. One day, after battling chilly headwinds and cycling endless miles up and down roller coaster terrain, a man appeared from out of nowhere as I crested the top of a hill.

"Hey", he yelled, "this is not a good day to be cycling."

From this rise, I could see a small town at the bottom of the hill.

"You're right about that," I huffed. Exhausted, I stopped and pointed to the intersection ahead. "Do you know which turn for Indian Springs Campground?"

"Take this road three miles," he replied, "it's all downhill. Where you riding from, anyway?"

"I'm just finishing an around the-world bike ride."

"You know," he said, "I've always wanted to travel overseas." Philip, a good-looking man probably in his late 30's, asked me questions about my bike ride for the next half-hour. He seemed friendly.

"Listen," he said, "you're welcome to pitch your tent in my yard. It's not much, but there's a garden."

Hesitantly, I agreed. I was too tired to think of alternatives.

I walked my bike with him down a dirt path to his rundown country home. It sat hidden from the road by an overgrowth of trees and bushes. We sat outside as he talked about the collection of antique jars that spilled from a weed-covered shed. We talked about his mother, who had passed away six months ago. He had inherited the house from her.

"Say, would you like to join me for dinner?" he asked. "I can thaw out some catfish."

"Sure," I answered as I watched Philip's lonely eyes light up. I walked with him into the kitchen. "Philip, you need a maid," I said as I looked at a drainboard piled high with a month's dirty dishes.

I looked in the refrigerator. Behind several six-packs of beer I saw a loaf of bread and some mayonnaise. "Do you have anything for a salad?"

"I told you, I have a garden," he said as he reached behind me and pulled out a beer.

"How about salad dressing?"

"No luck on that one."

"Let me run down to the store and pick up some things," I volunteered.

"No way; I don't want you going out. It's not safe." Philip's eyes followed mine as I looked out the window at some of his neighbors who were inspecting my bike.

"What the hell are they doing in my yard!" he exclaimed.

"Calm down, Philip. They're all right," I said. "Hey listen, you get the catfish going and I'll be right back."

"I don't want you going anywhere. That market is crawling with blacks just looking for a good time. It's not safe for you."

We went back and forth like this for the next 20 minutes.

"Suit yourself and go," he finally agreed. "Dinner should be ready by the time you get back."

On my way to the market, I thought about what Philip said. Everywhere I went, I was vulnerable to problems. But here I was,

16 months into my trip, and I had met good people all over the world. It was not unusual for me to meet someone on the side of the road.

I thought about my first night alone and the police officer who lectured me about traveling by myself. I recalled my time with Gaby and Monica, how wonderful they were yet how paranoid I was when I first walked into their home. I had been looking for good in people and I found good. Was the US really any different? If I acknowledged the good, then this country was no different from any other. It was up to me to see the good.

When I returned and put some groceries in the refrigerator, I noticed there was only one six -pack left.

We sat down to eat. The conversation changed. Philip began to ask strange questions. He asked if I carried a weapon and he wanted to know if I practiced self-defense.

"I still don't understand why you would take a trip like this," he said, with a puzzled look on his face. "There must be something wrong with you. What's wrong with you? Are you sick? No, I got it-you're dying, right? This isn't normal. Why in hell would you come to a stranger's house?"

Over the last five hours, I could see that the alcohol had changed his personality.

"Philip," I answered, "people have been good to me all around the world. I'm not sick or dying and I don't carry a weapon. I've been on the road now for 16 months and have found love and kindness in everyone I've met. There's no reason for me to be suspicious."

As I watched Philip's reaction, I began to sense that I had a problem. I had been too trusting, but I couldn't show him any fear.

Philip bolted to his feet, "What if I told you I was in prison eight years for five counts of rape and two counts of murder?"

Looking into his blue eyes, I replied, "It wouldn't change my first impression of you. I saw a kind man standing on the side of the road today. I know you're basically a good person."

I kept eating my dinner, even though it became harder and harder to swallow. Stay calm and act like this is nothing, I told myself. I worked diligently on visualizing a positive outcome. I kept God and Silva close at hand.

Suddenly, he reached into his wallet and threw some papers at me. I let them fall to ground.

He yelled, "Pick up the papers!"

"What for?" I asked calmly.

He reached under my chair and grabbed them. He held them in front of my face.

"This proves I was in prison eight years for manslaughter," he bellowed. "I've been charged with rape and attempted murder."

I sat and listened. My expression didn't change.

"Aren't you scared? Why don't you run? How do you know I won't rape or murder you? Read these papers," he demanded.

I looked up into his bloodshot eyes, "It's none of my business what has happened to you and I don't care about your past; it's unimportant."

He was getting worked up and I knew that I was in a serious situation. But I had to stay calm and reason with the man. I had to turn this around for my own safety. Fear and emotion would have triggered him immediately. I was certain he was trying to promote a reaction from me so that he could play his role.

"Philip," I said speaking softly yet confidently, "I met a kind, trusting person on the side of the road today, someone who was interested in my travels and was nice enough to invite me home. That was no different from the reception I have received all over the world. I think of you as a friend, and I know you respect my wishes to only sleep here for the night. I have a long day of cycling tomorrow in order to meet my father in Atlanta. Listen, I'm tired and I'm going to bed."

Thinking I could stop this from going any further, I stood up and walked over to my bike, pulled out my sleeping bag, and laid it on the extra bed. I climbed inside with my clothes on and pretended to fall right to sleep.

I lay there thinking of my alternatives. He had already padlocked the front door, and locked the rear door with a key he had on his belt. I considered breaking a window and running for help, but he could quickly catch me. And where could I go?

I wasn't willing to leave my bike and all my belongings inside. I reasoned that after spending so much time with this man, I still felt safer dealing with him rather than leaving and chancing this seedy neighborhood alone at night. I was pretty sure I knew who I had to contend with here, but I didn't know what dangers lurked outside.

Two hours went by as I listened to him move around the house. I heard one beer can open after another. Finally, he walked into the room.

He shook me. "Sally, wake up. I can't just let you sleep here for the night. I want you."

I didn't open my eyes. He kept shaking me. He laid down next to me.

Finally, I said, "Go to sleep, Philip."

He jumped up.

"What the fuck is this 'go to sleep Philip'? This is my house," he said as he stomped around.

He ripped the phone out of the wall. "And you ain't calling no police up here."

He threw an empty beer can across the room.

"Take off your fucking clothes," he roared.

"Philip, I don't want to know you this way. You're a friend." He calmed down a little. "What's going on here? Most women enjoy me when they see what I've got. What's wrong with you? I can make you happy."

I remained calm. I could see that he needed my fear to make his conquest exciting. Although I wanted to scream and run, I knew it would cause me more trouble. Inside I was trembling. Stay calm, I coached myself. Keep working with Philip. Show him he is not a bad person, that it's not necessary to revert to old habits.

"Philip, I don't want to lose a friendship. Believe me, I think you're an attractive man and I'll bet there's a lot of women that would like to have you. But I need time. I need a friend first."

"I don't believe you went around the world for this long and didn't sleep with another man. I am going to read your journal and I bet I find something in there," Philip demanded.

We talked for the next two hours while I struggled to disarm him psychologically. He alternated between being a madman and being the calm, normal person I had met beside the road. I tried every emotion on him, but he wouldn't let up. At one point he accused me of being a lesbian. Finally, I decided to try something radical. I let tears roll down my face, and in a make-believe sincere way I said, "OK, Philip, you want the truth?" I looked at him angrily because I was pretending to give in and tell him my secret: "I am dying."

"I knew it!" he exclaimed. "I knew something was wrong with you."

"Doctors have told me I have a contagious virus." I wiped the tears away.

Philip interrupted. "Oh, you have AIDS?" He sounded suspicious.

"No. I don't know what it is and neither do the doctors. All they know for sure is my white cells are overpowering my red cells. And it's fatal."

I paused for a moment. "I've wanted to travel for years and now with my life ending soon, I had to do it. What did I have to lose?"

Confused and suspicious Philip sat up and thought about my story. "I don't believe you," he finally said.

"I don't really care," I replied. "I'm only telling you to clear my own conscience in case something happens to you later. You will at least know where it came from. I have nothing to lose, remember?"

Philip looked distraught.

Then, all of a sudden, like a madman, he violently tried to rip off my clothes. His strong hands went right for my neck and almost immediately he had me in a choke hold. Proud of his strength, he said, "I could kill you right now. Try to move," he boasted.

I couldn't move. I did not react. Then he got on top of me and tried to force my legs apart, but I kept them squeezed together. I had to be careful not to fight too much or he would violently overpower me.

Finally, when I could see that he would not give up, I said, "Listen, I will make you a deal. I'll cooperate with you only if you wear a condom."

Thinking about his eight years in prison, and myself without birth control, I decided I could handle this type of rape. But to get pregnant or catch a dreaded disease would be a whole lot harder to accept.

"And anyway, Philip, beside the fact that you won't get me pregnant," I reasoned, "this protects you from my virus."

Earlier in the evening he'd told me he was so disgusted with all the sexual diseases going around that he'd invested in a box of condoms.

"Your virus, huh? How do I know that's not a bunch of bullshit."

"Go ahead and take your chances," I said. "I told you I don't care."

He left the room and returned wearing a condom. I let my body go limp as he climbed on top of me. Then, he sneakily removed the condom. "Philip," I yelled, "our deal is off. You get off me! We had an agreement and you already broke it." This seemed to be an opportunity to gain some control of the situation.

I picked up the abandoned condom and threw it across the room.

"OK, OK," he confessed, "you put it on."

Damn, I thought. Then, suddenly, I devised a plan. If I could destroy all but one of the rubbers, then I was certain this episode would soon be over. Now was my chance. So on the second attempt, I broke the rubber. I threw it down and retrieved another. I did it again and now there were just three left. Unfortunately, he picked up on my game, and put the next one on himself.

This time he penetrated me and I made my body to go limp. I lay there playing dead. He stopped; he couldn't stay excited.

"Come on," he yelled, "you said you would cooperate."

"How can I? I've lost respect for you because you didn't honor my wishes. I wanted a friend but you've acted like an animal. When I'm with someone, it's because I care for him and want to share myself."

He got off and sat there with a confused look on his face. I got up and walked into the living room.

"Where the fuck do you think you're going," he yelled as he stormed after me. He reached for my arm.

I yelled back at him, "No way! What kind of friend are you?" I was making him think that the only way to get a reaction out of me was to invalidate our friendship.

He backed off. His eyes shifted to the floor.

"And besides, Philip, I'm not tired anymore. I'm not going back to bed. You ruined my night. I'll make myself some coffee and watch the news."

I couldn't leave in the dark. Earlier, when I had gone off to the store, I had seen what I'd gotten myself into. Rusted cars sat on blocks along the road, their wheels removed, their windows broken. Weeds engulfed many of the yards. Men in T-shirts with large radical tattoos on their arms whistled at me when I rode by.

For the next few hours I wrapped myself in the only thing I could find, a dirty piece of plastic, while I sat in front of the television. I thought about my next challenge, getting out in the morning. Philip had threatened to lock me up for the weekend. My edge was still the friendship. I was sure I still had the upper hand, but I would need to handle it skillfully.

At daybreak I packed my bike and quietly walked into Philip's room. He popped up, "Hey," he exclaimed.

My heart stopped. I was startled that he was awake.

"Philip," I said, taking a deep breath, "it's morning and I must go. Are you going to come and say good-bye to me .

Knowing he held the key, I had to choose my words carefully. I didn't want to remind him that he was still in control of the situation.

"Oh, come on, Sally. I'll drive you to Atlanta. You can stay another day, can't you? We're just getting to know each other. Isn't that what you wanted?"

I could see that the beer had worn off.

"No, Philip, you blew it," I responded. "We could have been friends. I would have written to you, but you ruined my night. During my entire travels, I have not had a problem. It's too bad you had to ruin it for our country."

I could see the pain in his eyes as he opened the door. "Please call me and let me know how you're doing, OK?" He wrote his phone number on a piece of paper and handed it to me.

"OK," I said as I wheeled my bike out to the street.

A cold gray morning greeted me. I pedaled an hour before stopping for coffee at a quick-stop market. As I was leaving, a police car pulled up. Well, here's my chance, I thought. Do I turn Philip in? No, I decided. The cop would surely give me a hard time. Because I had voluntarily walked into Philip's house, and had chosen to travel this way in the first place, I knew he would only tell me that I'd asked for it. And anyway, if manslaughter could not keep him behind bars, then what good would my complaint do. Forget it, I said to myself as I pedaled away.

I kept a close watch in my mirror all day. I didn't know if Philip would follow me. I could only hope that my response to his actions had touched him in a way that prison had not. Recalling the pain that I had seen in his eyes when I left, I knew he had learned something from me. I had treated him like a real person.

It rained all day as I kept cycling toward Stone Mountain, near Atlanta. I was shaking as I pedaled. Scared and in shock, adrenaline kept me going. The odor of smoke and beer that was still in my clothes repulsed me and kept reminding me of my ordeal. I desperately wanted a shower and a way to wash my clothes but I needed to keep pedaling. Like a zombie, I was numb yet I kept my feet pedalling. I think if I would have stopped then the reality of what just happened would sink in and I might just fall apart. Instead, my mind moved into a survival mode as it did so many times on this trip. Just keep going I told myself as I had to shift my thoughts to the road and where my next destination was.

For days I thought about what this experience had taught me and how I had handled it. I had many choices and I played them over in my mind. Could I have completely prevented the rape? Did I have to allow it? Would he really have killed me if I had not cooperated or befriended him? Women always have to take extra care when out at night or alone. It was no different back home where I had to be on alert when leaving work late and living on my own. Did my travels toughen me up and give me more perspective? I clearly was able to separate my mind from my body during the ordeal and continued to do this as the days past. I felt different about rape now. I did not fear it as an unknown. I was still alive and able to walk away from my abuser. Somehow I found the courage to stay strong and calm which kept me in charge of my emotions and my ability to continue on. Feeling like I was straddling to stay upright on a balance beam, my fragile demeanor fought back the temptation to tip into a complete melt down.

I thought back about other fears and how I had handled them. When I began flying, I had a tremendous fear of an engine failure. I had practiced engine failures many times in training, but experiencing this for real would be completely different. In a real emergency our ability to make the right decisions quickly and stay calm is variable. And of course, I got what I feared.

One day while flying over the Santa Cruz mountains with my late brother, my engine quit. Without hesitation I calmly went through the procedure even though my heart pounded vigorously and I wondered if we would die. Regardless of my trembling hands, I stayed focused on my checklist while we spiraled down over the Palo Alto airport. Thankfully the engine started and we continued on our route home.

Fear can paralyze us in ways that create the actual thing we fear most. I was learning this on my trip as I reflected back on events like the leaches, rats, and my nightmares about traveling in Northern Ireland. It's important to cancel negative self talk and re-direct to a positive outcome. Using visualization is a powerful way to take a feeling of fear to a picture of possible.

Even though I had an ability to react calmly and quickly rather than to panic, I would remember that no matter how tired, fatigued, or anxious I was to find shelter, I needed to stay sharp. I could not set myself up in dangerous situations where someone like Philip may be tempted to hurt me.

My experience made me think about other women who had been raped. Many were emotionally destroyed sometimes for a lifetime. They became crippled and unable to return to the life they once had. Being kidnapped and raped was a serious and traumatic experience, yet I did not feel emotionally broken. Perhaps it was because I separated my body and mind in a way that helped me understand the violation was only a physical act. Separating the emotion gave me some control and allowed me to manipulate the situation so it was more difficult for him to escalate it. By connecting with him as a human being I dismantled his ability to completely control me. Although I was terrified and pissed at myself for my decision, I was now safe, alive, and much wiser.

I discovered that not everyone is honest and trustworthy. My trip was mostly positive over the past 400 days and one night went sour did not mean I should quit. I experienced so many good people. I had let my guard down which impacted my ability to listen to my gut. Traveling alone meant all decisions were mine to make. I did not have someone to balance a good or bad idea with.

I faced my fear in a way that reminded me the choices are mine and the consequences are mine to bear. Regardless of my mistake this would prove to be a life altering experience that would change my life and others forever.

Twenty-five miles outside of Atlanta is the city of Stone Mountain. I had looked forward to visiting this beautiful park and reading up on some of the Civil War history. Unfortunately my enthusiasm to play tourist was no longer a priority. As the rain drizzled down, I quietly checked into the campground, pitched my tent and found a shower and laundry room. I stood shivering under to hot water washing myself of the memories of the past night. Somberly, I crawled into my tent and curled my body into a fetal position. As the rain pounded on my tent, I closed my eyes and eventually drifted to sleep.

The next morning was like a new beginning. Blue skies, cool morning, and sun shining was a big change from the gloomy rain and nervousness of the day before. Feeling refreshed like I did on so many mornings, I jumped out of my sleeping bag packed up my tent and hit the road, anxious to see my father.

Entering Atlanta area, I pedal seamlessly with the traffic and arrived at the Holiday Inn just as my father and his wife Barbara were checking in.

"Dad," I called excitedly, as I walked across the plushly carpeted lobby.

"Sally, did you just get here?" my Dad asked as he walked toward me. His strong features, curly hair, and tailored suit accentuated his confident demeanor.

I stood there in my sweat-stained cycling clothes. The guests watched curiously as I hugged Dad and Barbara. In the sparkling lobby mirrors, I could see the hotel employees as they giggled.

"What do you say we check in, get cleaned up, and then we go out and have dinner?" Dad offered.

As we rode the elevator to our room, I could see that Dad didn't know what to ask me. Over the past year I had grown away from him too.

"So how do you like being back in the states?" Barbara asked.

I wanted to tell her about Philip. I wanted to tell her that since the experience, I had to watch what I said to men even more. But if I told her, it would be hard for her not to tell Dad, and I didn't think he would understand. So at dinner, we talked about the Everglades, the Epcot Center, and the ways different airports handled my bike.

Over the next two days the three of us went jogging together. We did many fun runs together over the years, including the Bay to Breakers in San Francisco and the infamous Garlic Festival in Gilroy, California. But my most memorable was when Dad and I ran 10 miles from our summertime 1920's cabin in Lake Almanor to Chester with the backdrop of Mt. Lassen inspiring us along the way.

During our stay in Atlanta, we also went shopping and dined out. My simple attire did not fit well with outings like this but

I had come to accept my ragged wardrobe and just enjoy the pampering. On our final night, Dad treated us to a horse and buggy ride. I loved horses and had always wanted to ride in a carriage. Wrapped with a blanket, we paraded down the street. It was a great way to end our trip together.

As we hugged and said our good-byes, I thought about the fun, laughter and reminisce we shared.

"Sally," Dad said as they got into the taxi for the airport, "you know that my offer still stands to fly you home. Please be careful." I was glad that I did not say a word about my kidnapping. Dad would have certainly pushed harder for me to stop.

"We think of you often," said Barbara. "Have a great finish to your trip."

Even though Dad had offered to pay for my room until the weather changed, I was ready to get back on the road. I headed east out of Atlanta in 22 degree weather. My clothing options were limited. I was not prepared for this cold. At times like this I would add my one pair of wool socks, my wool sweater and wind pants along with my gortex jackets and wool gloves. This was all I had to stay warm in the cold and in the rain. My light grey wind pant doubled as my tourist pants when I was sightseeing. At least they kept some of the chill off my legs and covered my bare skin when wearing just shorts was not appropriate.

At the bus stops and taxi stands along the way, I could see the breath of the commuters who waited in overcoats and scarves. They gawked at me as I rode by. Nearing the town of Madison, I found it harder and harder to breathe. As I inhaled the frosty air, the pain in my chest grew deeper. My cough returned.

After my 400-mile side trip to Atlanta, I retraced my steps eastward. In the next couple of days, the weather began to warm. Georgia's roller coaster terrain gave way to the gently rolling hills of South Carolina as I began to make my way north. Anxious to see my cousin Cheri and the rest of my cousins in Baltimore, I increased my daily mileage. During one three-day stretch, I logged 340 miles as I free-camped in the gardens of roadside markets.

I raced through North Carolina and Virginia and fixed my sights on Baltimore. Freeways and expressways complicated my riding routes. I spent a lot of time studying maps looking for a safe way around them.

I stayed with Carol, Cheri's older sister. She lived in Timonium, a suburb of Baltimore. Carol, Cheri and I shared many summers together. My parents would fly me across the country to vacation with my cousins. My visits always included a trip to Ocean City where we would dabble in innocent mischief.

Because Carol and I were the same age, single, and had similar life styles, we talked openly about my trip as a woman traveling alone.

"Honest, Sally, have you had any problems with men?" Carol asked as she brushed her long brown hair out of her eyes.

"I did have a problem with a man in Georgia," I answered.

"What happened?" Carol moved closer.

"Well, he raped me."

"Did you call the police?"

"No, he'd been drinking. Some people might say I set myself up for the whole thing. Maybe they'd be right."

"In what way, Sally?"

"I accepted an offer camp in his yard, something I had done all over the world. I trusted him and everything seemed normal, until he began drinking and locked me in the house. This area was off my route and I let my guard down. It would have been just as easy to figure out somewhere to stay and spend the money to be safe."

It's easy to look back on this and think about how I could have changed the outcome. I was learning that my deepest and darkest fears were surfacing on this trip and that we can manifest good and bad things. When visualizing good outcomes, I used a positive attitude. But when bad things happen, it was driven by fear. I don't believe we intend to bring negativeness to our lives. Our subconscious is a powerful tool that can be manipulated by love versus driven by fear. If we take responsibility for all aspects of our thoughts, we can realize our full potential and direct our lives beyond self-imposed barriers".

"Sally, that is a very interesting way to look at something as devastating as rape. I am not sure how other victims of abuse and rape would feel about this." Carol said.

"I agree with you Carol and it's is not for me to judge. But in my own situation, I am sorry it happened and I don't think this experience has emotionally hurt me at this time. Maybe it is because of my attitude about it and my separation of mind and body. Either way, I do think when we feel and act as a victim, we become one. Maybe this philosophy will help other women overcome their fears and handle something they encounter differently. I am not sure how I got the courage to deal with this and why I think as I do, I can only hope it serves to help others.

"You're a braver person than I am," said Carol. "I would have been in pieces."

"Watch your words, Carol, you get what you fear the most." I said softly.

My trip continued to test my beliefs and assumptions. Several months ago if someone had told me they created something tragic, I would have denied they could do that. But my trip was challenging everything I believed so it was natural for me to shift my views and way of thinking. The proof I needed to make this change in my mind was happening every day in so many ways.

The next day I stopped at the rehabilitation center to visit Cheri. Carol had told me a little about what to expect. She told me to try to keep the mood light. I looked across the way to the table where Cheri was seated. She wore a neck brace.

Cheri spotted me and slowly raised herself to stand. Her every move was deliberate.

"Sa..l..ee," she said as she started walking toward me. The legs that once carried this free-spirited person were limp and turned inward. She dragged them along to keep pace with the rest of her body as she held herself upright inside her walker.

She smiled and began to talk, her voice barely understandable. I listened intently, trying to maintain a smile while hiding the shock of what I was seeing. I opened up my arms to hug Cheri and embraced her fragile body next to mine.

"Cheri, it's so . . . good to see you," I smiled as I looked into her eyes. "Look at you! What remarkable progress. I knew you would pull through it all. We are both very determined people."

During my stay I spent as much time as possible with Cheri. We shopped, went out to dinner, and went to her rehabilitation classes. I enjoyed our relaxing conversations at her home. I watched intently as she mastered daily chores around the house like feeding herself and taking a shower.

One day I watched, biting my tongue, as she fixed us lunch. When she pulled out a huge butcher knife, my eyes grew large as she maneuvered it in the most awkward positions to slice a tomato. I knew this was part of her therapy. I prayed that she wouldn't cut off her finger.

Next she decided I needed a haircut. Oh, no, I thought. Cheri used to cut hair professionally and had always done a great job with mine. But I could see that even though she made her hands work, she still hadn't regained her dexterity.

"Cheri" I said, "you will spare my ears, right?"

We laughed.

She finished an hour later.

"How dush that . . . wook?" she asked as she held the mirror up for me to look.

"You are amazing, Cheri. It's great!"

"How a . . . bout a . . . mani . . . kew?"

I watched Cheri's deep concentration as she carefully worked on my nails. I knew that her determination and positive attitude would help her to get through this.

As we talked, Cheri shared her thoughts about the accident. "I choo . . . ose this", Cheri said. "I cawsed my own ac . . . ci . . . dent, I want..ed to chaynge my life. This is the . . . besht thing that's happen to me."

I listened carefully as Cheri's deep whispering voice tried to form the words.

"Sa..l.ee," she continued, "we aw bofh find . . . ing owshelves, our woles in l . . . ife and the mean . . . ing oph it aw. You con . . .

ches . . . ly made a de . . . chis . . . ion when you em . . . baw . . . ked on you juw . . . ney, and I sub . . . con . . . ches . . . ly caused my caw weck."

I couldn't believe what I was hearing. Inside of that crumpled exterior lived the sensitive Cheri I had known. We shared our struggles and our triumphs with each other. Soon we began to compare the insights that we were gaining. I told her about my struggles while learning the road; she told me about the difficulties she had experienced while learning to feed herself.

Soon, we began to see that both of us were on a path toward self-discovery. Our successes and triumphs, even our so-called failures, would achieve the same result.

After five days I forced myself back on the road. I was thankful for seeing that every experience, every difficulty, was an opportunity to grow closer to our own true selves. Inside our physical bodies resides the spirit that moves us all to any kind of action.

June 28, 1989: Bikecentennial Headquarters, Missoula Montana
Photo by Greg Siple

MY PORTABLE HOME

Camp/Bike Gear
- ❏ Eureka tent (2 person)
- ❏ Thermarest pad
- ❏ Ground cover
- ❏ Northface sleeping bag
- ❏ MSR multi fuel stove
- ❏ Cooking pot/lid
- ❏ Cup, spoon, fork
- ❏ Fuel bottle
- ❏ Matches/flashlight
- ❏ Swiss army knife
- ❏ Bike tool kit
- ❏ Michelin folding tires/tubes
- ❏ Misc bike parts
- ❏ Water bottles (3)

Personal Gear
- ❏ Cycle shorts/running shorts
- ❏ T-shirts (3), long sleeve (1)
- ❏ Sandals/journal
- ❏ Wool jacket
- ❏ Rain jacket/wind pants
- ❏ Sunglasses/suntan lotion
- ❏ Wool/cotton socks
- ❏ Cycle/running shoes
- ❏ Cycle gloves & helmet
- ❏ First aid/sewing kit
- ❏ Camera/film
- ❏ Shampoo/soap/towel
- ❏ Toothbrush/paste
- ❏ Money pouch/change purse

Chapter Thirteen
The Rhythm of Cycling

I left the rolling green countryside of Maryland and was only a few miles from our nation's capital, Washington D.C. Soon, I reflected, I would be starting on my route west to California.

While cycling around the District of Columbia, I thought about my trip there 14 years ago. I had been an appointed delegate to a Future Farmers of America convention. We had spent several days touring the sights. Although the monuments and museums like the Smithsonian were impressive, I really hadn't appreciated their significance. Now, many years later, I was pedaling through the city on a bicycle, after spending more than a year overseas experiencing other cultures and governments. I looked at the monuments and the White House with a different perspective and with a greater appreciation of what they stood for.

I thought about the war memorials I had seen all over the world, the senseless killings at Dachau, and bloodshed in Northern Ireland. I reflected on my visit to the Kremlin in the USSR, Buckingham Palace in England, and all the other capitals around the globe. I closed my eyes and prayed that someday peace and harmony would unite the world.

I left the District of Columbia and began pedaling southwest into Virginia. It was spring, and brightly colored flowers decorated the countryside. After fifteen months on the road, I had decided to trade in the sometimes hourly task of survival for the relative predictability of a network of roadways that cross the States, the Bikecentennial Trail.

Established in 1976 to celebrate our nation's bicentennial, this trail uses existing, often lightly traveled roads to form a bicycle route from one coast to the other. Bikecentennial, (now Adventure Cycle Association) is a nonprofit foundation based in

Missoula, Montana, which also offers a variety of other maps and routes around our country.

It was a nice break to have bicycle specific maps to navigate the US. These bicycle routes were popular with cycle tourist and I enjoyed a new world of meeting and riding with others along the way. My intention was to ride on these pre-planned routes so that I could spend the time in thought as I crossed the US. Instead, I became absorbed in the lifestyle of cycle touring that this popular system of routes is known for.

This series of trails and culture was similar to the backpackers of the Pacific Crest Trail and Appalachians. We did not have trail names, but the sharing of information, knowledge of others on the route and things to do or avoid were daily conversations. I enjoyed this change. Meeting other cyclists and riding together or meeting up at night was different for me. It was also interesting to see what gear others had that made their trip more comfortable, like good rain gear, touring specific bike, more cooking options. For those who rode in pairs, splitting gear meant a lighter load and in some cases more clothing and gear options.

I had become accustomed to my minimal choices. The one exception was my tent. By the time I arrived in Portugal, my tent was trashed and I had to order a new one from the States that would take over a month to receive. I was already carrying a two person dome tent that as needed I could squeeze my bike in upside down and next to me, barely . . . But after the long winter, and lots of rain, I felt I needed a bigger tent. So I purchased a larger tent with a vestibule .

The larger digs was exciting until I packed it on my bike and carried it across the US! As I rode with other cyclists they stared in disbelief as I pitched this nearly eight pound tent. Their tents were one or two person minimal lightweight backpacking tents. However, the larger tent was helpful when dealing with the amount of inclement weather across the US. There were times the high winds and storms would flatten my old tent, laying it to one side or the other. My first tent was a two pole system, and a lower end tent. It fit my budget. This time, I wanted more. My new tent was a four pole system which added the structure to withstand higher winds, heavier rain and a snow load. Still I was tested.

The weather in the east was scary at times. One night while sleeping in a campground amongst a lot of trees a huge thunder and lightening storm hit. I looked outside my tent door to see that I was truly alone in the storm with nowhere to go. I sat in my tent hoping for the best. At least I felt safer in this sturdier tent.

After a while I found myself going through the motions of bicycle touring. And yet, even though my heart was no longer completely in the ride, I felt driven to be home by late July. Family and friends were tracking my progress across the country and wanted to pull together a welcome home party. This could have been any date, but somehow I became fixed on finishing on a predetermined date.

On the trail I stopped eating for performance or for coping with the climate. Instead, I began to eat at roadside cafes or in other social situations with fellow travelers. I adopted many other habits that distracted me from the almost animal-like keenness I had developed overseas. I stopped meditating. I listened to the radio and let myself get caught up in the daily soap opera of who was doing what on the trail. My fellow travelers provided me with a wealth of entertainment and cycle touring resources. It was interesting how easily I exchanged one lifestyle for another.

Stormy, rainy weather persisted as I pedaled across Virginia. I was rescued repeatedly from the wet weather by local residents, churches, and even a free night at a motel. Americans were kind, loving people, and my trust was being strengthened once again.

I left Virginia for eastern Kentucky. The weather remained unchanged and the terrain continued to test my endurance as I pedaled up one steep mountain after another. Unfortunately, this part of Kentucky featured roadside trash, abandoned cars, and attacking dogs. The dogs kept me alert and ready to draw my water bottle within a second's notice. These ferocious creatures were not your typical house pets. Dobermans, German shepherds, and pit bulls came charging at me full speed. I had to be quick to squirt them, or I was certain to be dog food.

I laughed as I thought back to a day in Portugal. While staying in Monte Gordo, I frequently took day rides up the mountain to outlying villages. One afternoon, as I entered a small town, a pack of dogs came charging for me. Unlike the Dobermans, these dogs were a mix of everything, but their teeth were just as sharp and they were after me! The wild pack of dogs had descended on me before I could draw a water bottle. Happily, their bark was worse than their bite, except for one ambitious dog who grabbed my rear tire with his teeth. He had Buddy slowed almost to a stop. Stunned by his aggressiveness, I pedaled harder. A man called the dogs off and I prepared for my next problem, a flat tire. Surprisingly, it never came.

After spending a night at a Kentucky hostel at Pippa Pass, I cycled a mountainous route through Hindman to Buckhorn Lake. This is coal mining country. Trucks drove at high speeds in convoys. Pieces of coal and rocks lined the side of the road. Truck drivers sped by me without moving to the left at all. The exhaust, noise, and near hits tempted me to give up for the day.

Suddenly, someone in an old pickup truck driving in the opposite direction shot at me! The loud bang deafened my ears and my right foot came out of my toe clip. I stopped, not believing what had happened. Was this a shot or a loud backfire? I questioned this and kept a watchful eye in the area. Shaking my head, I knew of the trouble cyclist had with drivers and I too had some. Considering how many miles I had cycled, my encounters were very few. Using my protective light no doubt created positive outcomes that had kept me safe.

I patted Buddy, assuring us both it was OK. I climbed back on and slowly pedaled away.

Several miles later I came upon some major road construction. I inched my way forward and saw a large ditch stretching over two feet wide and several feet deep. I asked the men working on the project if there was another way around.

"Nope. This is it," replied the foreman. "It'll be at least two hours before we get the ditch filled." I wondered if I would reach my destination by nightfall.

Looking for a way out of my predicament, I tried to figure

out if I should dismantle my bike and attempt to carry the 110-pound machine over in pieces. Then one of the construction workers interrupted my thoughts.

"Hey lady, come on," he said. "We'll get you over the ditch."

Everyone helped lift Buddy over to the other side. Gratefully, I shook their hands and took snapshots of everyone. They cheered as I pedaled away.

After I crossed the Ohio River into Illinois, my mileage increased and I really began to cover ground. Buddy and I caught a lot of attention and we passed through one town after another. Just looking at the worn bike and panniers told a story. My clothing and my load confirmed the story; that our travels were beyond the groups traversing the country along the Bikecentennial.

In the weeks ahead, I felt apprehensive about returning home. I didn't have some of the answers I had hoped for. People began to ask me more questions about my future, and it was the same answer, "not sure". Interesting that many questions came in the form of "What's your next adventure?" Almost like what will top this one?

After all this time on the road, all the miles of cycling and thinking, I did not have any more answers. Perhaps I was approaching this with too much thought. Maybe my lessons were more subtle and laid deeper inside of me in the form of stories and examples. That my journey was not about what's next, but awakening an inner spirit and shaking up beliefs and assumptions in ways that could be shared with others.

It's really difficult to change a mindset that has been ingrained in us for years. But maybe my trip could help others see how powerful our thoughts really are? That we can create outcomes by visualizing them first. And that we can also sabotage something by negative self talk, fear and doubting behaviors.

Still I wondered why I had so much rain and inclement weather? How did that help or hurt me? There were times when my clothes were soaked, my skin was shriveled and my bike was full of dirty road spray, that I wanted to quit. I felt I could not go on another day. Then, like a miracle, someone would come into my life. Almost like I was being saved. These amazing encounters energized me and inspired me to keep going. They were little reminders from the universe that I needed to continue on. And so I did.

Buddy and I camped at Cave-in-Rock State Park after pedaling 109 miles in hot weather and hilly terrain. I sat outside my tent and looked at the clear, midwestern sky.

"Soon we'll be home, Buddy," I said sadly. "We've shared so much together. I can't imagine not waking up each morning ready to start cycling with you. When our trip's over, I promise I'll always keep you close to me. You don't have to worry about being forgotten in a cluttered garage or being sent to the local dump. You're my friend, and we'll still go places together."

I arrived in Carbondale, Illinois, for a brief layover while I repaired some of Buddy's worn parts. Then, anxious to be on my way and moving, I began riding during a vicious storm. Rain soaked me in a minute as thunder and lightning charged across the sky. Visibility was nil. What the hell was I doing? Somehow my intuition was telling me to keep going.

After following my instincts to continue in the storm, I arrived at a small post office to mail a package home. There I met Bev, who was just getting off work. When she invited me to her house, I happily threw up my arms and said, "OK, I give up!"

We arrived at her home and were greeted by her two teenage sons, Rob and Eric. After I had a hot shower and changed into dry clothes, we sat down to dinner. Bev's husband, Bob, came in from work and joined us. I felt an immediate connection to Bev and her family. It almost felt like I already knew her. That evening was a special night for the family. In less than an hour we would all be sitting in the high school auditorium watching Eric receive one honors award after the next.

We watched the small graduating class of 65 receive their diplomas. I was touched by this group of students. I could feel that they were really close to one another. They had shared four years of high school and now would be making choices about their futures. The energy in the air was positive. There was something very touching about the simplicity of this Midwestern celebration. The wholesomeness and self-sufficiency of life reminded me of the families I had met in New Zealand. Love and happiness seemed a natural outcome for these families. It was an honor to be a part of this family's special night.

I crossed the Mississippi into Missouri and pedaled toward the Ozarks. The weather had gotten progressively hotter and the afternoon humidity was grueling. I pushed through the area averaging 90-mile days without the full use of my gears. Something was amiss. I couldn't shift through my middle gears; I had to jump from high to low. "Come on, Buddy," I pleaded, "not now. Why do you have to do this out here, of all places? I need all of your gears."

During my travels it seemed there were times when Buddy just wouldn't work right. And yet, looking him over, everything checked out OK. At times like this, I would scold him for playing around when I needed him the most.

I recalled a day in Florida when I was pushing to get to my destination by nightfall. The rain had started and we were 25 miles away. Without warning Buddy's gears would slip. I was making very little progress. Finally, I stopped at a bike shop. Explaining to the owner that I couldn't find anything wrong with the shifting, I asked for his help. We unloaded Buddy and put him on a bike stand. The owner went through the gears and found nothing wrong. By then I was furious with Buddy. I loaded him up and continued on. The slipping never occurred again.

I crossed into Kansas at Pittsburg. It was Memorial Day weekend, and I was encountering one scorching day after another. The intensity of the sun's rays reminded me of New Zealand and how badly I had burned. Now I wore a number 40 sun block. It helped, but not completely.

I left early one morning from Toronto State Park in Kansas, anxious to get a jump on the heat. A 16-mile stretch on route 54 to Cassoday proved very dangerous. The narrow, two-lane road had absolutely no bike lane. Two large vehicles passing simultaneously were forced onto the gravel shoulder. Recreational vehicles raced by, oblivious to the danger they were causing. They passed me with inches to spare and generated a tremendous gust of wind that left me swerving into traffic that followed close behind—generally another RV.

I thought I had already been through the worst. Certainly the coast of Spain was no Sunday ride in the park, and Rome had challenged my courage to be aggressive, but this was just plain suicidal. More than ever, I needed my protective light. I visualized for my safety and kept on pedaling. Exhausted and frazzled, I ended my stretch of route 54 still in one piece.

The wind persisted across Kansas. Although I had heard about the summer southwesterly winds and their demoralizing effect on cyclists, I was looking forward to some flat riding, especially after the Ozarks. The flat terrain never came, but the wind did. The wind and repetitive scenery forced me to find distractions. I listened to the radio for hours and began to play mileage games. How far could I get by 8:00 am? By noon? I rarely took breaks in the mornings and just raced the clock.

Buddy's gears finally gave out. His cracked housing unit was barely hanging in, and the derailleur was sloppy. We arrived in Hutchinson, Kansas, for repairs. A new derailleur, chain, freewheel, and minor miscellaneous parts ran up a bill of $162. But I was pleased with Buddy's performance and felt that at 17,000 miles, I had certainly gotten my money's worth.

When I pedaled away the next morning I was shocked at the ease of shifting and how everything responded so well. I had become accustomed to the inefficiency of Buddy's worn-out parts. Buddy felt like a new bike again!

Just outside of Larned, the wind blew progressively stronger. My legs were weak and my body fatigued. Farms were few and far between, and most were off the main road down sandy driveways. Not listening to my intuition, I stopped at the first farm I saw on the main road. Although it didn't really feel right, I was tired and didn't care. A woman came out before I could dismount from my bike and told me I couldn't stay.

Exhausted from 90 grueling miles of wind and heat, I somehow continued to pedal west. I came upon another house.

This time I listened to my inner voice. It didn't feel right, and I continued on. Three tiring miles later, I came over a hill and saw a group of white buildings in the distance. Excitedly, I pushed on, hoping it wasn't a mirage. A man in a field driving a tractor tooted his horn and waved. I smiled and waved back. A sense of relief filled me. I knew this was the right place.

I rode up to the house and knocked on the door. A brunette woman in her 50s opened it and smiled.

"Hello, dear," she said. Her eyes were warm and welcoming.

"Hello," I answered. "I'm passing through and was hoping to pitch my tent somewhere nearby for the night."

"My goodness," she exclaimed, "you've been on the road a while."

I smiled and told her I was completing an around-the-world trip. She stood there shocked. Her brother-in-law and his wife joined her at the door. Not wanting me to camp under the threatening sky, they invited me in for dinner and offered a place to sleep.

"Pat," I said, "rain and stormy weather has followed me around the world, if I sleep outside, it's guaranteed to rain!"

They all laughed at the thought that my presence would bring rain to their serious drought conditions. But sure enough, by morning rain had fallen. We sat for hours talking about farming and the prolonged drought that were ruining Midwestern farmers. While crossing Kansas, the only station I could get on the radio was farm reports. I was desperate to listen to anything to distract me from the long days. This information became useful. It helped me in times like this to follow conversations with the farmers.

From Pat's house I began a gradual ascent into the high plains where I entered eastern Colorado. Climbing one foot per mile would hardly be noticeable to most recreational cyclists, but I certainly was aware of it with 70 pounds of gear packed on my bike. After three days of this, I hit the Rockies.

Traveling along Colorado Highway 285, I pedaled across Kenosha Pass at 10,000 feet and several miles later Red Hill pass at 9,900 feet. I continued on to Fairplay, where I joined Highway

9 over Hoosier Pass, topping out at 11,543 feet. I felt strong as I conquered one pass after the next.

Hoosier pass was the highest point of my trip but certainly not the toughest climb. Northern England's terrain was the most difficult, recalling the cars struggling to climb. It was the only place where I was forced off my bike and somehow managed to brace my body against Buddy and push us uphill. The Missouri Ozarks were absolutely stunning, but the constant steep short climbs wore on me.

I had come to enjoy climbing because I could set a pace and allow my mind to wander. This was true when climbing passes similar to the Rockies where the grade was gradual. If the climb was ten miles then I knew it would take me two or more hours to summit. I would settle in with a pace and be in it for time. There was no use in rushing a climb. Endurance, pace and mindset were key. When climbing the Ozarks, the ups and downs were relentless and I could not escape inward. In the Ozarks, I struggled over each climb making a 90 mile day in these conditions feel more like 150 miles.

Weather in the Rockies was predictably unpredictable. It seemed every morning started out sunny but by 11:30, the skies would darken and stormy weather including thunder and lightning would hit. This delayed my progress but it was not safe to ride in the mountains during lightning storms. I learned to recognize the approaching storms and plan ahead by ducking into any building or shelter I could find and wait it out. I became keenly aware of the sky and somehow learned which storms to ride in and which to take refuge.

After summiting Hoosier Pass, I coasted down a quick thousand feet to the Breckenridge area. That afternoon I arrived at the home of Dave and Meg. Friends in Florida had told me about this adventuresome couple, and thought it would be fun for us to meet. Now married for 23 years, Dave and Meg had set off on an around the-world bicycle adventure nearly 15 years ago. With little prior training and no money, they finally had to give up in Australia and ship their bikes home. They continued their trip by train.

A narrow road led to their beautiful pine home sitting at 10,500 feet. Surrounded by forest and running creeks, it was an absolutely picture-perfect place.

"You must be Sally," Dave said when he opened the door. "Please come in, and let's bring in your bike, too. It's ready to rain-or even snow."

Meg put the kettle on and we got acquainted.

Dave was a county judge and Meg was self-employed in the marketing business for ski resorts. The atmosphere was comforting and easy. We had so much in common. They immediately picked up on the personal growth aspect of my trip and we began to have lengthy and enlightening conversations.

We could relate easily because of our extensive travels overseas. They too had sold everything and were faced with the realities of starting over when they returned home. Since that time, they had taken smaller trips in an effort to balance their personal desires to travel with living in the real world.

"Sally," Dave counseled, "you'll be faced with many decisions when you get home. Sometimes they might seem overwhelming. But always bring yourself back to your trip. Remember the growth, the challenge, and the personal insight you gained. No one can ever take this trip away from you."

Dave stood up and put another log on the fire. Snow had begun to fall outside. It felt like Christmas.

"We had a tough time adjusting," Meg said. "Everyone expected us to begin our lives where we left off, almost as if the trip hadn't happened. It's difficult for others to understand what you've been through. We found that we couldn't share much about our trip or our feelings with our family and friends. But at least we had each other. I don't know what I would have done without David."

"The sad and also exciting part of it all," continued Dave, "is that life moves on. You might return home to the same place, but your friends and social activities will change. You may want to surround yourself with other people who have gone through similar transitions and will understand you better."

That night I lay in bed and watched the stars through an

overhead skylight. In six weeks I would be home. For the past month or so, I had purposely ignored thoughts of returning home and how my life would be different. I was suspect that adjusting back into the community and society expectations would be difficult. I was not even sure how to prepare myself. I found it easier to just keep pedaling and not think too much about my future. I buried myself into cycling long days and high miles to pass the time away. I was excited to get home and see everyone but beyond that I had no plan of how I would re-settle. It was a confusing time for me and I had to start seriously thinking about the reality of coming home.

Chapter Fourteen
Coming Home

My route took me along beautiful rivers, then across the Continental Divide several times, over innumerable mountain passes, and into the jagged jaws of the Grand Tetons. I arrived at Jenny Lake and was so taken by the dynamic scenery all around me. It was a perfect place to camp for two nights before heading north. The weather turned on me once again as I pedaled through Yellowstone National Park. There were very few tent campers at this time of year and no one anywhere near me. I thought the bears would be my big concern, but as it turned out, it was the snow. I woke up to several inches of white fluff on the ground. I was thankful to have my huge tent that could hold a snow load.

Although my pace increased as home grew closer, I still enjoyed meeting new people and seeing our country's treasures. I met a couple of cyclists in Missoula and decided to join them for a week to cycle north through Glacier National Park and into Waterton National Park in Canada.

Going to the Sun Road towards Logan's Pass captivated me. Winding up the pass, I felt like I was climbing to the sun. Rock walls lined very narrow switchbacks while water dribbled across the road making each bend a bit mystical. After passing through the tunnel, the climbing really started. The route veered east and the cold mountain wind began to blow. The snow covered the peaks and numerous waterfalls could be view all around me. Although I was exerting myself as the terrain continued to increase, my head spun from left to right trying take it all in. To feel on top of the world and witness this amazing geological area was truly unforgettable. This was one of my favorite passes around the world.

I thought back to my first days of this trip, wondering how I would pedal my loaded bike up a hill or even a mountain. And yet it was the mountains that brought me confidence and connection to the outdoor world. My senses would awaken with the smells, the air and the sounds of the ecosystems around me. I would get absorbed by my surroundings. It became one of my favorite parts of cycle touring.

On this iconic day, I left the states once again as I made a chilling descent from Logan's Pass, heading to Canada. With Jackson Glacier as a backdrop, I pedaled to St. Mary's Lake and began a 14 mile cold windy climb to the border and then into Waterton National Park. It was 10pm by the time I pitched my tent and had dinner. Exhausted, I crawled into my tent, closed my eyes and smiled, knowing this would be a day to remember.

The Rockies were now just a memory as I returned to the states. I gathered supplies in Missoula and headed south over the beautiful highway 12. The weather was hot as I ascended Lolo Pass. My stomach ached as my body fought to digest the food I had eaten before climbing. Nauseas and wobbly, I scolded myself for eating lunch before a serious climb like Lolo.

Crossing the Snake river, I left Idaho and entered eastern Oregon through Hells Canyon. The air was hot and blew like a furnace against my face. The canyon temperatures were forecasted at 115 degrees. I thought my tires could melt onto the asphalt so I kept moving to avoid the peak heat of the day.

As I pedaled the high desert toward the Cascades, I biked many hundred-mile days and averaged 10 to 13 hours of cycling. With the longer days I stopped to camp sometimes as late as 9pm and then back in the saddle by first light. This gave my legs less time to recover. My butt was sore and my skin was raw. To cushion the chafing I started wearing two pairs of shorts.

Accompanied by jack rabbits and barbed wire fences, I cycled along pondering the reality that I was actually heading home. When I left the US in January 1988, I wasn't sure if I would return. Perhaps, I had mused, I might find somewhere else to live. Maybe there would be a better place for me to start over.

I had found lots of places I could live and jobs I could have, but what did I really want to do? Why was this decision so hard for me? Did I want to escape, like Jack in Australia? Running away did not feel right either. I knew that unresolved issues would simply follow me.

By now, I was almost certain that I would stay in the States, but what about California? Could I find a new life and a fresh start surrounded by my old life? Small towns with slower paced lifestyles were appealing. But was it enough for me? As a single woman would I get lonely or feel out of place in a smaller community? Returning to my hometown would be difficult. Falling back into old habits and behaviors could easily happen. Did I have the courage to stand up for my new beliefs to help make life more meaningful? I knew I could commit inward, but could I have an impact with my family and friends? Would sharing my experiences be enough for them to contemplate their own lives?

My stomach knotted as thoughts of returning home continued to race through my mind. I missed home, but how would it be after the initial visiting was over? Would the gap that I had sensed between my parents and myself during the trip continue to widen? Would I also distance myself from everyone else? When my mother came to Portugal we had a great week together, but conversations lacked depth. This was rare. My mother and I were always able to talk about anything. I felt even more alone.

What about working again? I knew I wasn't ready to start a job, but I would need to find a place to live which would cost money. My mind was dizzy thinking about all the decisions I would need to make. A part of me felt overwhelmed and against returning home. It occurred to me that maybe returning to my life could be avoided. There was an inner peace and sense of wisdom deep inside of me that I wanted to keep forever. How would I protect myself from the complexities I left? How would I be sure to not repeat the behaviors and lifestyle that I dismantled?

Crossing the Cascades was now a day away. I stopped in the town of Sisters to stock up on supplies and inquire about the route ahead. Road crews were clearing the snow and the locals assured me that the pass would be open by mid morning the next day.

Heading out of Sisters, I settled into my familiar pace as I pressed into my pedals to adjust to the terrain. A sea of lava rock covered this area as far as my eyes could see. My body worked together with my arms and legs as I rounded one switchback after another, until the summit was near.

Reaching the top of Oregon's Mackenzie Pass, I stopped alongside the wall of snow that was just plowed. I glanced out at a sea of black lava. The snow-capped volcanic mountains stood proudly in the distance. Inside I was bursting with excitement knowing that MacKenzie, represented the last major mountain pass of my trip and the final peak separating me from the Pacific Ocean.

"God, give me anything-wind, rain, snow, the steepest mountain you can find, and I will do it!" I yelled. "There are no limitations, I faced my fears, I have conquered the world!"

Descending down this steep, rugged pass was thrilling as so many descents had been around the world. But descents like this one still required focus and concentration. Steep terrain like McKenzie was daunting on the hands. It took synchronizing my hands from right to left to keep my speed in check and not heat my brakes. Just like driving a car down a steep mountain, pacing the brakes were important.

I also learned the value of layering when descending a mountain. Although I did not have much to wear, I often had to stop at the top and cover my sweaty body with enough to block the wind from cooling me and causing hypothermia.

Everything else was anticlimactic as I coasted into Eugene. I thought about the mountain passes around the world, and reflected back to the Auckland airport and how I couldn't imagine pedaling my loaded bike up a hill, much less a mountain pass. As I pedaled west toward the Pacific Ocean, I thought about my first flat tire, the police officer in New Zealand who had scolded me for being alone, and China, with its cockroaches, spitting, squat toilets, and incredible challenge of just surviving. I thought about Russia and my trust in the universe that the right train ticket would come to me there. I recalled the families who had shared their homes with me. They had come into my life at times I needed them most. They offered their love unconditionally, supported me, and gave me the strength to carry on. They taught me about what really counts, the simple things in life that I had lost sight of before my trip.

But why did I have so much cold wet weather? It seemed the ultimate test of endurance. Yet somehow I just kept going. My trip became so much more than traveling, cycling and seeing the world. When I left seventeen months ago, I knew it would be life changing, but what did that mean? Nothing could have prepared me any differently.

I had tested everything. I had called into question my femininity, my values, my fears, and my belief systems. I even wondered if I would ever buy a car again. Maybe I would live in my tent for a few months while the weather was still good.

When I left on my trip, I couldn't imagine being out of work for such a long time. Now I couldn't imagine myself spending the rest of my life working only to make a living. I needed more. I needed to make a difference in people's lives and this trip helped me discover that.

Buddy had witnessed my growth. My companion had shared my fears and triumphs. I couldn't imagine imprisoning either of us inside a house where we would be deprived of the rising sun, singing birds, or the magic of a star-filled night. I wondered if I could ever settle down now that I no longer felt bound by rules or expectations.

As I turned down Highway One, I embraced the beauty of the Pacific Ocean. Its familiarity called to me as if it were an old friend. We had shared a lifetime together, and I had not realized how bonded the two of us were until I took my first breath of its distinctive, salty mist.

Heading south along the Oregon coast, I thought about the rising prices of real estate in California. What could I have sold my home for in today's market? Had I forsaken another $60,000 to make this journey? But could I put a price tag on this trip? I knew I could not.

And what price had I paid with my health? Even though I had grown spiritually, I had been hard on my body. I still coughed and wheezed. My shoulders slumped inward, constricting my breathing. My fingers had almost grown arthritic from supporting my body for all the countless miles of riding. My skin was brown and felt like leather. My face had aged from the sun, more wrinkles had appeared. I was still heavy and bulky.

Even though I had thought I would be in great shape from all my cycling, I wasn't. My strength was on a bicycle. I had failed to address my overall fitness. I could barely do a sit-up. I could hardly touch my toes. In different parts of the world, my diet had changed to what was available. What about parasites; would something develop later?

I knew I had paid a high price for my journey and yet I would not have done it any other way. My experiences taught me lessons that I might never have learned if I had chosen a different path. I would use my experiences to help me help others deal with difficult situations that life would surely present.

Making my way down California's rugged and challenging coast confidently was proof of how far I had come as a cyclist. But there was more to the this coast than its beauty and familiarity. I was seeing the coast through a different lens, almost like I had been in a time capsule. It was an eerie feeling as my mind seemed to separate from my body. Somehow, my legs just kept pedaling anyway, keeping Buddy and I moving forward.

My final days along the coast were surreal and incredibly emotional. I tried to stay strong and engaged but inside I was tormented, vacillating between a feeling of accomplishment to fear.

As I crossed the golden gate bridge in San Francisco, I thought about my life back then. I had been on this bridge many times before but I never felt this way. The wind howled so strong that Buddy and I could barely stay upright as we crawled around each massive pole. Crowds of people huddled together to keep from falling over as they competed for limited space to navigate the bridge. As I crossed, the view of the city took my breath away. It's a picture that never gets old. I cried looking across the bay at the towering buildings I once worked in. The life I left behind to pedal around the world was in view while my 18 month bike ride was coming to an end.

When I entered Santa Cruz, tears filled my eyes again as I thought about the new direction my life would take. My goals would be about being true to myself. And yet the trip was not about me. It was about using my life more meaningfully. And I could do that right here. Seeing the world had shown me that life is really about people, love, and sharing.

As I pedaled down Beach Drive in Aptos, "The Stars and Stripes Forever" played, and my family and friends welcomed me home. Horns honked and people cheered. Banners announced my arrival. Champagne flowed freely. Toshia my dog jumped up and down and licked my face. My precious nieces clung to me in between hugs from friends old and new. The media people crowded around me. I laughed. I cried. I was glad to be home.

Epilogue

Can life be reviewed? Like a movie we settle in and watch as a plot unfolds. What about our own life? How often do we really get a chance to replay and revisit something so personal as our past? And what's the point of doing that anyway. It's history, it's done and we can't change our past. Can we?

In 2016, I decided to walk a section of the Camino de Compostela. This was not a trip I had planned or a walk that was a must do, but somehow I was directed to this Pilgrimage.

Like many who make this trek, and like the journey I embarked upon 30 years ago, I did not have expectations nor did I think I would find answers to my tough questions. By walking every day I was pushing my physical boundaries, connecting with nature and giving my mind a chance to regroup. I chose to walk most days alone and allow myself space. However, sharing bits of time with fellow pilgrims also helped remind me that we are never alone in our quests and that we have a common connection as we seek guidance and direction.

As it turned out walking the Camino gave me the renewed perspective and confidence that I needed to trust God and listen to the universe. It's a message I know all too well. And one that continues to test me and provide me with valuable lessons.

Making a life of meaning and purpose that serves others exists in everything we do. It's not a title, a lifestyle or a job, it's a way of life. It comes in the most subtle ways every day. Sometimes we look too hard for these answers when they often are right in front of us.

Disrupting a 24 year career was not a conscious choice; I hadn't intended to leave my job. Yet looking back, something inside of me had become dissatisfied. It felt a lot like the discontentment in my life in 1987. Again I asked myself, "Is this it? Is this all my life will be?"

Approaching sixty made me think more about what my next years would look like. I was constantly strategizing on ways to add value and purposed work back to my demanding schedule. I grew more frustrated as I struggled to see a clear picture of my future.

Dismantling my life in 2016 put me back on a trajectory to re-explore my around the world bike ride of 1988 and subsequent book, *Seeing Myself, Seeing the World,* published in 1990.

As I was directed back to the book, I thought it would be a simple task of bringing it into the digital world. It became clear that it was much more. Again, I jumped on a new journey of reflection and self-discovery as I dug into my past with a perspective and wisdom of today.

So why I am I back to this path? What did I miss? Was my life to take a different direction? It seemed each choice I made over the past thirty years was validated by its value, its meaning and ultimately its success. All my endeavors in my career, raising a family and creating a healthy lifestyle were met with purpose and conviction. Making a difference in the lives of people, in my community, my staff, my family always drove my decisions and actions. Even when they were not the popular ones, I always made sure I stood up for what I thought was right. I pushed boundaries and encouraged others to do the same. I honestly believe I had been on the correct track. So what's up now and what is my new destiny to be?

All I know for sure is that my around the world bike ride is a critical part of what's next and retelling the story thirty years later builds that foundation. Today feels a lot like winter of 1987 when I sold all my belongings to cycle around the world.

Again there is an element of excitement but there is also a pressure of the unknown. Change is difficult to manage because it often takes us to a place we are unfamiliar with. To trust something that we cannot see, measure or control creates a feeling of disorientation. Regardless of how disruptive and confusing these times can be, I firmly believe they are callings that need to be answered.

Epilogue

This leap of faith, if we surrender to it, can direct and reward us beyond imaginings. I have learned that when we let go of our comforts, we can create an indifferent view that helps us detach from the very barriers that block change. This philosophy has been ingrained in me for years and I believe has helped me muster up the courage to disrupt my life in search of purpose. Additionally, I believe there are consequences for ignoring these chances and that a higher power can intervene and force us into unfavorable directions. Regardless of the path, it's not easy and it is full of surprises for us to uncover.

Upon returning home in July of 1989, I struggled to integrate back into society. I was lost, I was vulnerable and I was lonely. I searched outside myself for answers hoping to be directed to building back the life I once knew. But that felt just as awkward as something new and unknown.

I went through the motions of adjusting by visiting friends and family and doing things together that we used to do. Yet it was awkwardly fun and deeply lonely. I am sure it was for them too. I grew depressed and lost as the days went by.

The road called again; I cycled down the Pacific Coast Highway to the Tijuana border where I met up with friends to participate in an organized bike ride in Ensenada. I could not bring myself to sit in a car for the eleven hour drive, so I opted to take a week and pedal there.

Reconnecting to the road engaged me and helped to ignite a fire within. Returning home, I began the journey of public speaking which led me to write a book. Writing and self publishing was never even a remote possibility or desire. Yet neither was riding a bike around the world. People came into my life and directed me to writing my story, just as people came into my life on my bike trip and helped me continue on. Where would I be today without their guidance and love?

When I think back on my bike ride with the perspective of today, I wonder how I survived. Where did I get the courage to even go, let alone keep going under such difficult circumstances? Somehow I was meant to succeed and come back to share my learnings in ways that would help others. But why me? My bike ride did not cure me of fear or equip me with confidence in all my pursuits. I have come to learn that courage and confidence is learned over and over again as we progress through the different phases of our life. It never ends. Nor do we want it to. Each journey, every barrier sets us up for something better.

Following the publication of my book, my next chapter began. I met my wonderful, loving husband and began a long career in the Outdoor Industry. Raising children and pursuing a career grounded me. The greatest gift of my life has been the privilege of being a mom. I could have never predicted this. I had always feared that this type of life would entrap me. By replacing fear with love, I was able to create a life of purpose and meaning which helped complete me. My children have taught me so much through their lens. I love them both deeply!

Returning to a more predictable life fulfilled me at the time because my view changed. I could see life differently. This seemingly small change made a huge difference. Working within a corporate structure was not as confining because I was passionate about doing work that mattered: Making a difference in my community and helping people realize their dreams.

Looking back on the past with a perspective of today is daunting and enlightening. I wonder how often we might rearrange our future with the information we learn going backwards. Aging naturally forces us to converse and reflect with ourselves, but do we always take action to replay and relearn? Either way we must recognize the importance of feeding not starving the burning need we all have within us.

Today more than ever we seek answers to tough questions. Life has become more complex, stressful, confusing and, in some cases, unfulfilling. Yet I see a trend beginning to unfold where people are disrupting the status quo in search of meaning. Looking for answers and observing our common struggles, I realize that our journeys might look different but our lessons, our triumphs and our challenges look alike. Ultimately our bond with each other lies within our common lessons. Those we might know and those we have yet to discover. Our attraction to people around us are not always clear, but its purpose begins to unfold as we listen and follow our gut down new paths. And it's no surprise that we get called back to events in our life that will continue to shape our future.

The technology of today had not been invented when I first published this story. I now have the privilege of reaching audiences around the globe. The power of a click, a share and a like engages people worldwide to participate and communicate in ways that matter to them.

I am inspired and excited to take this journey forward with my readers and audiences around the world. Thank you for being a part of this adventure as we explore the future together.

As I promised before and I renew this today, that my life's accomplishments are not about me. That somehow the disruption of 1988, the unplanned change of 2016 and all the experiences in between were orchestrated for today's work.

As I venture forward to next, I find my message from thirty years ago is not that different than today. That we need a purpose and we want our life to matter. We want guidance that will help us through our challenges, find love and ultimately be happy with the life we have or make the change we seek. When we discover the simplicity of our quest we find our peace and we nurture our soul.

About the Authors

Sally Vantress-Lodato, a national speaker, author, adventurer and business leader has over thirty years of experience traveling, managing businesses, developing people and building community outreach. She is a graduate of Cal Poly San Luis Obispo, worked for Crocker National Bank as a AVP in Sacramento and San Francisco, CA, VP for Vantress Designs Associate in Santa Cruz, CA and Store Manager for REI in Spokane WA. Sally currently operates Vantress-Lodato Enterprises, a consulting and publishing company and serves on the Spokane Park Board and Riverside State Park Foundation. Website: www.Sallyvantresslodato.com

Martin Krieg, a graduate of Cal State University Hayward and former accountant, crossed the US twice on a bicycle after his rehabilitation from paralysis, clinical death and a seven week coma. He has published several articles and books including the CARD (Cycle America Resource Directory) and Awake Again (1994). Martin is the founding director of the National Bicycle Greenway (NBG). Learn more about Martin and his work at www.bikeroute.com/Martinkrieg.

Larry Pearson graduated from Stanford University with a degree in creative writing. He has worked for the textbook division of Prentice-Hall and edited college texts published by McGraw-Hill. Pearson was also head of administrative services for the Stanford University Libraries. He has published short stories, essays and programmed reading materials-and has been a sports columnist for the Santa Cruz Sun. He is a retired City Planner living in Santa Cruz, CA.

www.ingramcontent.com/pod-product-compliance
Lightning Source LLC
Chambersburg PA
CBHW071223080526
44587CB00013BA/1479